The Author is Not Dead, Merely Somewhere Else

DATE DUE

The Author is Not Dead, Merely Somewhere Else

Creative Writing Reconceived

Michelene Wandor

palgrave
macmillan

© Michelene Wandor, 2008

First published 2008 by
PALGRAVE MACMILLAN
Houndmills, Basingstoke, Hampshire RG21 6XS and
175 Fifth Avenue, New York, N.Y. 10010
Companies and representatives throughout the world

PALGRAVE MACMILLAN is the global academic imprint of the Palgrave Macmillan division of St. Martin's Press, LLC and of Palgrave Macmillan Ltd. Macmillan® is a registered trademark in the United States, United Kingdom and other countries. Palgrave is a registered trademark in the European Union and other countries.

ISBN-13: 978–1–4039–3419–2   hardback
ISBN-10: 1–4039–3419–3   hardback
ISBN-13: 978–1–4039–3420–8   paperback
ISBN-10: 1–4039–3420–7   paperback

This book is printed on paper suitable for recycling and made from fully managed and sustained forest sources. Logging, pulping and manufacturing processes are expected to conform to the environmental regulations of the country of origin.

A catalogue record for this book is available from the British Library.

A catalog record for this book is available from the Library of Congress.

10   9   8   7   6   5   4   3   2   1
17   16   15   14   13   12   11   10   09   08

Printed and bound in China

Contents

Acknowledgements

Thanks to the Arts Council of Great Britain for a writer's grant, 2006-2007, to help complete this book; to the Royal Literary Fund for providing me with a Fellowship from 2004. Thanks also to Anne Cluysenaar, Susanna Gladwin, David Craig and Jon Cook for giving me interviews. Finally, thanks to Anna Davin and Sam Hodgkin, for searching conversations on the nature of creative writing. This book is in tribute to Julia Briggs.

Introduction
Creative Writing – a Success Story

Creative Writing (CW) is one of the success stories of the late twentieth century in the UK. In 1992 Malcolm Bradbury wrote in *The Times Literary Supplement* that 'a subject that not too long ago was regarded as a suspect American import, like the hamburger – a vulgar hybrid which, as everyone once knew, no sensible person would ever eat . . . has turned into one of the subjects of the season'.[1] Since then, many more universities have added CW, as (a) options within undergraduate English, (b) major/minor options within combined degrees, (c) full undergraduate degrees, and expanded the number of MAs and PhDs.

A report produced by the English Subject Centre in 2003 pointed to CW as a 'rapidly expanding province of activity'.[2] The Centre's 'Survey of the English Curriculum and Teaching in UK Higher Education'[3] was sent to all 135 higher education institutions running English degrees in the UK. The report suggested that 'the exponential growth of creative writing courses (as separate awards or as pathways or pedagogies within English) has had significant effects on the shape of English nationwide.'[4] Creative Writing is the final art form to enter the academy, taught as a university 'subject', a 'discipline', with its own methodologies and pedagogic principles, with courses leading to degree qualifications.

CW was established in American colleges from the early twentieth century. It took longer to register as a significant presence in higher education in the UK. Residential courses and community-based writing groups are widespread in the UK, part of the thriving amateur arts

---

[1] 17 January 1992.
[2] *Creative Writing: Good Practice Guide* by Siobhan Holland, Report Series no. 6 (February 2003), p. 1.
[3] Halcrow Group Ltd, with Jane Gawthorpe and Philip Martin. English Subject Centre, Report Series no. 8 (October 2003).
[4] Ibid., Foreword.

culture. A recent directory of Writers' Circles listed about a thousand groups and courses.[5] Made-to-measure magazines, such as *Writers' News* and *Mslexia* (the latter aimed at women), cater for the large number of people who write fiction, poetry and drama with passion and commitment.

Teachers of CW in the UK come from two professional groups: (a) career academics (generally within English), and (b) professional writers, brought into higher education to parallel musicians, performers, painters, etc. (professional practitioners) who have for many decades taught their arts expertise to students. This new incursion of professional writers into the academy is on a different basis from Writer-Residencies, or short-term Fellowships of various kinds, where writers have minimal institutional responsibilities, with time and money to help support their writing. CW has generated a new group of academic professionals.

I am one of this second group. I began writing poetry, plays and journalism at the end of the 1960s, at an extraordinary cultural moment. For over ten years (1971–81) I edited the Poetry Column in a London listings magazine, *Time Out* (which started in 1968). I reviewed literally hundreds of poetry magazines and books, theatre and films, and wrote articles and news stories. I edited the first anthology of Women's Liberation Writings in Britain, *The Body Politic*, in 1972.[6] My plays were produced in the post-1968 theatre, newly freed from official censorship. I began writing short stories in the mid-1970s, and, since the end of that decade, have been writing drama for theatre, radio and TV. It was an enormously exciting cultural and political time; one of the most vibrant promises it carried was the possibility of some explicit debate, if not rapprochement, between art and politics.

However, this was no apocalyptic moment of reconciliation, despite the passionate commitment of those engaged on both sides of the divide. While the idea of the Death of the Author was beginning to nest in the academy, the secular political world had its own puritanical political disapproval of individual authorship. I will never forget (or forgive, actually) an occasion when I 'submitted' some poems to *Red Rag*, a socialist-feminist journal on which I was one of the editorial group. One of the other members of the 'collective' pronounced in very public-school tones that 'all poetry was moribund'. Some years later I saw that she had capitulated to bourgeois decadence and published her first novel. Well, at least it wasn't poetry.

---

[5] *Directory of Writers' Circles, Courses and Workshops 2005*, ed. Diana Hayden (Diana Hayden, 2005).
[6] *Stage* 1 (1972).

My socialist and feminist politicisation during the 1970s was grafted onto a love of theatre which dated from my undergraduate years at Newnham College, Cambridge, where my teachers were passionate Leavisites, and where I spent far more hours than were academically respectable, performing in enterprising undergraduate-run drama productions. Steeped in 'close reading', my literary perceptions continued to be deeply engaged with language and form, and this, to me, felt natural, easy and exciting. I added an MA in the Sociology of Literature at the University of Essex in 1976, partly to explore the art/writing and politics axis, although this was the most vexed and inconclusive aspect of the course. However, my dissertation gave me the chance to revisit the sources of my own 'English' education, and see them in broader social and political contexts.

Apart from this brief return to the academy, my contact with higher education was sporadic: little more than occasional visits to universities for readings or guest lectures. I had no interest in teaching. This began to change in 1983, when I was asked to teach a playwriting class to acting students at the Guildhall School of Music and Drama. Like the vast majority of CW teachers, I basically made it up as I went along. Then two things happened; they appear to be quite discrete events, but each, in its different way, led me to an engagement with pedagogy (teaching and learning) in some rather interesting and surprising ways.

First, in the early 1990s, I went to one of the London conservatoires as a 'mature' student to study my other great passion (after literature), Renaissance and Baroque music. A four-year professional performance degree was followed by a one-year MMus. My experience on the receiving end (as a student) of conservatoire teaching was musically rewarding, and pedagogically shocking. The second event was taking a 0.5 post (half a job is better than a whole job for a professional writer) to teach CW at one of the London polytechnic-turned-universities. This I found exciting – and also pedagogically shocking. Not only was I teaching a 'new' subject, but I was now seeing a university from the inside, and finding a very different beast from my own undergraduate and, later, graduate experiences, some decades earlier.

Still making it up as I went along, I discovered a real enthusiasm for teaching CW. Developing what I considered appropriate methods, I began to realise that my approach was very different from that of other CW teachers. I found the vast array of CW 'how-to' books limited and frustrating, and never used any of them. I became convinced that it was important to look searchingly at CW pedagogy (its processes of teaching and learning), in order to generate some much-needed arguments about the nature of CW as an academic discipline, and to pose some fundamental questions about its relationship to Literary Studies and Literary Theory. I was certain that it was important to theorise the principles which underpinned CW teaching, to explore its methodologies and pedagogic principles, and – particularly – to address the workshop format in which it is conventionally taught.

Creative writing needs more than an alternative 'how-to' book. There are plenty of those. It needs an account of its history, and an analysis and explanation of why it has come to take its current form. Its very success and recognition as a university 'subject' means that it has reached a point where it can benefit from a trenchant critique of its principles and practices. I am passionately committed to the potential of CW, the latest art form to enter the academy as a 'subject'. I am completely convinced that 'creative' (i.e., imaginative) writing can be taught, and can be productive and exciting for teachers and students. However, I am equally passionately convinced that it needs to be historicised, theorised, problematised, and finally, reconceived.

The Author is Not Dead, Merely Somewhere Else augments three other books. *The Elephants Teach,* by D. G. Myers, *Creative Writing and the New Humanities* by Paul Dawson, and *Creative Writing: Education, Culture and Community*, by Rebecca O'Rourke.[7] Myers' account is a taut history of the relationship between English, Composition and Creative Writing in the United States, since 1880. Dawson recasts that history, adding information about CW in Australia, and suggesting a major role for CW in the humanities and intellectual life. O'Rourke's book concentrates on the vital political history and presence of CW as part of grassroots cultural education and production in the UK, linking this with an analysis of arts and educational policy in recent decades. The books offer different emphases on the configuration and purpose of CW, with differing agendas, and suggestions for its future.

This book constructs the first history of CW in formal, higher education in the UK, situating it in sometimes overlapping historical, cultural and political contexts and influences. I have traced lines of influence through the rise of English Literature, the autodidactic movement, aspects of educational philosophy which impinge on notions of 'creativity', the rise of literary criticism and theory. CW's methodology may have come to us from America, but the UK has its own distinctive influences and cultural formations, which raise rather differently inflected questions.

---

[7] University of Chicago Press, 2006 (first published 1996); Routledge, 2005; NIACE, 2005.

There is no shortage of CW 'how-to' books, DIY nuts-and-bolts texts. While they might be recommended for the classroom, they are mainly presented as self-help support, addressed to individuals who want to develop their writing at home. In recent years, as particular universities establish their CW reputations, compendia 'handbooks' or 'workbooks' have appeared, covering different kinds of writing which might feature on courses. These books tend to be generically practical, incorporating writing 'exercises' to generate words on the page, rather than texts which explore the principles underlying the implications and pedagogies of CW – they do not, in other words, theorise its practice.

Since the 1960s and 1970s, cultural/literary/critical theory has pursued discussions about the author, the text, the act of reading and linked social, cultural and literary creations of meaning. Poststructuralism, postmodernism, intertextuality, reception theory, cultural identity and the nature of the self, with emphasis on the reader/audience as the arbiter of meanings, have generated concepts which are in direct contradiction to earlier, Romantic-based notions of the writer and the writing process. This has had some important impact on the teaching of literature, and a vexed relationship with CW.

In an apparently brilliant move, CW seems to offer a solution to, or at least reconciliation between, the imponderable differences between literary criticism, theory and literary practice. It seems to bring creativity onto the university campus in new and exciting ways. Scattered throughout its own 'literature' are a series of claims for the importance of its role:

1 that it is training for would-be professional writers
2 that it is therapeutic self-expression
3 that it is a better (the best?) way to study and understand literature
4 that it is the solution to the crisis in English Literature
5 that it is the answer to the sterility of 'Theory' – indeed, that it operates 'against' theory
6 that its own 'theory' constitutes a poetics of writing
7 that it has put the 'Author' (*pace* Barthes) back into the text
8 that it has reinstated the text as an object in the classroom, along with intentionality and subjectivity into the study of literature
9 that it has revived literary criticism
10 that it teaches criticism
11 that it encourages reading
12 that it is the solution to problems of literacy

13   that its pedagogical methods (the workshop) are unique, and challenge traditional academic methodologies
14   that it is a training for employment in the cultural industries
15   that it is a new form of patronage for professional writers
16   that it is popular, and therefore one of the solutions to university recruitment crises
17   that it is a 'subject' in its own right.

Its opponents, critics and sceptics tend to have a shorter list of objections:

1   Genius/talent/creative writing cannot be taught.
2   It is not an academic subject.
3   It is not intellectually rigorous enough.
4   It is a soft option.

This book takes both claims and counter-claims seriously. Within its own literature and accounts of its practices, CW has contradictory and conflicting purposes. At the same time, it is undoubtedly here to stay, to join the other art forms – music, drama, dance, the visual arts – in a rightful place in the academy. Its success is not due to the fact that it is a maverick interloper; the contrary. It *belongs* in the academy. Where it belongs is dependent on answers to more over-arching questions: what is creative writing? What does it do, or what is it for? How is it taught, and how should or could it be taught?

This book offers theoretical and material foundations for an alternative approach. I argue that there are better, more productive ways in which CW can and should be taught, in order to position it in a four-way symbiotic structure with the study of language, the study of literature, the role of literary and cultural theory in relation to these, and the relationship of all these to creative/imaginative writing.

The history of CW threads through a number of other histories, the sum and product of a much wider range of multi-origin narratives. Literacy provides the preconditions; concomitant struggles for education across age and class ranges, and the establishment of English literature as a subject to be studied, lay the foundations for reading and writing pedagogies. Belletrism gave way to literary criticism and later literary theory, and these provide crucial cultural contexts for CW's arrival in the UK. Socio-educational developments after the Second World War created receptivity for new subjects and pedagogies. Any understanding and critique of CW only makes sense in the context of these varied histories, and the ideological, institutional and cultural legacies which have infused it. It is a kind of detective story, a what-dunnit, in order to produce a better understanding of the current configuration of CW, its contexts, practitioners and futures.

What is creative writing?

What exactly is creative writing? asked the undergraduate son of a friend at dinner. Can you really teach it? followed up the journalist sitting to my right. I turned first to the latter and pounced on his subtext: It's not about genius. Ah, he said, I didn't use the word 'genius'. No, but you implied it, I countered. Well, he said, have any of your students gone on to publish successfully? There you are, I triumphed. You *do* think it's about talent and genius. It isn't either of those, and neither is it about commercial publication success. But then, pressed the young man sitting on my left, what is it? I waffled a bit, as one does after two glasses of wine; not inaccurately, I think, but also not succinctly. At the end of my waffle, he (the young man) said: so it's a mode of thought, then? That's exactly it, I said. It's a mode of thought. It's a mode of imaginative thought.

1
First Histories: Creative Writing as Cultural and Educational Intervention

Postgraduate pioneer: University of East Anglia

In 1970 Malcolm Bradbury and Angus Wilson set up the first MA in creative writing in the UK. During the 1950s and 1960s, Bradbury had regularly visited and taught in American universities. In the early 1960s he was also involved with the new Centre for Contemporary Cultural Studies (CCCS) at the University of Birmingham. This postgraduate centre was set up in 1964 under the Directorship of Richard Hoggart, then Professor of Modern English Literature. Its aim 'was to inaugurate research in the area of contemporary culture and society: cultural forms, practices and institutions, their relation to society and social change'.[1]

In 1965 Bradbury joined the University of East Anglia (UEA) in Norwich, one of the 'new' universities founded in the 1960s; here his internationalism and multi-genre writing found a productive home. The School of English and American Studies was set up in 1968, and Bradbury became Professor of American Literature in 1970.

In the US, Bradbury had found that 'nominal teaching posts are widely available. . . . In the years after the war, it would seem just to say, the primary focus of the American intelligentsia and the would-be intelligentsia was the university campus. . . . The academic as poet or as novelist has been vindicated.'[2]

---

[1] *Culture, Media, Language*, ed. Stuart Hall, Dorothy Hobson, Andrew Lowe and Paul Willis (Hutchinson, 1980).

[2] *The Times Literary Supplement*, 25 November 1965.

In 1967, a domestic literary concern preoccupied him. With reservations about the state of recent British fiction, he argued that 'it is writers like Bellow, Barth, Mailer and Heller who are producing the English fiction that has genuine scope, intellectual and psychological tension, and aesthetic curiosity'.[3]

The MA aimed to combine the reading and study of literature with its writing, and was set up as a self-conscious cultural intervention to correct what was feared might be the death of the high-art English novel. As at the Iowa Writers' Workshop in the US, a 'creative dissertation' (i.e., a work of fiction) could be submitted for the final MA degree. UEA also hosted a writer's residency on campus from 1970 to 1971, the Henfield Fellowship (funded by the local East Anglian Arts organisation), where a writer spent six months of the year on campus, with little other commitment than to write. As Jon Cook, then a graduate student at UEA, later commented: 'The idea was that the university was a place where literature might be created as well as interpreted'.[4]

Students on the MA who could demonstrate a serious commitment to writing, were given an opportunity to develop their skills in an academic environment, and thereby also earn a postgraduate qualification. The course was consciously created to produce professional writers. This theoretically enabled academic tutors to intervene by constructing a new contemporary canon before the event, as it were. It was, significantly, a vocational course of a new kind, bringing literature, as a verbal art, into the academy at postgraduate level.

Undergraduate pioneer: the University of Middlesex

The first full CW undergraduate degree in the UK ran at Middlesex University in 1991–2, under the title of 'Writing and Publishing'. Susanna Gladwin had been teaching English Literature there since the 1960s, when it was Middlesex Polytechnic. In 1984, dissatisfied with traditional English teaching – 'the syllabus, the structure of lectures and seminars, the students writing essays and so on', which kept 'students at a distance from what literature was all about . . . the students seemed to me to have no connection with the authors they were studying' – Gladwin went to a conference organised by the Verbal Arts Association.[5]

---

[3] *The Times Literary Supplement*, 19 October 1967.
[4] Interview with the author, 2004.
[5] Interview with author, 2004.

Here she encountered other writers and teachers with similar concerns.

Back at Middlesex, she set up a 'Verbal Skills' course, in which the students wrote a weekly creative writing exercise and log report. This led to a module called 'The Practice of Writing', for second-year English students, with fictional and non-fictional modes of writing. At the end of the 1980s she began the longer institutional process of setting up what became the 'Writing and Publishing' degree. She found resistance within the English department – 'I think it was seen as not academic enough.' The degree was finally placed outside the English School, in a cross- media/cultural studies department.

This resistance, if not hostility, from teachers of literature has been a recurring experience for those wanting to incorporate CW into their work, dating back to the 1960s. When David Craig introduced CW into his undergraduate English teaching at Lancaster University in the later 1960s, it was scorned as 'Yankee', and informally 'allowed in on sufferance'.[6]

There were two additional aspects to Gladwin's work. First, she was aware that the initial degree was 'validated, because of the tie-in with industry; the idea was that in the final year the student would do a – what we now call an Internship – a short work placement, and that was an essential part of the whole structure. . . . There was a sense that it was going along with the enterprise culture, and making links between the university and the workplace.'[7] Secondly, the emphasis was on writing skills which extended beyond English studies: 'writing was the kind of thing which could enhance every endeavour – mathematics, engineering, medicine . . . '.

Two definitions of the 'vocational' are encapsulated here: the application of CW writing skills in the cultural industry, as against the aesthetico-theological notions underpinning UEA's specific 'vocational' aim of training professional writers. That the aims were also divided between under- and postgraduate degrees was significant at this early point.

The university and writers

In 1981 Alan Brownjohn completed a report, commissioned by the Arts Council of Great Britain, on 'Writers in Education, 1951–1979'. In it he

---

[6] Interview with author, 2006.
[7] Gladwyn, ibid.

described a new kind of patronage which developed after the Second World War, enabling writers to become a presence in, and boost their income from, higher education. He noted that:

'There were creative courses in art colleges, and composition courses in colleges of music: professional sculptors, painters and composers of the highest reputation had long been employed in them as essential components of the teaching programme and permanent members of staff. But in 1951 . . . there were no creative writing courses leading directly to, or contributing to, diplomas or degrees in British colleges or universities; no history at all of the employment of writers in these institutions for the purpose of teaching students to write poetry or fiction. It was only later, in the expansionary years of the 1960s, that a few writers, temporarily and rather accidentally, found teaching posts in another sector of higher education: the teacher training institutions, or Colleges of Education. But even there they were employed simply as academics with school teaching experience, and could only make use of their creative capacities if they specially contrived to do so.'[8]

There had been a small number of artistic residencies before 1951. In 1943, for example, a Bradford businessman, E. C. Gregory, donated money to set up artists' residencies for a sculptor, painter, composer and poet to bring 'younger artists into close touch with the youth of the country'. The Gregory Fellowship in Poetry began in 1960, at the University of Leeds.

As Brownjohn pointed out, it was the Regional Arts Associations in the mid 1960s which formalised the presence of writers in educational institutions. In 1967, Northern Arts set up a Writer's Fellowship at the Universities of Durham and Newcastle, followed in 1968 by a Fellowship at the University of Hull. In 1967–8 a Writers-in-Schools initiative was launched by the Arts Council, supported by the Department for Education and Science. Money came from a mix of arts and educational organisations. In 1971, a Poets-in-Schools scheme was set up by the Poetry Society (founded in 1909), and financed by the W. H. Smith chain of newsagents and bookshops. Under this last scheme, during 1979, 593 visits were made to schools by 167 different writers.

By the end of the 1970s, 'Writers' Fellowships had . . . become one of the principal means, alongside the important Writers' Grants scheme, of assisting writers through the Arts Council Literature Department. . . .

---

[8] 'Writers in Education', unpublished, p. 5.

The Fellowship would form a useful part of any larger plan to raise the status of the writer, enhance his [*sic*] rewards and widen his readership. And yet they can scarcely be said to have been firmly established in the educational institutions.'[9]

These residencies were designed to subsidise writers – in a useful shorthand, to 'buy time to write' – a modern form of patronage, academically hosted. Some writers gave readings, some also did informal 'guest' teaching or offered consultations to students – but the primary responsibility of the writer was to write. Any *quid pro quo*, as it were, for the financial support received, was justified by the recognition that making a living as a professional writer was/is a precarious business, and that the presence of a creative writing presence on campus was recompense enough. In keeping with this approach, Brownjohn's conclusions were that:

'There has been hardly any connection between fellowships and creative writing degree (or other) courses in the educational institutions. . . . Even if such courses WERE established (and logically they SHOULD exist) a system of writers' fellowships which did NOT require prescribed teaching would be desirable. The rigorous demands of creative writing teaching (as well as incorporation into the teaching force of an institution) would be fulfilling for some writers, but anathema to others.'

Alan Brownjohn's report marks a transitional moment. As long as writers were financed by Arts organisations, their presence as working artists was ideologically justified. However, once writers began teaching as a matter of course, and the money and terms of employment began to come from the universities, more conventional academic imperatives and parameters were inevitably set. The academy was helping to expand the professional security of writers, augmenting their intellectual practice, and demanding 'academic' services in return. Writers were being offered degrees of financial security, and the chance to expand their artistic expertise into the development of pedagogic skills.

The Arvon Foundation

After running a poetry day for Devon schoolchildren in 1968, poet John Moat combined forces with fellow poet John Fairfax, and persuaded

---

[9] Ibid., p. 17.

John Butt, a Devon drama organiser, to let them tutor 15 schoolchildren in poetry for five days' residency 'in a remote rectory':

> 'By coincidence, just at that time the Arts Council had begun to look for ways to involve writers in education. . . . Several of those we first approached have said that the whole idea seemed so barmy they don't know why they went along with it.'[10]

Poet Ted Hughes (later one of the signatories to the Verbal Arts Manifesto) was a guest reader on the first course, and then 'for years gave his house in Yorkshire, Lumb Bank, to Arvon, on a peppercorn lease'. Arvon centres have retained their original format: two tutors and up to 16 students live together for a week. There are group writing/discussion sessions of different kinds, a strong emphasis on one-to-one tutorials, and a guest reader. The students cook and wash up, so that bonding (and sometimes lifestyle co-operation and conflict) is domestic as well as artistic.

Moat's assessment of the Arvon 'values' highlights a tenet which commonly underpins CW pedagogy:

> 'In my view Arvon works simply became it has reverted to the most practical, perhaps the only real educational dynamic – something which contemporary culture has lost sight of. Something that imbued traditional apprenticeship in the same way that it imbues the oriental idea of guru and pupil . . . the idea of the spiritual friend and friendship – something that Fairfax and I had experienced in our own apprenticeships – were absolutely constitutional to Arvon from the start.'[11]

Arvon's intensive and informal combination of professional writers and 'students' offered a model which deliberately differed from the traditional teacher/pupil relationship; these principles extended to the adult courses.

The Verbal Arts Association

Poet and teacher Anne Cluysenaar initiated the Verbal Arts Association (VAA) in the early 1980s, and was its first Director. Cluysenaar graduated

---

[10] *Resurgence*, no. 121 (March/April) 1987, p. 37.
[11] Ibid., p. 37.

in English and French Literature at Trinity College, Dublin, in the 1950s. She joined the University of Lancaster (one of the new universities) in the late 1960s to teach linguistics, and introduced stylistics and CW, though not on the same course. Her book *Introduction to Literary Stylistics* is a lucid presentation of many of the arguments and approaches which fed into the VAA.[12]

Like Gladwin and others, she found the strongest resistance to CW from people in English departments; by contrast, there was support from people with a Classics background 'because they knew about rhetoric', and from 'people like engineers, who thought, how can you study a subject without learning how to do it?'[13]

When she moved to Sheffield Polytechnic in the late 1970s, she encountered questions such as: 'Are you going to teach everyone to be Shakespeare? Are you just going to have people sitting around listening to Beethoven and writing?' Her determination to construct a serious course combining a stimulating variety of 'new' disciplines led to an 'English degree with literature, linguistics and CW . . . the only thing we didn't have is literary theory, and I considered that a serious omission'.[14]

The Verbal Arts Association was formed after a 1982 seminar on 'The Arts and Higher Education', funded by the Calouste Gulbenkian Foundation, and chaired by Anne Cluysenaar. A group of professional writers and radical academics (including Raymond Williams and Richard Hoggart) called for 'Urgent reforms . . . in the teaching of English if the practice of verbal arts is not to remain for most people a missing subject.' (The phrase 'missing subject' recalled Stephen Potter's witty and passionate disquisition on the state of English in the 1930s, *The Muse in Chains* – see Chapter 3.)

The VAA held its first conference in 1984 in Manchester, and the organisation boasted an impressive list of literary patrons, including William Golding, Doris Lessing, Ted Hughes and Iris Murdoch. It was out of the Verbal Arts Association that the Northern Association of Writers in Education was formed in 1987; in the summer of 1991 it became the National Association of Writers in Education (NAWE), whose journal *Writing in Education* is currently an important forum for CW across the educational spectrum.

Anne Cluysenaar later wrote of the VAA: 'Members of the seminar took the view that literature is an art whose medium, language, is man's [*sic*]

---

[12] Published by Batsford, 1976.
[13] Interview with the author, 2004.
[14] Ibid.

most important, and universal, communication system. We were struck therefore by the almost total absence in higher education of productive as against receptive, historical or analytical studies in verbal arts. Literacy is a continuum.'[15] As a result, one of the VAA's key recommendations was that all literature courses should include CW elements.

A manifesto letter with 43 signatories in *The Times Higher Educational Supplement*, on 21 October 1983, argued: 'It is an unfortunate anomaly that verbal arts as part of the discipline of classics were not carried over into the study of English when this became a major academic area in the early years of the century.' Claiming that 'Precise and creative use of language is of major importance for the maintenance of our complex intellectual, industrial and democratic structures,' the letter resonates with some of the concerns which later infused Gladwin's work at Middlesex, seeing that through its focus on the practices of writing, CW could extend to being of value to other disciplines, as well as to applications in employment.

CW, argued the VAA, 'helps students appreciate the achievement of writers of the past and take an informed interest in contemporary writing. It provides an intimate and practical insight into how language works, so acting as the ideal bridge between literary and linguistic concerns.' Answering accusations that CW lacked intellectual rigour, the letter denied that 'verbal creation is somehow more self-indulgent, undisciplined or easy than other forms of creation . . .'. It referred to 'art as a form of knowing', making a clear connection with the cognitive features of other arts – music, painting, drama, sculpture, which 'include practice as an essential component'.

Schools and teacher training

Peter Abbs, poet, teacher, and one of the most indefatigable campaigners for CW, argued that the '. . . intrinsic concerns of English as a discipline are literary, expressive and aesthetic'.[16] Abbs taught at Filton High School between 1965 and 1968, getting children to write poetry and stories. This experience led to his first book, *English for Diversity*.[17] In the early 1970s he worked with students training to be school teachers, and in 1976 he set up an MA in Language, the Arts and Education, at

---

[15] *The Times Literary Supplement*, 31 December 1982.
[16] *English Within the Arts* (Hodder and Stoughton, 1982) p. 1.
[17] Heinemann, 1969.

Sussex University. This course was renamed 'Creative Writing, the Arts and Education' in the early 1990s, 'but the content remained identical and included all the genres of expressive writing'.[18]

Abbs called for a 'new synthesis', drawing on 'the three great traditions which struggled to provide a more comprehensive and demanding understanding of English: the Progressive School, the Cambridge School and the prevailing Socio-Linguistic school . . . each of them formulated certain elements of good practice, and . . . it is these elements which we must now take into a new synthesis, the radical reconstitution of English as art. . . . What is the nature of art? Why is art of educational value? How can art be taught? What is an aesthetic education?'[19]

Abbs' convictions were in line with the recommendations of the Gulbenkian report, *The Arts in Schools* (1982). This

> 'offered a framework for an aesthetic education. The bold philosophi-
> cal arguments derived from a central European tradition in aesthetics,
> going back through the work of Herbert Read and Louis Arnaud Reid,
> to Susanne Langer and Ernst Cassirer, to the philosophical work of
> Kant. The arts were seen to provide a unique and valuable kind of
> knowledge and thereby formed an indisputable part of any complete
> curriculum. The emphasis was on knowledge, but this aesthetic
> knowing was understood as materialising largely through the practice
> of art-making, through the pupil's direct engagement with the forms
> of art. . . . The educational distinctions should not be between cogni-
> tion and affect, between thinking and feeling, but between different
> kinds of intelligence, different kinds of knowledge, different kinds of
> symbolic form.'[20]

Characterising English as a 'literary-expressive' discipline, Abbs spelled out the 'common and everyday' nature of creativity – 'the condition of our existence',[21] together with its epistemological validity, as asserted/acknowledged in the Gulbenkian report and stressed in the VAA's manifesto, the 'concept of art as a form of knowing'.[22] This report argued for 'the teaching of the six great arts – music, literature, dance, drama, film and art – in our schools.'[23]

---

[18] Letter to author, 3 September 2006.
[19] *English within the Arts*, p. 1.
[20] *A is for Aesthetic* (The Falmer Press, 1989), pp. 53–4.
[21] Ibid, p. 2.
[22] Ibid, p. 27.
[23] Ibid, p. 27.

Adult and community education

Fuelled by a passionate belief in the importance of literacy and education for all, of whatever social and class origin, community writing groups have long been part of the rich tradition of adult education in the UK.

Self-organised meetings of this kind date back at least to the first half of the twentieth century. A still lively example is the annual Swanwick Summer School, first organised in 1949 by members of some of the thriving Writers' Circles in the British Isles. Nancy Martin's affectionate and evocative history, *Venture of Faith*,[24] described Swanwick's beginnings in a former prisoner-of-war camp outside Derby. At the first school they still needed to collect ration books (used during the Second World War) from the 'student' arrivals. As well as lectures and talks from guest writers, the staple of these British amateur residential courses, familiar to all those who have been on similar events, were home-made bread and rock cakes, country dancing, and evening entertainments of various kinds. Martin's account affords two clearly articulated – and contrasting – notions which fuelled these events – indeed, still do. The School (and the Circles, by implication) were for 'People who write, whether they do it for a living or as a spare-time occupation'. At the same time, they afford 'a fellowship for writers who are alone'.[25]

Further examples of adult education traditions are Morley College and the City Literary Institute, in London. Morley began in what is now the Old Vic Theatre, near Waterloo Station, running series of lectures in the early 1880s. In the early twentieth century it developed a reputation for its extraordinary music education, led by composers such as Gustav Holst and Michael Tippett.[26] The City Lit (as it is known) began in 1919, also with a wide range of courses, with strong emphases on drama. From early on, it encouraged poetry writing for its monthly magazine and annual arts competition, which was started in 1925.[27] During the 1980s it 'ran one of the largest and most ambitious writing programmes within liberal adult education in the British Isles'.[28]

The community arts movement across the UK has been supported by the regional Arts Associations since the 1960s. Some writing groups have tutors and others are run by the groups' members. The social and educational importance of literature, and the convictions about the impor-

---

[24] Published by Swanwick, 1983.
[25] Ibid., p. 85 and p. 82.
[26] Denis Richards, *Offspring of the Vic* (Routledge, 1958).
[27] T. G. Williams, *The City Literary Institute* (Saint Catherine Press, 1960).
[28] Rebecca O'Rourke, *Creative Writing: Education, Culture and Community* (NIACE, 2005), p. 48.

tance of publishing this work, were foregrounded in the Federation of Worker Writers and Community Publishers (FWWCP), formed as an umbrella organisation in 1975, and still functioning. (See Chapter 6.)

Conclusions

These historical snapshots provide a roving chronology which marks the beginnings of the formal arrival of CW in the UK academy, delineating two quite distinct approaches to its 'content' as a subject, and to its pedagogic aims.

The UEA project, in its aesthetic-vocational aim of making a cultural intervention in the creation of a contemporary literary canon, privileged 'talent', if not 'genius', aiming to train professional writers – a cultural end in itself. Middlesex's undergraduate degree, on the other hand, proposed a wider educational intervention: first, into practice-based ways of enhancing the teaching of literature, and secondly, as a functional 'vocational' skills-base for other university subjects, as well as for the wider world of cultural employment. Students spent a period of time on work placements – as they still do. Middlesex's project shared with the VAA a concern for literacy and expressive literary skills, for a varied form of writing instruction in higher education, which would be available to all students, not just those who may already have evinced literary 'talent'. In addition, the VAA's manifesto and campaigns touched on deeper epistemological questions: art seen as a specific form of knowledge, acquired by 'doing' – and shared as an aesthetic practice with the other arts.

Beyond the distinctions between under- and postgraduate training (clear at this early stage, but more vexed as the decades progress), a central issue is heralded by CW in its very nomenclature: the now heavily overused term 'creative', and its oppositional uses: on the one hand, to identify the rare, exceptional (talent, genius), and on the other, the democratising, expanding, enhancing faculty which some argue is possessed by all, and should be a central part of educational philosophies and practice, at all levels.

The new subject brought with it not only new methodologies in the seminar/workshop, as we shall see later (Chapter 12). It brought with it the principle that the art must be taught by those expert in it – i.e. professional writers, thus bringing writers onto campus in new ways, asked to slot into an already-formed academic structure and set of practices. While this might have been (and might still be) a cause for celebrating the increased presence of arts practitioners, it has also generated problems on both sides of the pedagogic fence. As we shall see later (Chapter 15), these are already issues of some longstanding in the US. The arrival of CW in the UK performed (intentionally or not) two rather different functions: to work as a reform within English pedagogy, and as a discrete subject in the academy.

From its beginnings, this uneasy, bifurcated relationship with 'English' has been one of CW's legacies. The following chapters chart the histories which fed into the immediate arrival of CW: beginning with the fundamental prerequisites of the development of literacy, and the establishment of English as a university subject.

2
Autodidacticism and the Politics of Literacy

Literacy – the ability to read and write – is closely connected to individual and social power. The right to literacy for all took centuries to achieve. In the West, education was initially controlled by the Church, a monopoly which curtailed access to literacy – which, before widespread printing, meant reading the Bible:

> 'A 1539 proclamation limited discussion and reading of Scripture to graduates of Oxford and Cambridge universities, and the 1543 Act for the Advancement of True Religion dictated that "No women nor artificers, prentices, journeymen, servingmen of the degrees of yeomen or under, husbandmen nor labourers" were permitted to read the English Bible.'[1]

English translations of the Bible in the fifteenth and sixteenth centuries were controversial, and it was not until the 'Authorised' version of the King James translation was published in 1611, that direct access to its contents was theoretically available. However, the majority of the population was still illiterate, with campaigns for literacy led by the more enlightened clergy, who, through the Sunday School movement, taught people to read and write, in order to encourage them to read the Bible.

Gradually, access to literacy was joined by a wider access to education at all levels. In 1823 Dr George Birkbeck launched London's first Mechanics Institute, dedicated to the education of working people. This

---

[1] Jonathan Rose, *The Intellectual Life of the British Working Classes* (Yale University Press, 2002), p. 13.

became Birkbeck College in 1907, and it is now part of the University of London, still dedicated to providing part-time higher education (mostly in the evening) to those already out at work.

Mutual improvement

The name 'Mutual Improvement' was first used of educational meetings for working people in 1731; by the early nineteenth century, Mutual Improvement Societies and Working Men's libraries proliferated:

> 'The mutual improvement society was a venture in cooperative educa-
> tion. In its classic form, it consisted of a half dozen to a hundred men,
> from both the working and lower-middle classes who met periodically,
> sometimes in their own homes, but commonly under the auspices of a
> church or chapel. . . . In turn these collaborative cultural activities were
> but one branch of a vast popular movement of voluntary collectivism.
> Nineteenth-century working men organised an array of friendly soci-
> eties, clubbing together to offer basic health and unemployment bene-
> fits, savings banks, job referral services, and burial plans.'[2]

Similar organisations included the London Working Men's Association in 1854, linked with Christian Socialism. The Sheffield People's College, provided day and evening classes from the early 1840s.

University extension

The University Extension Movement dates from the middle of the nine-teenth century. Many of those teaching at Oxbridge (all men, since these institutions did not admit women until much later and after much campaigning) were keen to extend educational opportunities beyond the walls of the Oxbridge colleges, by providing extra-mural classes: 'The primary object of the new association was to be the extension of univer-sity teaching through an ultimate alliance between the universities and working-class movements.'[3]

'During the 1870s this unofficial work was put on an official basis by

---

[2] Ibid., p. 58.
[3] Robert Peers, *Adult Education* (Routledge, 1959, 1972), p. 64.

the universities as an organised University Extension scheme. Cambridge was first in the field in 1873, followed by London in 1876, followed by Oxford in 1878, and by 1889 there were more than 22,000 students attending some 200 courses. . . . By this time, of all the subjects offered, English literature was certainly the most popular: out of 104 courses offered by the London Society for the Extension of University Teaching in 1889, 25 were on English literature, far more than on any other subject.'[4]

Literacy and schools

Before the Elementary Education Act of 1870, the only formal education available for children apart from the Sunday Schools, was through the 'ragged school' movement. The new Act created state schools, known as 'Board schools', because they were run by locally elected Boards:

'Compulsory education for all was enacted by Section 74 of the Education Act of 1870. This legislation was the inevitable result of the success of schools founded for the education of the children of the working poor in England after the Industrial Revolution. Such schools were founded almost entirely as a result of religious determination to spread as far as possible the ability through reading and writing in particular to enter into greater fullness of life. The State made its first grant in 1833 through the National Society for the Education of the Children of the Poor in the Principles of the Established Church, which had created National Schools in the bulk of English parishes. . . .'[5]

These institutions could charge fees, if they wished. Unusually for the time, women were allowed to vote for the School Boards, and two of the first women thus elected, Elizabeth Garrett and Emily Davies, were later active in the campaigns for women's suffrage. Attendance at the elementary schools was voluntary, until 1881, when education for children up to the age of ten became compulsory. In 1890–1, state education became free. Here the teaching of English Literature became of immediate importance: 'Undenominational Board schools proliferated after the Education Act of 1870. English literature became their most widely taught subject, especially after 1882, when readings from Shakespeare,

---

[4] Anthony Kearney, *The Louse on the Locks of Literature* (Scottish Academic Press, 1986), p. 37.
[5] Albert Mansbridge, *The Trodden Road* (J. M. Dent, 1940), p. 252.

Milton, Defoe and other "standard authors" were mandated for the higher grades. In response, publishers churned out numerous school editions of Scott, Goldsmith, Cowper, Bacon, Pope, Byron, Lamb and Gray.'[6]

Since there was not yet a through line from state primary school to university, and since the main stress at Oxbridge was on Latin and Greek in the classics, teaching literature in the vernacular (i.e. English) was a very radical educational move. While the direct campaigns to establish English teaching at university were conducted by university men, it is important to stress the line back through school-based literacy, as well as via the adult education movement; both provided great power and impetus for the formal teaching of literature in English.

Changes in printing, publishing and bookselling at the end of the nineteenth century meant that lending libraries, both those set up by working people, and those, such as Mudies, patronised by the already-reading classes, were able to share the same texts: 'First editions of books in nineteenth-century Britain could be very expensive, but eventually they would pass out of vogue and end up in the *2d* bookstalls.'[7] The increasing demand for books was boosted by publishing companies who produced the 'classics' (in English) for this new market. What is sometimes seen as a literary canon established only in the twentieth century, was already significantly in place.

Joseph Dent, the founder of the Everyman Library, was a bookbinder's apprentice; enterprisingly, he made his way by buying second-hand books and rebinding them, publishing the Everyman Library in 1906. Dent's Everyman Library was 'the largest, most handsome and most coherently edited series of cheap classics', though it was certainly not the first: 'By 1975 more than 60 million copies of 1239 Everyman volumes had been sold worldwide.'[8]

The links between oppositional politics, literacy and the autodidact adult education movement continued well into the twentieth century. The mass-circulation of Dent's publishing achievement took a further revolutionary step in 1935, when Allen Lane published the first ten titles in Penguin paperbacks. That first year, 800,000 books were printed, rising to nearly twenty times that number in the early 1970s.[9]

---

[6] Rose, p. 33.

[7] Ibid., p. 121.

[8] Ibid., p. 131 and p. 135.

[9] Diana Laurenson and Alan Swingewood, *The Sociology of Literature* (Paladin, 1972).

The Workers' Educational Association and the Oxbridge tutorial system

The Workers' Educational Association (WEA) was founded by Albert Mansbridge and his wife, in their house, in 1903. In his memoir, *The Trodden Road*, Mansbridge described himself as 'a compound of the effects of early chapel, co-operative and University Extension influence'.[10] He married in 1900, and he and his wife set up a Christian Economics Society in their house:

> 'It was partly as a result of that society that the great adventure of our life, the Workers' Educational Association, was undertaken a little later. . . . My wife and I, together with our immediate friends, were convinced that the future of England would depend largely upon the development of education in the widest possible sense among working men and women, who constitute by far the largest proportion of the population. . . . That very evening, in a completely democratic meeting attended by both of us and no-one else, she appointed me honorary secretary pro tem, contributed half a crown out of her housekeeping funds and the movement was on foot. We called it "An Association to promote the Higher Education of Working Men". The awkward title, which certainly did not satisfy women, was, in the course of time, altered to the Workers' Educational Association, and has since been generally known as the WEA.'[11]

Interestingly, the WEA derived its approach in part from the Oxbridge principle of the tutorial system: 'The centrepiece of the WEA was the University Tutorial Class. Under that scheme, university-trained lecturers came to working-class communities to teach . . . courses, ostensibly at the university level. With a maximum of 32 students, each class met for twenty-four two-hour sessions each year. One hour of lecturing was followed by an hour of discussion, with fortnightly essays assigned. These courses were funded mainly by universities, the Board of Education and local education authorities.'[12]

As Jonathan Rose has indicated, in the 1930s the WEA had over 60,000 students, and this autodidactic tradition was of importance for the Welfare State's education policies after the Second World War:

---

[10] Mansbridge, p. 36.
[11] Ibid., p. 45, p. 48 and pp. 60–1.
[12] Rose, p. 265.

'Building on a long autodidact tradition, the WEA had produced an army of postwar Labour politicians passionately committed to education, and thus constituted an all-party consensus for government aid to the arts.'[13]

While it is undoubtedly the case that the monied privilege of the post-medieval Oxbridge mainstream contrasted starkly with the poverty and limited prospects of much of the population, the active educational links between the two extremes were important and effective. For example, R. H. Tawney, the socialist and economist historian, was president of the WEA between 1928 and 1944; he gave its first tutorial class in 1908 in the Potteries town of Longton. According to Rose, he 'strove to educate British workers toward an Arnoldian ideal of a "common culture". . . . WEA classes were designed to open up communications across class lines, to allay working-class distrust of the universities, to educate the "educated classes" in the realities of proletarian life, and to train workers to exercise power in a democracy.'[14]

Jonathan Rose has challenged any crude assumption that 'ordinary' people were attracted only to 'inferior' (i.e. low-brow, populist) literature. On the contrary. His book is seamed with long quotations from working-class autobiographies and memoirs, and it is clear again and again that the literary 'classics' were avidly read. Radical working-class intellectuals read Proust and Macauley; tailoring factories in the Jewish East End created their own universities of reading matter. Often at work 'one labourer commonly read aloud while the others divided his share of the work. . . . Autodidacts widely recognised that . . . canonical literature could produce epiphanies in common readers, and specifically, only great books could inspire them to write. . . . We must therefore break the habit of treating high culture and popular culture as two distinct categories with mutually exclusive audiences. In fact, a promiscuous mix of high and low was a common pattern among working-class readers of all regions, generations and economic strata.'[15]

The autodidactic tradition took a more explicit political edge in the 1930s when organisations opposed Fascism in Europe, in '. . . a diffuse cultural and political association which included the documentary film movement, the Workers' Film Movement, the Workers' Theatre . . . Documentary writing projects such as those initiated by

---

[13] Ibid., p. 293.

[14] Ibid., p. 266. Despite a very different approach to industrialisation and politics, F. R. Leavis considered Tawney an important educational and social analyst, particularly in *Religion and the Rise of Capitalism* (London: Pelican, 1969).

[15] Rose, p. 84 and p. 371.

Mass Observation, Unity Theatre and ... Left Review and New Writing'.[16]

The Left Book Club was founded by publisher Victor Gollancz in 1936. At its peak, in 1939, it had 57,000 members and 1500 discussion groups,[17] consisting of groups which 'ranged from members of the universities to the miners and the organised unemployed, from social workers and parsons to city clerks and research scientists'.[18] Poets, artists, actors and musicians also lent their energies, with 250 Left Book Club Theatre amateur companies in different parts of the UK. There were Left Book Club meetings, reading groups set up to discuss the books published by Gollancz.

There was also a Readers and Writers Group 'because they felt that the appreciative and critical *reader* was inseparable from the writer'. The Poets' Group announced that they were 'trying to restore the traditional link between poetry and the people, going out to the people and letting them hear poetry that had some connection with reality and their daily lives, poetry which by its clarity and compactness of expression stabs like a searchlight into the confusion and contradiction of our experience'.[19]

Conclusions

The notion that the literary canon dates from the end of the nineteenth century is given the lie by the knowledge that the secular literacy movement, the working people's autodidactic organisations and the campaigners to widen access to the privileges of Oxbridge, drew on the same range of 'great' poets and novelists.

With the development of the mass media in the twentieth century, debates about 'high' versus 'popular' culture became more polarised. In addition, in both the adult education movement and the University Extension courses, the stress on the smaller tutorial class to maximise participation is the forerunner of the university seminar, and, in terms of CW pedagogy, one of the strands of influence behind the 'workshop' structure. As we shall see later, however, the assumptions behind the seminar and the workshop also derive from other, rather different social and educational sources.

---

[16] *The Republic of Letters*, ed. Dave Morley and Ken Worpole (Comedia Minority Press Group, Series No. 6, 1982), p. 69.
[17] John Lewis, *The Left Book Club* (Gollancz, 1970).
[18] Ibid., p. 12.
[19] Ibid., p. 77 and pp. 78–9.

3
Walking with Swinburne: English at Oxbridge

E. M. W. Tillyard's insider story of English at Cambridge, *The Muse Unchained*, contains a line which is a fitting comment on the story told in Chapter 2: 'Naturally,' he wrote, 'innovation was best tolerated in the lowest ranks of the hierarchy.'[1] Primary schools, alongside the autodidactic adult education movement, decisively (if not always consciously) supported English literature in its journey to become a university 'subject'.

Two decades before Tillyard's book, in *The Muse in Chains*,[2] Stephen Potter had written his own account of university English. Potter identified the first important shift to the study of English literature with the widespread acceptance of Shakespeare and Spenser, thus breaking with the concept that only Latin and Greek texts were worthy of study: 'in the 17th century, English was further dignified by the discovery of the merits of the English translation of the Bible. . . . Before the end of the 18th century middle class parents were sending their children to those private schools known as "Academies" . . . [where] there was a new specialisation in modern studies, including English Grammar and Composition; including sometimes the reading of English literature.'[3]

By the end of the eighteenth century, lectures on logic in Scottish universities included references to literature written in English. Dr Hugh Blair lectured in English at Edinburgh, where he was Regius Professor of Rhetoric and Belles Lettres, and a Professor Nichol was appointed to a Chair of English in Glasgow in 1862.

---

[1] Bowes & Bowes, 1958, p. 21.
[2] Jonathan Cape, 1937.
[3] Ibid., pp. 100 and 103.

London University was the first to introduce English literature into its examination system. University College was founded in 1826, Kings in 1829, and both were amalgamated into London University in 1839. The concept of English 'set books' was initiated by F. D. Maurice at Kings, after he became Professor of English Language and Literature there in 1840. In 1850, Royal Commissions of Enquiry were set up to suggest improvements for Oxford and Cambridge, and new subjects were advised: this meant, among other things, Modern Languages – and in the intellectual landscape of the time, English was (by contrast with Latin and Greek) clearly a Modern Language. In 1859 there were already specified English texts for study as part of the examination for the BA degree.

In this context, we can see how the potential for the University Extension Movement was growing: 'The reading public of the 1850s was ten times that of the 1750s – hence the exoteric quality of the great Victorian writers. A Dickens does not create, but is created by, his public. The idea that our literature was great and dignified began to permeate the nation. There was a reaction against the adulation of the classics at the expense of our own writers.'[4]

John Churton Collins – pioneer of English at Oxford

John Churton Collins was the man most directly responsible for getting English onto the curriculum at Oxford University. Born in 1848 and arriving at Oxford's Balliol College in 1868, he became a formidable literary and public figure. At Balliol he apparently went about in a velveteen coat, accompanied by a deerhound called Prince.[5] After Oxford, he worked in London as a Classics' coach, and literary journalist. He edited and prepared for publication scholarly editions of Tourneur and Tennyson. He knew Carlyle and Browning, and walked and talked with Swinburne. After writing an adverse review of one of Swinburne's books, the men's friendship ended, despite Collins' conviction 'that a man and his book are apart: that if you attack a man's book, you do not attack the man. You may criticise a man's work unfavourably, and yet be the best of friends personally.' [6]

---

[4] Ibid., p. 183.
[5] *Life and Memoirs of John Churton Collins*, written and compiled by his son, L. C. Collins (John Lane, 1912).
[6] Ibid., p. 114.

Collins gave his first course of lectures on contemporary literature for the University Extension Society in Brixton, in 1880 – 'English poetry from 1830'. He researched, wrote and lectured tirelessly; he was both prolific and popular, and his son estimated that he might well have delivered over 10,000 lectures during his lifetime, often up to five lectures in a single day. During the 1890s he campaigned for English to be taught in its own right at Oxford. The university was planning a School of Modern Languages, similar to the recently set up Medieval and Modern Languages Tripos at Cambridge. English was already being offered at Cambridge (though not yet at degree level), with the main emphasis there on language and early literature. In an article called 'English Literature at the Universities' published in the *Quarterly Review* in 1886, Collins lamented:

'Why Oxford and Cambridge should not deem the interpretation of our national literature as worthy of their serious attention as the study of our national history – how it has come to pass that, while the most liberal and enlightened views prevail with regard to the teaching of history, the teaching of literature is either neglected altogether or abandoned contemptuously to dilettantes and philologists . . .'[7]

In 1887 he wrote an article called 'Can English Literature be Taught?' followed in 1891 by *The Study of English Literature*,[8] a book which was used as the basis for the Cambridge Tripos some thirty years later. By 1893 the campaign was successful, and Oxford set up a Final Honours' School in English Language and Literature; students could now take the subject as an undergraduate degree. Collins was rejected for a teaching post at Oxford, but then appointed as Professor of English Literature at Birmingham University in 1904. Here, in 1907, a year before his death, he set up a School of Journalism, the first such university course in the UK.

Collins felt strongly that a school of English Literature should not be included with other 'modern' language literatures. Nor did he think it belonged with modern history. Ideally, its place was 'with the literatures which are at the head of all literatures, with the literatures which nourished it, which moulded it, which best illustrate it'.[9] In other words, with the Greek and Latin Classics. He canvassed support from many people –

---

[7] Ibid., p. 93.
[8] Macmillan, 1891.
[9] Collins, *Study of English Literature*, p. 95.

including Gladstone, the Archbishop of Canterbury and Matthew Arnold, who had some sympathy for the English–Classics combination:

> 'I should like to see standard English authors joined to the standard authors of Greek and Latin literature who have to be taken up for a pass or for honours at the universities. . . . These seem to me to be elementary propositions, when one is laying down what is desirable in respect to the university degree in Arts. The omission of the mother tongue and its literature in school and university instruction is peculiar, as far as I know, to England.'[10]

English at Cambridge

E. M. W. Tillyard wrote his stimulating, first-hand account of the establishment of the English Tripos (the name of Cambridge degrees) at Cambridge. Written while the author was Master of Jesus College, Cambridge, it was first published in 1958,[11] and is an 'intimate account of the revolution in English studies at Cambridge' after the First World War:

> 'The newer universities, unable to compete with the old in the great established subjects of Pure Mathematics and Classics, had their chance in the newer ones like Modern Languages; and a main incentive to English studies in Cambridge was the thought that they were being better exploited elsewhere.'[12]

The campaign for English at Cambridge had begun in the last part of the nineteenth century. In 1878 W. W. Skeat, 'the first great Senior Common-Room editor',[13] was appointed as the first Professor of Anglo-Saxon, a post he held until 1912. In the same year, a Special Board for Modern Languages was set up at Cambridge, and when it reported in 1881–2, it included a minor, but nevertheless important, suggestion to include English:

> 'Cambridge had less predisposition to English Literature – or to Rhetoric, its forerunner – than Oxford. Its concentration on mathe-

---

[10] Ibid., pp. 96–7.
[11] Bowes & Bowes.
[12] Tillyard, p. 20.
[13] Potter, p. 177.

matics was greater than Oxford's on classics ... with the founding of the Medieval and Modern Languages Tripos in 1886, Skeat agitated for a University Lectureship in English.'[14]

Spurred by a sense of urgency following the experience of four years at war, Tillyard's account shows how the personal and economic combined to influence new peacetime thinking about education:

'In and behind the trenches in Flanders I found that the only reading that satisfied me was of English poetry and that there and not in Greek vases my true aesthetic interests lay. ... By learning the solid things (from Milton, this phrase) and not just the languages, men would fit themselves for careers in business and the public services, and something would be done to break down the insularity of most educated Englishmen which the war had revealed.'[15]

Until the middle of the nineteenth century, the only degrees at Cambridge were in Mathematics and Classics. Moral and Natural Sciences were added, then Theology, Law and History. From 1890–1, when the Cambridge syllabus included old English and grammar, there was little literature studied after Shakespeare. However, 'In 1900 ... the Special Board advised giving more attention to Eng Lit ... as far as the year 1832 ... the word, "essay", suggesting something other than grammatical or linguistic comment, had crept unobtrusively in. ...'[16]

Cambridge degrees were taken in two parts during the student's three years (as they still are), making it possible, in effect, even at this stage, to take a combined degree in two subjects. The concept of a combined, interdisciplinary degree was already a part of the principle of Cambridge study. Tillyard summed up the rapidity and radicalism which marked the establishment of the English Tripos in 1917 and first examined in 1919, overtaking approaches to the subject already in place:

'English at Cambridge ... was no more than a small province of Modern Languages. ... But in 1917 there came a change. English was given a Tripos of its own ... freer than the scope of any School of English in any British university. ... Those who belonged to the Cambridge English School in its early days knew that they were doing

---

[14] Ibid., p. 179.
[15] Tillyard, p. 16 and p. 59.
[16] Ibid., p. 33.

something fresh, that they were leaders. . . . Most sweeping was the entire abandonment of compulsory language or philology. . . . English at Cambridge thus took a violent leap from a marked archaism to a hitherto undreamt-of modernity . . . there was a new orientation of early studies which not only substituted the history of culture and civilisation for philology but made a big change in the units of time and space included.'[17]

English at Cambridge, already teaching literature from the first part of the nineteenth century, was fertile ground for further modernising. The contributions of I. A. Richards, F. R. and Q. D. Leavis and the group which produced *Scrutiny* (the journal they published for nearly twenty years, between the 1930s and the 1950s) shaped the ways in which English was taught, across the educational spectrum. (See Chapter 5.)

The Missing Subject

Much of the opposition to English literature as an academic discipline in the early days was uncannily similar to the suspicion of CW in later decades. Scepticism about whether 'it' could be taught at all led to the assumption that it certainly could not be examined. As Potter quoted: 'You can't teach taste, or examine in taste';[18] literature was 'Chatter about Shelley', English language and literature were 'the school of the intelligent postman or the village schoolmistress'.[19] The origins of the subject, from lower down the educational, class and gender scales, were used to diminish its value and scoff at its pedagogic potential.

Towards the end of his book, Stephen Potter ventured a radical, if not revolutionary, exhortation: 'The layman might have thought that litera-ture, the art of self-expression in writing, was the one thing that a written examination could test. . . . To draw an analogy it would be necessary to invent an impossible situation – e.g., a student violinist whose work consisted in the attending of a series of violin recitals, but who was never asked to lay bow to string himself . . .'[20]

Prophetically, Potter entitled his final chapter 'The Missing Subject':

---

[17] Ibid., p. 11 and p. 58.
[18] Potter, pp. 195–6.
[19] Ibid., p. 196.
[20] Ibid., pp. 121–2.

'The Principles of . . . the Art of Writing? That would be a misleading title, though it is extraordinary that outside Diploma courses in Journalism the art of writing is nowhere taught to those past the age of eighteen. . . . A School of self-expression is nearer to it perhaps – self-expression through words.'[21]

He added that

the opportunities Literature gives for training in the use of the imple-ment of writing, in the art of the use of words, is obvious. . . . First, it must never again be a School of reading-for-the-sake-of-reading. It must be Reading in order to know how to write. Writing and reading must go hand in hand. No student should . . . study the . . . Elizabethan sonnet . . . without himself [*sic*] attempting these forms, using as theme his own experience.'[22]

As a consequence, 'Gone also will be the hard-and-fast distinction between creators and critics, the implication that writing is possible only for the God-visited few, criticism for everybody.'[23]

Conclusions

The story of 'English' – the study of literature in the English language – was finally achieved at the end of a long and strongly-contested struggle. Many of the objections levelled at its campaigners were remarkably similar to the reservations about CW, listed in the Introduction: a soft option, just a matter of reading and 'taste', difficult, if not impossible, to evaluate. Directly and indirectly, these accusations were countered by the development of literary criticism, principles and a vocabulary which established a critical discourse for the new subject. The legacies of philol-ogy in textual scholarship helped to divert attention from what might have drawn the US and the UK together, in programmes of writing instruction. As it was, the USA was the first custodian of this aspect of higher education.

---

[21] Ibid., p. 254.
[22] Ibid., pp. 256–7.
[23] Ibid., p. 264.

4

Watching the Elephants: Creative Writing in America

English, Composition and creative writing

Stephen Potter's call for the Missing Subject had already, it transpires, been anticipated across the pond. D. G. Myers, in his book *The Elephants Teach: Creative Writing since 1880*,[1] gives a cogent historical and ideologically interesting account of the arrival of CW in American universities. The 'elephant' metaphor in the title derives from an apocryphal anecdote about Vladimir Nabokov, who was proposed for a Chair in Literature at Harvard University. Linguist and literary theorist Roman Jakobson is supposed to have objected: 'What next? Shall we appoint elephants to teach zoology?' Behind the anecdote lurk two questions: the first is the familiarly sceptical 'Can literature/creative writing be taught?' which strongly implies the answer 'no'; if the answer is 'yes', the question which follows is: 'If so, what is it that is taught, and who are the best people to teach it?'

Rhetoric

In nineteenth-century America, English as a university subject retained its ties with Rhetoric (from Classics) more closely than it did in the UK: 'English literature had adorned college registers and catalogues since the first quarter of the century . . . taught by professors of rhetoric, oratory

---

[1] Prentice-Hall, 1996 (New edition with Afterword, University of Chicago Press, 2006).

and English literature. Not until the final third of the century was English permitted to stand apart from rhetoric and oratory.'[2]

At Amherst, in New England, a Chair in Rhetoric, Oratory and English Literature was created in 1825; in 1875 Johns Hopkins offered a Chair in English to Francis J. Child, and 'English first appeared in the Harvard catalogue to designate a separate course of study in 1868–1869.'[3] In 1872 Harvard appointed a full-time instructor in English composition, and the following year adopted its first entrance requirement in English. 'Between 1872 and 1885, English composition was taught twice weekly to sophomores, and after that, three times a week to freshmen . . . and freshman English was born.'[4]

The link with Rhetoric and Composition from its beginnings is the crucial divider between English in the US and in the UK. In the US, the bridge between the old and the new (between Classics/Philology and English) remained, to re-emerge as Composition/Rhetoric in the English language. While 'composition' was taught in the US before the 1880s, it was normally understood as 'Latin composition' and based on the foundations of rhetoric: 'Writing as such was subordinated to grammatical exercises, spelling drills, and the memorisation of rhetorical concepts.'[5] Thus, in the US, the arrival of English literature as a subject for university study was accompanied by the subject of writing *as* writing, deriving initially from Classical studies.

Gerald Graff has supported this argument: the 'earliest methods of teaching English literature were copied from those used to teach the classics. Literature was subordinated to grammar, etymology, rhetoric, logic elocution, theme writing . . . and recitation.'[6] Initially, then, 'Under the influence of philology, literature was studied, and taught as a source of knowledge about language – or, at best, as factual backgrounds to reading. . . .'[7]

Post-rhetoric composition gradually sloughed off some of these approaches: 'It was the creation of a new discipline altogether. . . . Writing and not speech became the customary discourse situation.'[8] The study of 'literature' itself was at first merely lectured about – '. . . the actual reading of it was extracurricular.'[9]

---

[2] Myers, p. 16.
[3] Ibid., p. 19.
[4] Ibid., p. 46.
[5] Ibid.. p. 37.
[6] Gerald Graff, *Professing Literature: An Institutional History* (University of Chicago Press, 1987), p. 36.
[7] Ibid., p. 29.
[8] Myers, pp. 37–8.
[9] Ibid., p. 22.

Advanced Composition

Myers claimed that 'the true beginnings of creative writing' date from later in the 1880s, when Barrett Wendell ran a course in 'advanced composition' at Harvard, 'including elements we would now recognise as CW'. By the end of the century Harvard composition had become the dominant mode of writing instruction in American universities.[10]

John Churton Collins' book *The Study of English Literature: A Plea for its Recognition and Reorganisation at the Universities* (1891) was widely read and discussed in America. In part as a reaction against the technical study of language within philology, 'Polemics on behalf of criticism begin to show up in professional literature as early as the 1890s, at which time we can already detect most of the disciplinary and pedagogical themes of what would later be called the New Criticism.'[11] Gerald Graff suggested that a course in 1895 at Yale was the first dealing with contemporary fiction in English.[12] In 1901, a course on 'Great Books' was taught at Berkeley, and in 1919 a US college anthology was published called *The Great Tradition*, containing selections from American and English prose.

Progressive education and creative writing

Myers also pin-pointed the influence of the early twentieth-century Progressive Education movement: 'Creative writing was first taught under its own name in the 1920s. It began in a junior high school where it was originally conducted as an experiment to replace traditional English – grammar, spelling, penmanship, even literature classes – with something more appealing to young people.'[13]

Teacher and pedagogue Hughes Mearns wrote two influential books: *Creative Youth* (1925) and *Creative Power* (1929). The first of these coincided with Mearns' '"deliberate experiment" of replacing English with creative writing at New York University, as part of a postgraduate class . . . the phrase "creative writing" was used for the first time to refer to a course of study. It was not called creative writing until Mearns called it creative writing. And then it was rarely called anything else. . . . '[14]

---

[10] Ibid., p. 46 and p. 55.
[11] Graff, p. 122.
[12] Ibid., p. 124.
[13] Myers, p.101.
[14] Ibid., pp. 103–4.

Founded in 1919, the Progressive Education Foundation was influenced by John Dewey. He was appointed in 1894 as Chair of the Department of Philosophy, Psychology and Education at the University of Chicago, developing ideas for teaching children which incorporated play: 'lessons and recitations were replaced by what would come to be known as the "workshop method". In English study its subordination of materials to the student led inevitably to a reconception of literature: no longer a record of what has been said, it became a means of saying something; no longer a subject of historical and linguistical examination, it was now . . . a course in personal development by means of self-expression for its own sake, not for the sake of demonstrating mastery of concepts in English language and literature.'[15]

Myers called this a 'constructivist' approach, because it involved 'constructing' forms of literature, as well as studying it in its already-published forms. The formalisation of writing instruction is also linked to the professionalisation of journalistic training in the early twentieth century: 'The first school of journalism unlocked its doors at the University of Missouri in 1908, and perhaps the most famous – Columbia's, which had initially been endowed in 1903 – opened in 1912. Between 1908 and 1915, in fact, seventeen accredited university programs in journalism were founded. . . . Genius had been detached from craft by the early years of the century.'[16]

Writers' groups and teaching

Formal writers' initiatives were another distinctive feature of the American literary landscape at the turn of the twentieth century. Writers' Colonies influenced the Iowa School of Letters, which later became the Iowa Writers' Workshop. In 1905–6 George Sterling founded the first rural artists' colony at Carmel, California (later famous also as the town in which Clint Eastwood became mayor). According to Myers, the Carmel colony 'was a serious attempt to create an ideal working environment for artists . . . soon the Carmel experience was duplicated . . . .a compromise between a bohemian retreat and an academic program; what was offered was a temporary accommodation – the summer conference. The most famous was the Bread Loaf Writers' Conference, inaugurated in 1926, which grew out of a summer school in English language

---

[15] Ibid., p. 105, p. 121.
[16] Myers, p. 76.

and literature held at a rambling three-storey inn on the slopes of the Green Mountains about 12 miles away from Middlebury College.'[17] In the 1920s other retreats were started – the MacDowell Colony and Yaddo, the former Trask estate in Saratoga Springs, New York.

Poets and novelists also moved into the universities, to teach literature: 'the recruitment of poets as university professors received its strongest boost when the most popular living poet – Alfred Noyes . . . was recruited to teach at Princeton (1914–1916). . . . The first two poets in residence were Robert Frost, who taught at Amherst from 1917 to 1920, and Witter Bynner, who taught at Berkeley for one semester in 1919.'[18]

Composition (as part of 'freshman English') at undergraduate level, 'progressive' educational approaches in schools, and the explicit presence of working poets as teachers of literature, together prepared (if perhaps unwittingly) the ground for CW, as a postgraduate forum for training professional writers. According to Myers, this was how 'they started the business of making professional poets by drawing up a partnership between criticism and creative writing. Although the partnership was short-lived, it led to the establishment of a new literary and academic institution – the graduate writers' workshop.'[19]

New Criticism

With literature established as an object of study, new concepts and vocabulary were created – the development of literary criticism: 'Calls for aesthetic criticism continued to punctuate professional literature between 1900 and 1915. . . . Criticism was becoming a common rallying cry for a diffuse number of interests and attitudes not always having much in common except dissatisfaction with the alternatives of pure science and pure impressionism.'[20] In 1917, Joel E. Spingarn (who founded the publishing firm of Harcourt, Brace in 1919), one of the most vocal proponents in favour of 'the theory that works of art were unique acts of self-expression',[21] published a collection of essays called *Creative Criticism.*

The codification of New Criticism in the US took until the 1930s to

---

[17] Ibid., p. 85 and p. 88.
[18] Ibid., pp. 95–6.
[19] Ibid., p. 121.
[20] Graff, p. 126.
[21] Ibid., p. 127.

appear in the form of guided textbooks and literary criticism. *Understanding Poetry*, by Cleanth Brooks and Robert Penn Warren, which Myers calls 'the syllabus of the new critical movement', was published in 1938. In their Postscript to the 1950 reprint, the author/editors commented retrospectively that even when the book was first published, it was still the case that 'the ordinary college course in poetry made little or no attempt to teach poetry except by paraphrase, by the study of biographical and historical material, or by didactic interpretation.'[22]

Understanding Poetry is an anthology of poetry, compiled for classroom use, punctuated by sections providing a 'close reading' of the poem 'as poem' – the focus intensively on the text and its language. John Crowe Ransom's book *The New Criticism*, of 1941, gave the approach its name, although the phrase 'new criticism' had already been used earlier – in an essay by Spingarn in 1910.[23] Myers acknowledged that their aims have been partly misunderstood:

> 'The new critics did more than anyone to advance the cult of autonomy but their conception . . . has been badly misinterpreted. It was set forth in the Letter to the teacher attached to *Understanding Poetry*: "though one may consider a poem as an instance of historical and ethical documentation," Brooks and Warren said, "the poem itself, if literature is to be studied as literature, remains finally the object for study."'[24]

However, Myers interestingly suggests that the impetus to look at the internal structure of poems and their language developed as a direct consequence of the presence of poet-teachers: 'the key point is that their criticism grew out of their practical interest in writing poetry. The method that came to be known as "practical criticism" or "close reading" was founded upon the sort of technical discussion of poetic problems that would occur among a group of poets.'[25] This is perhaps an over-idealistic view of the kind of conversations which prevail among poets; however, the fact that poets were also literature teachers may well have helped to direct attention to language in more urgently practical, and creative ('constructivist') ways.

---

[22] Cleanth Brooks and Robert Penn Warren, *Understanding Poetry* (Holt, 1950), p. xxi.
[23] Graff, p. 153.
[24] Myers, p. 130.
[25] Ibid., p. 131.

Creative writing after the Second World War

After the Second World War the university population in the US expanded: 'Under the GI Bill – officially the Servicemen's Readjustment Act of 1944 – veterans were allotted 48 months of free education at the college or university of their choice . . .'[26] Over two million former service personnel took advantage of this in 1947–8, and, with more students receiving state aid for study, student numbers rose: 'From 1930 to 1957 college enrolments more than doubled, going from just over a million, to over two and a half . . . between 1960 and 1969 they doubled again, to seven million.'[27]

Postgraduate CW courses increased, with programmes set up at four universities after the Second World War: Johns Hopkins in 1946, Stanford and Denver in 1947 and Cornell in 1948. After that, the increase was rapid. By 1970, according to Myers, there were '44 post-graduate programmes, by 1980 over 100; and, by the early years of the twenty-first century, between 300 and 400.

In 1967, the Association of Writing Programs (AWP) was founded at Brown University by R. V. Cassill, an Iowa University graduate. The AWP runs annual conferences and has evolved guidelines for the employment of CW teachers, advising on qualifications for teaching, as well as campaigning for the national profile of CW. English Studies are organised within the Modern Languages Association (MLA), thus organisationally separating CW from English, even though in most universities CW is part of the English department. In an ironic historical twist, in the same decade that the AWP was founded, literary theory began to challenge the New Criticism. In the 1960s, 'The New Criticism was caricatured as an extension of technological domination, explication being now seen as at best an evasive activity, at worst a form of manipulation . . . .'[28]

Writers' groups and the Iowa School of Letters

The Iowa Writers' Workshop is generally seen as the model for the development and pedagogy of CW on both sides of the Atlantic. Stephen Wilbers, chronicler of Iowa's history, described the strong 'spirit of

---

[26] Ibid., p. 159.
[27] Ibid., p. 160.
[28] Graff, p. 240.

regionalism' which overlapped with a tradition of writers' clubs on the Iowa campus. There were similar clubs on other college campuses, 'tailored for young men and women who wanted to learn and actually practice the craft of writing'.[29] A Verse Making course was planned at Iowa in 1895–6 and first taught in 1897; a short-story writing course was listed in the university catalogue of 1900–1. In 1905, Edwin Ford Piper arrived; a passionate folklorist, he also taught CW courses for 34 years, and was a leader in informal 'workshop' sessions in the early years.

In 1922–3, the University of Iowa took the important step of allowing 'artistic production, the performance of a project' to be eligible for credit: 'This arrangement . . . made the University of Iowa one of the first institutions in the country to accredit creative work for advanced degrees in all the arts.'[30]

Norman Foerster was appointed Director of the Iowa School of Letters in 1930, a post he held until 1944. He extended the accreditation of CW in 1931, when he 'persuaded the university administration and the Board of Education to accept the creative dissertation for the Doctor of Philosophy degree', a step which distinguished Iowa's from other CW programs.[31] The first such Iowa PhD was awarded to a woman.

It is important, for historical accuracy and discussions about the future of CW in the twenty-first century, that Foerster's work is appreciated in its breadth: 'The growing reputation of the University of Iowa's Department of English was another factor in the program's development. Foerster . . . was responsible for shifting the department's emphasis from a traditional interest in historical scholarship and literary history to a concentration on literary criticism. . . . In the field of literary theory, the department soon became one of the most highly esteemed in the country.'[32]

D. G. Myers drew together the disciplinary implications of this: 'Criticism and creative writing went hand in hand at the Iowa School of Letters . . . the aim was comprehension: creative writing was an effort of critical understanding conducted from within the conditions of literary practice. It was the acquisition of a certain kind of knowledge entailed in a certain type of practice.'[33]

In 1939–40 the term 'Writers' Workshop' appeared officially for the first time in the Iowa University Catalogue. The phrase had already been

---

[29] Stephen Wilbers, *The Iowa Writers' Workshop* (University of Iowa Press, 1980), p. 20.
[30] Ibid., p. 39.
[31] Ibid., p. 45.
[32] Ibid., pp. 50–1.
[33] Myers, p. 133.

used to refer informally to Piper's graduate writing seminar, which also ran as a summer school. Paul Engle then ran the Writers' Workshop from 1942 until 1966. 'In 1949, there appeared for the first time in the University Catalogue the "Undergraduate Writers' Workshop" . . . .also the first year that the Department of English offered an "English Major with emphasis on Creative Writing".'[34] Engle consolidated Iowa's reputation during the 1950s and in the 1960s, providing the prototype of what is now widely characterised as the distinctive form of CW: 'creative writing programs or "writers' workshops" became commonplace in universities and colleges across the country. Many of these programs were founded, directed and staffed by Iowa Workshop graduates.'[35]

Conclusions

The history of CW in the USA is important, because it pioneered the subject at postgraduate level, and has provided the dominant pedagogic model for the UK. Undergraduate English also included writing instruction, via the survival of aspects of Composition and Rhetoric from Classical studies, augmented by the Progressive Education movement; the 'workshop' became the form in which CW found its distinctive place.

The presence of writers' groups, part of whose priorities were to generate new regional/national literatures at the turn of the twentieth century, influenced CW methodology. Thus the creation of a new university 'subject' in the USA in the early twentieth century was in part fired by a spirit of cultural interventionism, just as it was decades later in the UK. At the same time, on both continents, the arrival of English literature as a new subject for study generated new conceptual approaches and analytical vocabularies for the analysis of imaginative writing.

---

[34] Wilbers, p. 97.
[35] Ibid., p. 105.

5
From Belles-lettres to Literary Criticism

Before English scholarship settled in the academy, such work took place as part of a wider intellectual climate: 'There were closer links between literature and public life in Victorian England than can readily be realised in our own more complex, more compartmentalised world. Statesmen wrote learned works in their spare time; authors were lured into party politics'.[1] Styles of reviewing bridged the late nineteenth-century 'aesthetic' into increasingly analytical approaches to fiction and poetry pioneered in literary journals, such as *Pall Mall*, *The Saturday Review*, *The Nineteenth Century* and *The Westminster Review*, for which George Eliot and George Henry Lewes both wrote.

At the end of the nineteenth century, a new approach was developing. E. M. W. Tillyard was part of this transitional moment: 'the dominant trend was towards gossipy, and often highly metaphorical description and unspecific praise; unspecific, for, since imaginative writing was an affair of the emotions alone and the emotions do not lend themselves to analysis, you merely evade the issue if you enter into greater detail . . .'.[2]

Nevertheless, what John Gross described as 'verbal upholstery which could be passed off as serious criticism'[3] still held attraction as an inspirational approach to literature. This was partly exemplified by the figure of Sir Arthur Quiller-Couch, who was appointed as King Edward VII Professor of English at Cambridge in 1912. Already established as a journalist and novelist, 'He was . . . intensely patriotic, and indeed his whole

---

[1] John Gross, *The Rise and Fall of the Man of Letters* (Penguin Books, 1973), p. 113. The book was first published in 1969.

[2] E. M. W. Tillyard, *The Muse Unchained* (Bowes & Bowes, 1958).

[3] Gross (p. 197).

conception of English literary history was bound up with a romantic notion of thatched-and-timbered Englishry.'[4]

Quiller-Couch, or 'Q' as he was both affectionately and acerbically known to those around him, depending on whether they accorded with his tastes or not, is interesting not merely because of his relaxed attitudes towards his teaching responsibilities (turning up late, sometimes not at all, commuting between Cambridge and his Cornish home), but also because of what were then relatively uncommon ideas about teaching writing alongside teaching an appreciation of literature:

> 'Q believed that however humble the kind of writing, the way you wrote was part of what you said. . . . He lectured in his early days on the art of writing, but, having lectured, he could not be troubled to begin a campaign for getting his doctrines put into action. This among others is the reason why the chief sin of the Cambridge English School is that it has never insisted on a high enough standard in the writing of English.'[5]

E. M. W. Tillyard and F. R. Leavis were both educated in Cambridge, first at the Perse School and then at the university. Tillyard, returning from army service after the First World War, became one of the first English Tripos teachers 'with the weakest professional qualifications . . . at the Perse School (in Cambridge) I had a teacher . . . who . . . linked up the Classics with other literatures . . .'[6] Tillyard's undergraduate degree was in Classics, from Jesus College, Cambridge, in the early 1890s.

Matthew Arnold, I. A. Richards, F. R. and Q. D. Leavis

Matthew Arnold was a poet and critic, a religious thinker and a lifelong campaigner for the democratisation of access to education. His father, Thomas Arnold, was the headmaster of Rugby School, 'and the principal creator of the modern English public school system'.[7] In 1851 Matthew Arnold was appointed as an Inspector of Schools, a post he held until 1886. Arnold's passionate arguments for educational reform were based on a belief in the value of literature as a force for the improvement of

---

[4] Ibid., p. 206.
[5] Tillyard, pp. 91–2.
[6] Ibid., p. 13.
[7] Matthew Arnold, *Culture and Anarchy* (Cambridge University Press, 1963); Introduction by J. Dover Wilson, p. xii.

both the individual and the national culture. The modernity (in many ways) of his reforming arguments is indicated by Dover Wilson's comment in 1963 that 'Nothing would strike him (Arnold) more about modern England than the ubiquity of state activity and the acquiescent temper of the people who rejoice to have it so.'[8]

Arnold's influential book *Culture and Anarchy* was first published in 1869; in it Arnold defined literature as a 'criticism of life', arguing for a spiritual notion of 'culture': 'In thus making sweetness and light to be characters of perfection, culture is of like spirit with poetry, follows one law with poetry.'[9] The Arnoldian belief in the saving importance of culture had been shared by the campaigning Churton Collins: 'The remedy proposed was also Arnold's: namely the acquisition of Hellenic sweetness and light through a study of Greek literature and Greek ideals. . . . Arnold, along with Carlyle, had done more than any other contemporary to insist on the ethical and spiritual values of great poetry which provided the main basis for Collins' earnest campaigns for literature in education.'[10]

These convictions were later reasserted by I. A. Richards and F. R. Leavis in rather different ways. Richards laid the foundations of what was formalised as practical literary criticism:

'It is not too much to say that *Principles of Literary Criticism*, which I. A. Richards published in 1924, contained a programme of critical work for a generation . . . the *Principles* and the shorter *Science and Poetry*, published in 1926, offer and depend upon a particular idea of culture which is essentially a renewed definition of the importance of art to civilisation.'[11]

Richards began teaching at Cambridge in 1917, the year the English Tripos was announced. His radicalism was shared by Tillyard; he 'wanted . . . to supplant the easy-going and vaguely laudatory criticism that was still largely the vogue by something more rigorous, and . . . to adapt the things that were vital in philosophy to the criticism of literature.'[12]

Richards had a larger cultural, and semi-religious, aim, which he linked to the experiences of reading literature, and responding to its language: 'The arts are our storehouse of recorded values. . . . They record

---

[8] Ibid., pp. xxxiv–xxxv.

[9] Ibid., p. 54.

[10] Anthony Kearney, *The Louse on the Locks of Literature* (Scottish Academic Press, 1986).

[11] Raymond Williams, *Culture and Society 1780–1950* (Penguin, 1961; first published 1958), p. 239).

[12] Tillyard, p. 89.

the most important judgements we possess as to the values of experience.'[13] His method of 'Practical Criticism' listed the categories of 'Sense', 'Feeling', 'Tone', 'Intention', in order to explore and establish a 'close natural correspondence between the poet's impulses and possible impulses in his reader . . .'.[14]

Tillyard drew out the connection between this approach, current philosophical trends, and Freudian ideas:

> 'Richards was the main instrument in this country, and perhaps anywhere, of developing in literature the seminal ideas of Moore in philosophy. . . . The effect of the psychology that Richards learned at Cambridge was twofold. First, through Freudian insistence on underlying motives it reinforced the influence of Moore in seeking multiple meanings in literature. And, second, it led Richards to attempt a change parallel to the change he attempted in the criticism of texts: a change from the old a priori type of aesthetics to the scientific examination of what actually went on in the mind and also in the body under the impact of a piece of literature. . . .'[15]

Moore's 'concentration on problems of meaning, on, for instance the frequent ambiguity of apparently simple statements, were to have their analogue in the turning away of criticism from a mystical emotionalism to the practice of linguistic analysis . . . [involving a] distinction between a poetic and a logical use of words.'[16] As a consequence, Tillyard 'began to vary essay questions with detailed discussion of the texts themselves'.[17]

Richards gave students unattributed (i.e. no author's name) extracts from literature (poetry and prose), asking them to describe/analyse their responses. It is partly from this exercise (and the later incorporation of a more highly developed form of analysis, identification and dating of extracts in the Cambridge examinations) that the fallacy has arisen that the 'Cambridge school' believed in the study of texts without any regard for their social or historical contexts.

This was never actually the case; the genuine radicalism involved in homing in on a detailed study of the language of literary texts (close reading) and giving an account of readerly responses was the precondition on the basis of which critical discourse could be developed. The

---

[13] I. A. Richards, *Principles of Literary Criticism* (Routledge, 1924) p. 32.
[14] Ibid., p. 29.
[15] Tillyard, p. 90.
[16] Ibid., pp. 89–90.
[17] Ibid., p. 87.

close textual focus directed attention to language, and to the specificity of its applications in fictional discourses (see also Chapter 10).

Literary journals: *The Calendar of Modern Letters*

In London, poet and critic T. S. Eliot edited *The Criterion* between 1922 and 1939; his essays on seventeenth-century poetry, on concepts of literature and tradition, and on the nature of imaginative writing, were all taken up by academics teaching English in the 1920s and the 1930s, although he himself never held a university post. F. R. Leavis championed Eliot's poetry and criticism in the 1920s, and continued to do so in later decades.[18]

From an Oxbridge collaboration came a short-lived, but influential publication, *The Calendar of Modern Letters*. Published between 1925 and 1927, the journal spanned what later became an oppositional line-up in the 1930s, between *Scrutiny* and *Left Review*. F. R. Leavis respected and acknowledged the *Calendar* as a precursor to *Scrutiny*, editing a selection of pieces from the *Calendar* in *Towards Standards of Criticism*, published in the politically conscious cultural 1970s, by Lawrence and Wishart, a radical press which supported the Communist Party – the very Marxists against whom Leavis had inveighed so heavily during the 1930s.[19] The title of *Scrutiny* was itself borrowed in tribute from a series of evaluative articles published in the *Calendar*, and called 'Scrutinies'.

The *Calendar* was founded through 'a concern with the changes in English university teaching, and with the demands made on modern criticism by the emergence of the new work of T. S. Eliot (*The Waste Land*) and James Joyce (*Ulysses*) . . .'. The editors were Edgell Rickword, Bertram Higgins and Douglas Garman, the first two, Oxford graduates, the third from Cambridge. As well as publishing reviews and criticism, the *Calendar* included poetry and stories (by D. H. Lawrence and T. F. Powys, among others). Garman and Rickword both joined the Communist Party in the early 1930s, and Rickword was editor for a short time of *Left Review*. The *Calendar* included articles about the commercialisation of literature, the effect of industrialisation on 'feelings' and aesthetic response, T. S. Eliot's notions of the relationship between 'personality' and literature, and applications of psychoanalytic theory to reading poetry and fiction.

---

[18] See *English Literature in our Time and the University* (Chatto & Windus, 1969).

[19] First published in 1933 by Wishart, and reprinted with a new Introduction by F. R. Leavis, by Lawrence & Wishart in 1976.

Scrutiny

Like E. M. W. Tillyard, F. R. Leavis was also educated in Cambridge, first at the Perse School and then at the university. Leavis, too, served in the army during the First World War. He was closely associated with *Scrutiny*, published between 1932 and 1953, joining its founders L. C. Knights and Donald Culver, both Cambridge graduates, in the third issue. *Scrutiny* was based in Cambridge, centring round Leavis and his wife, Q. D. Leavis. The latter's name was never formally on the editorial masthead, but M. C. Bradbrook, who was also at Cambridge at the time, spoke on BBC Radio 3 (14 July 1975) of the fact that the Leavises were 'in every sense partners in *Scrutiny*'. It was also in 1932 that Q. D. Leavis's PhD thesis was published: *Fiction and the Reading Public*, whatever its ideological idiosyncracies and limitations, remains an important example of the historical and cultural analysis of literature, which later developed as the sociology of literature, in the 1970s.[20]

Leavis combined Arnold's, Richards' and Eliot's notions of a 'cultural heritage' encapsulated in an age's 'best' literature, where a 'tradition' in the form of the most important values or meanings is preserved. It is easy to see how such a 'theory of literature' and its values went hand in hand with the consolidation of the literary canon.

There were three ideas being explored during this period: the process and importance of 'criticism' (i.e. of discernment, interpretation and evaluation), which 'is as inevitable as breathing'.[21] It can be clearly seen how the criticism followed the literature, as it were – modernism and the avant-garde poetry generating thought and 'criticism' for its exegesis. The second was an insistence on 'the historical sense',[22] and the third, the link between the social and cultural significance of poetry within Eliot's concept of tradition – codified in the concept of the canon:

> 'No poet, no artist of any art, has his [sic] complete meaning alone . . . what happens when a new work is created is something that happens simultaneously to all the works of art which preceded it. The existing monuments form an ideal order among themselves, which is modified by the introduction of the new (the really new) work of art among them . . . the *whole* existing order must be, if ever so slightly, altered; and so the relations, proportions, values of each work of art

---

[20] Chatto, 1968.
[21] 'Tradition and the Individual Talent', in *Selected Essays* by T. S. Eliot (Faber & Faber, 1932), p. 13.
[22] Ibid., p. 15.

toward the whole are readjusted . . . the past should be altered by the present as much as the present is directed by the past.'[23]

Bearing in mind that these were pre-(articulated)-theory decades, and that many cultural conservatives (with a small 'c') have taken these ideas to support arguments for elitist culture, it is useful to see the force of an argument which placed literature in a broad context of history, culture, with a serious attempt to construct a poetics, an aesthetic theory, based on descriptive evaluations of the canon. The enterprise was self-consciously a cultural intervention. For the Leavises and those around them, the study of English was *the* key to a revived set of values, which, they argued, had been lost with industrialisation. The study of English was to be a humane centre of education, reviving and re-establishing 'civilising' values. It is salutary to compare these aims with their echo in the lengthy claims for CW, made by David Fenza at the turn of the twenty-first century (see Chapter 15).

Scrutiny's first editorial, 'Scrutiny: a Manifesto', deplored the 'general dissolution of standards', and promised to combine 'literary criticism with criticism of extra-literary activities'.[24] Cautiously they announced: '*Scrutiny* will also publish original compositions. Since, however, more people are able to write good criticism than good verse or short stories, we commit ourselves to no large or constant proportion of creative work.'[25] In the event, the journal published little imaginative writing.

Left Review

Left Review first appeared in 1934, the same year the first Soviet Union of Writers' Congress was held in Moscow.[26] Concerned to create an 'association of revolutionary writers', it published campaigning articles as part of the anti-fascist movement in the 1930s particularly during the Spanish Civil War, in support of republican Spain.

Reporting on the Soviet Writers' Congress, Amabel Williams-Ellis wrote: 'Write about our lives, write about what is going on now.' Socialist-realism was considered as the form which represented working-class life most recognisably; the journal conducted debates in its pages about the relationship between art and society, art and ideology, art and

---

[23] Ibid., p. 15.
[24] *The Importance of Scrutiny*, ed. Eric Bentley (Grove Press, 1948), p. 1.
[25] Ibid., p. 5.
[26] Lawrence & Wishart, 1977 (first published by Martin Lawrence Ltd, 1935).

political commitment. *Left Review* invited readers to send in stories and poems, as well as autobiography. Unlike *Scrutiny*, they regularly published imaginative writing.

Criticism, evangelical and methodological

The Leavises were highly critical of the secular literary world and its cliquishness, as well as hostile to the social benefits of industrialisation, mass education, popular culture, and the influences of 'Americanisation'. In her book *Fiction and the Reading Public*,[27] Q. D. Leavis expressed concerns about the 'debasement of language', invoking 'values' associated with former times, in the interests of creating (or, rather, recreating) an 'organic' cultural coherence or wholeness. The combination of these resulted in a cultural elitism, which has been the object of much criticism of their work.

The second charge often levelled against them is on the grounds of the practice, the methodology of literary study – the practical criticism, or close reading, which has been criticised as entailing attention only to 'texts' at the expense and/or exclusion of 'contexts'. Robert Eaglestone's book *Doing English* is symptomatic of such extreme dismissal. Aimed to encourage (particularly A-level) students to think about wider social and cultural issues in relation to the study of literature, the book is immensely stimulating, but it seriously misrepresents some of the Leavises' ideas. Eaglestone acknowledges the Leavises' 'quite astonishing vigour and dedication',[28] but then claims that practical criticism involves 'concentrating on the words on the page and disregarding the work's context. . . . A literary text is free from history and time.'[29]

Ben Knights has highlighted one of the contradictions that resulted from the radicalism of 'close reading' entailed in practical criticism: 'While it has always been an ill-informed slur that the Leavises and their followers were formalists, careless of history, it was nevertheless the case that in pedagogic terms the grounding of the subject in practical criticism could create this appearance.'[30]

There is no doubt that the Leavises' ideas and legacies were complex and often vexed. In *Mass Civilisation and Minority Culture*,[31] F. R. Leavis wrote:

---

[27] Pimlico, 2000. First published in 1932.

[28] Routledge, 2000, p. 15.

[29] Ibid., p. 16.

[30] Ben Knights and Chris Thurgar-Dawson, *Active Reading* (Continuum, 2006), p. 12.

[31] Gordon Fraser, 1930.

'In any period it is upon a very small minority that the discerning appreciation of art and literature depends: it is (apart from cases of the simple and familiar) only a few who are capable of unprompted first-hand judgement. They are still a minority, though a larger one, who are capable of endorsing such first-hand judgement by genuine personal response. The accepted valuations are a kind of paper currency based upon a very small proportion of gold. To the state of such a currency the possibilities of fine living at any time bear a close relation . . . *such capacity does not belong merely to an isolated aesthetic realm: it implies responsiveness to theory as well as to art, to science and philosophy in so far as these may affect the sense of the human situation and of the nature of life.* Upon this minority depends our power of profiting by the finest human experience of the past; they keep alive the subtlest and most perishable parts of the tradition. Upon them depend the implicit standards that order the finer living of an age. The sense that this is the direction in which to go, that the centre is here rather than there.'   (my italics)

There were undoubtedly profound contradictions at the heart of the Leavisite project. The elite minority, leading 'judgement', was closely tied in with F. R. Leavis's aims for an English School at the centre of the university; at the same time, he could not and did not deny or ignore (in however qualified a fashion) that there is always a cultural/educational/intellectual context and relationship between literature and its society. The concept of 'Life and Thought', the title of one of the examination papers of the Cambridge Tripos, aimed to demonstrate the foundations of studying literature which went beyond mere 'text'. Whatever theoretical and political limitations there were, there was always an acknowledgement of the interplay between 'society' and its literatures. As Leavis wrote: 'If you do a critique of *Little Dorrit*, that book won't be all of Dickens you've read. . . . And if you know Dickens, you won't be content with knowing Dickens alone. And Dickens leads you into the study of Victorian civilisation, leading you on at the same time into extended and still further extended, acquaintance with the novelists.'[32]

There was profound political and cultural opposition between *Scrutiny* and *Left Review*. In practical terms, *Scrutiny* was more immediately successful, in their influence on university teaching, and the development of a methodology of critical response which filtered down into

---

[32] F. R. Leavis, *English Literature in our Time and the University* (Chatto & Windus, 1969), p. 5.

schools and A-level teaching. It could be said that *Left Review* had the theory, while *Scrutiny* had the practice, and it was the latter which had the more enduring educational legacy. After all, there can be no analytical relationship to any text without some close attention to it; put more simply, one does not have to support the Arnoldian–Leavisite claims for literature's moral or religious purpose, or to champion the literary elite, to endorse some form of textual criticism/close reading.

Conclusions: text, presence and absence

The establishment of English literature as an object for study called for a methodology, a system and a vocabulary; this development has been briefly outlined here. The men [*sic*] of letters outside the university, and the new academics, shared an interest in the tumbling accumulation of new, difficult, modernist writing. The mix was heady: Virginia Woolf and the Sitwells, Eliot, Pound and James Joyce, the first translations of Proust. 'In literature the connection between creation (which takes place, in the main, outside universities), criticism and scholarship is apt to shift and be uneasy. Nevertheless an uneasy connection is better than none at all. In the first years of its existence the Cambridge English school succeeded in maintaining such connections in a way rarely achieved in universities.'[33]

Further, as Tillyard noted, the 'change of taste typified and promoted by Eliot, the reaction from Romantic emotionalism to a more cerebral type of poetry, fostered the urge towards practical criticism because it directed attention to a kind of literature for which minute exegesis was especially apt'.[34]

The emphasis on the text was dual: at one level, the functional consequence of the material objects for a new university subject (books, texts – the canon), at another level, attention to the language out of which the text was composed – the materialities and meanings of the writing. In relation to the first, the intense work of literary scholarship, editing and publication animated many literary intellectuals in the last part of the nineteenth century, and the early part of the twentieth. In the work of textual rehabilitation, attention to language was intense, and careful reading and editorial decision-making were essential: 'Until the closing years of the century the notion of a *critique universitaire* scarcely existed

---

[33] Tillyard, pp. 134–5.
[34] Ibid., p. 100.

in England, while even the labours of exhuming and annotating texts were as often as not performed by private enthusiasts far from the universities. . . .'[35]

The professionalisation of literary study and scholarship in UK universities developed together. Interestingly, this was an area in which some of the legacies of philology necessarily survived. The symbiotic links between philology and English informed the scholarly skills applied to textual rehabilitation, making texts available for study, rather than generating the separate Classics-derivative of Composition, as happened in the US. The Early English Text Society was founded in 1864, reprinting early English texts, especially those from manuscript. Philologist Walter William Skeat was one of the Society's founders, producing editions of Chaucer and Langland. As Stephen Potter commented, 'The editor has his own genius to express.'[36]

Part of this 'genius' helped to confirm the literary foundations on which the canon later rested. George Saintsbury produced compendious histories of French and English literature between the 1880s and the early twentieth century, and Q, apart from writing poetry and novels himself, edited a number of new editions of Shakespeare (with Dover Wilson), as well as the influential and successful *Oxford Book of English Verse, 1250–1900* (published in 1900).

In the UK, literary excavation, the political struggles to establish English, which resulted in its separation from Classics and Philology, and then the development of literary criticism, took up the intellectual and cultural space. However, the very active presence of all these new activities also generated a noticeable absence – as was observed by some literary intellectuals. Quiller-Couch was concerned about writing instruction (see Chapter 10), and, as we have seen, Stephen Potter returned to the argument in the 1930s. The absence of formalised writing instruction which accompanied the establishment of English – the Composition which became essential for CW in the US – meant the absence of an institutional context for writing instruction of any significant kind, discursive or imaginative, in UK universities, until after the Second World War.

---

[35] Gross, p. 186.
[36] Stephen Potter, *The Muse in Chains* (Jonathan Cape, 1937), p. 176.

6
Secular Intellectuals after the Second World War

Government and culture

In 1945, after the war ended, a Labour government was elected. In power until 1951, it established the Welfare State and the National Health Service. The 1944 Education Act raised the school-leaving age to fifteen and enabled everyone who qualified to benefit from higher education. Local authorities paid fees and give grants to students. The fighting armed service had consisted almost entirely of men, with women largely in servicing roles. As a consequence, wartime patterns of domestic employment had changed, with many women working in industries which the men had left. The peace-time economy involved reversals in this gender-based employment, with women leaving jobs which men took over again.

With the establishment of the Welfare State and improvements in housing, health care and education, gradually material prosperity improved. However, these were far-ranging social changes, with ideological consequences for traditional class allegiances. One of the most moving and important accounts of this, spanning the pre- and postwar periods, was Richard Hoggart's *The Uses of Literacy*.[1] In this *tour de force* of personal reminiscence, memoir and sociological description, Hoggart wrote about the changes affecting the young industrial (male) working-class in the 1950s:

---

[1] Penguin, 1971 (first published in 1957).

'I have in mind the kind of milk-bar – there is one in almost every northern town with more than, say, fifteen thousand inhabitants – which has become the regular evening rendezvous of some of the young men. Girls go to some, but most of the customers are boys aged between fifteen and twenty, with drape-suits, picture ties and an American slouch . . . those who, for a number of years, perhaps for a very long time, have a sense of no longer really belonging to any group. . . . Almost every working-class boy who goes through the process of further education by scholarships finds himself chafing against his environment during adolescence. He is at the friction-point of two cultures. . . .'[2]

This class dislocation was at the heart of much of the new fiction being written in the 1950s and 1960s by a generation born before the war; novels such as John Braine's *Room at the Top* (1957), Kingsley Amis's *Lucky Jim* (1954) and Alan Sillitoe's *Saturday Night and Sunday Morning* (1958) were all popular successes, generating fresh literary voices.

New drama (even if still under official censorship) introduced different content and experiences onto the stage. Joan Littlewood at the Theatre Royal in London's Stratford East, as well as directors in regional theatres, began to stage plays about ordinary people, in contrast to the middle/upper-class drawing room theatre of London's West End. At the Royal Court Theatre, John Osborne's *Look Back in Anger* (1956) became emblematic of a new generation of playwrights, initiating a contemporary canon.

Theatre historian John Elsom commented that 'Within ten years suave actors had been replaced by rough ones as heroes, metropolitan accents by regional ones, stylish decadents by frustrated "working-class" heroes.'[3] All these were challenges to the cadences and contents of the middle-upper-class literary world; from America came the exuberance of the Beat generation, with its fierce political, poetic and performing energies. There is an interesting tension between these new cultural events and the dissatisfactions voiced later by Bradbury and Steiner et al. (see Chapters 1 and 7) about the apparent 'decline' of British fiction. The cultural interventionist ambitions of Malcolm Bradbury's MA in 1970 turned out to have its own class-based bias.

---

[2] Ibid., p. 248, and pp. 292–3.
[3] *Post-War British Theatre* (Routledge, 1979), p. 34.

The postwar generation and new media

By the late 1950s, new generations of university graduates were working in an expanding white-collar sector, servicing material expansion in manufacture, industry and housing. With the increase of consumer goods, alongside the BBC (which began radio broadcasting in the 1920s), there developed a mass-distributed culture, through commercial TV, cinema and popular music. Again, the US was an important influence, through the 'American inspired paperback revolution of the early 1970s. Novels were promoted on TV and radio, writers sent on nationwide tours, and dump bins began to appear in supermarkets and bookshops.'[4]

At the same time, there were new kinds of political and social discontent. The Campaign for Nuclear Disarmament (CND) and the university-based New Left, which both formed during this period, wanted more than mere material and leisure improvement. CND, in the aftermath of the consequences of the nuclear bomb in the 1940s, attracted people from all classes in political protest. The New Left revived interest in Marxist theory, and Continental Marxist writing; young intellectual professionals criticised a training which (as some saw it) fitted them into a bureaucratised and technologised capitalism. This combined a politics of protest against militarism, with a questioning of social values in an affluent society – questions which, ironically, were askable precisely because of relative economic security.

Domestically, social and sexual divisions of labour – the different occupations and responsibilities of men and women – were also highlighted. The technology of domesticity – fridges, washing machines, cookers – made life easier for women in the families. New housing provided better services. However, these very benefits separated extended families and groups. The individual 'nuclear' family became more self-sufficient, and as a consequence, more autonomous and isolated. Discontents which led to a revival of feminism were brewing.

Gender, the public and the private

More efficient contraceptive methods, in particular, the pill, made it easier for women to separate sex for pleasure from sex for procreation (in theory, anyway). However, such potentials for greater freedom of choice

---

[4] *The Republic of Letters: Working Class Writing and Local Publishing*, ed. Dave Morley and Ken Worpole (Comedia/Minority Press, 1982), p. 37.

collided with postwar messages of hearth and home as the ideal role for women, promulgated by advertising and women's magazines. The readjustment of gender-based social patterns (men at work, women at home) after the war, created new pressures.

Of course, women have always worked outside the home and always will – but the reality of two 'jobs' for many women highlighted discrepancies between aspiration and reality. Whether they saw themselves as working- or middle-class, the first generations of postwar university-educated women found that they shared this gender imbalance.[5]

Legislative reforms during the second half of the 1960s came from strong earlier demarcations between private and public life. In 1967 an Abortion Act and an Act partially legalising male homosexuality were passed (female homosexuality has never been illegal – popular myth has it that when the first anti-homosexual legislation was passed in 1885, Queen Victoria was so horrified at the mere thought of lesbianism that the ban applied only to men). In 1968, after much campaigning, theatre censorship ended. In 1969 the Divorce Reform Act eased conditions for divorce, and in 1970 the Equal Pay Act proposed that equal pay for men and women should become a reality by the end of 1975. It still hasn't. However, the movement was towards a lessening of State intervention in private, single or family life: an acknowledgement that the cultural expectations of the new generation were for greater lifestyle freedoms.

Cultural politics

During the 1950s and 1960s Britain's imperial role in the world loosened, and large numbers of people came to Britain from the West Indies, India and Pakistan (see Graham Hough's observations in Chapter 7). Rock and roll music challenged the pop ballad in the 1950s, and what was dubbed as 'Swinging London' blossomed in the 1960s. Flower-power culture affirmed liberal, 'permissive' lifestyles; massive outdoor pop festivals on both sides of the Atlantic appeared, and the Beatles battled it out with the Rolling Stones. Young people were not only a new affluent economic factor, but were creating a culture of their own. Whether it was called the counter-culture, the 'underground', the 'alternative' arts – the

---

5 See Betty Friedan, *The Feminine Mystique* (Norton, 1963; Penguin, 1968); Hannah Gavron, *The Captive Wife* (Pelican, 1966); Juliet Mitchell, *Woman's Estate* (Pelican, 1971), *The Body Politic: Women's Liberation in Britain*, compiled by Michelene Wandor (Stage One, 1972).

decade of the 'Swinging Sixties' crossed institutional boundaries, and generated books, pamphlets, theatre, film, poetry.

The student movement, parts of the traditional labour movement and the Campaign for Nuclear Disarmament protested against world events during the 1960s – the American war in Vietnam, the Soviet invasion of Czechoslovakia. While the hippies and the politicos had distinctive styles, there were overlaps and shared ideas. The later development of Cultural Studies at universities was the academic outcrop of this. As Michael Green noted:

> 'In the 1970s the consolidation of cultural studies . . . relates also to the astonishing proliferation of radical journals and their accompanying left and feminist network . . . .this new higher education 'movement' developed an important confidence in its own distinctive intellectual production, support networks, and even in its forms of insertion into political groups and parties.'[6]

At the centre was a shift in the very notion of what the term 'politics' could mean. Traditional political struggle, particularly in the British labour movement, had largely been focused at work, organised at the point of industrial production by men. What we now identify as gender, race, post-colonial, and/or identity politics were markers of the crossovers between different aspects of life and thought, as it were, which were beginning to be strongly articulated: the relationship between public and private, between the personal and the political, between art and politics.

Some new culture also emerged from contradictions within the radical movements themselves. While the New Left and the counter-culture asserted democracy and equality, within their own ranks women remained mainly second-class participants, and even the so-called sexual permissiveness of the Sixties reflected this double standard. Feminism, which had been relatively dormant as an explicit political force for around half a century (after the struggle for full women's suffrage was finally won in 1928), re-emerged. The Women's Liberation Movement (WLM) and the Gay Liberation Front (GLF), both of which started in 1969–70, addressed these issues: the position of women at home and at work, of sexual choice, and of the oppressive and exploitative aspects of the division of labour at home and at work.

---

[6] *Re-Reading English*, ed. Peter Widdowson (Routledge, 1982), p. 87.

Cultural production

Critical attention was given to the way the dominant ideology (the 'message' in the interests of those in power) was conveyed through the arts, media, education and communications of postwar society. This was cast in sometimes crude terms, with the individual consumer seen as passive; but it also led to exciting radical critiques of the mass media, suggesting that these were sites of political struggle; while they were channels for dominant messages, they also had the potential to be used to disseminate alternative culture and literature.[7]

The counter-cultural, hippie slogan of 'do your own thing' was supported by new technologies; portable cassette-recorders, super-8 cameras and printing technology: 'The new offset litho technology has made it possible for many people to learn basic printing and plate-making on small A4 and A3 machines. Similarly, access to an electric typewriter with a carbon ribbon makes elementary typesetting easy. Also it was very much part of the ideology then that campaigning groups, ethnic groups, tenants' associations and so on should do the whole typing, layout and design and printing processes themselves. . . .'[8]

In this digital age, these developments may seem negligible, but at the time they made self-publishing into a political act in itself. I gained experience of typesetting, layout and publishing on a socialist-feminist journal called *Red Rag* at the beginning of the 1970s. This gave me the expertise to self-publish two pamphlets: *Sink Songs* (1975), a collection of short plays by Dinah Brooke and myself, and *Cutlasses & Earrings* (1977), a collection of poetry by women. It was time-consuming, celebratory rather than vanity-work; the politics of publishing for some became a means and an end:

'in recent years working class people, particularly women and black people, have begun to develop new forms of writing, new modes of local, collective publishing, and alternative distribution networks – the elements of a movement which aims to 'disestablish' literature, making writing a popular form of expression for all people rather than the preserve of a metropolitan or privileged elite . . . adult education and literacy classes . . . community publishing projects . . . writers' groups and local history workshops came together in 1976 to form the

---

[7] *Power without Responsibility: The Press and Broadcasting in Britain*, James Curran and Jean Seaton (Routledge, 1993; first published in 1981).

[8] Morley and Worpole, p. 49.

Federation of Worker Writers and Community Publishers . . . produced outside the established field of "Literature" and the market economies of commercial publishing.'[9]

The 'politics of representation' meant that the voices of ordinary people could be written down and produced, unmediated, unjudged and uncensored by the literary 'establishment'. One of the paradoxes, of which the Federation of Worker Writers amd Community Publishers (FWWCP) was aware, was that, while they claimed to operate 'outside' and 'against' the system, they relied for survival on public subsidy.

However, the community publishing movement had (and still has) marked successes, and a great deal of influence. A pamphlet of poems by a black schoolboy, Viv Usherwood, published in 1972, sold over 10,000 copies, and if anyone thought grassroots writing a safe activity, the reverse was proved when teacher Chris Searle was suspended for editing and publishing a collection of poetry by schoolchildren, *Stepney Words*, in 1971.

The FWWCP, some of whom were university graduates, saw their work, in part, as a critique of dominant practices in English teaching: 'English is a training in reading, not writing, literature. . . . In this, literature is unique in this country. Those interested in music at schools, playing, composing . . . can at least compete for the opportunity to go to a full-time college of music. People who have a particular interest in painting, sculpture or other arts, can go to a full-time art college. The same is true of dance, theatre, film-making, television production and so on. The exception is writing. It still seems to be believed that you can either do it or you can't. . . .'[10]

Authorship and authority

The Republic of Letters ironically manifested one of the contradictions inherent in its own philosophy. The book's cover has no editors' names on it, and the sections are not credited to individual authors. While the worker-writers encouraged by the FWWCP all had their names attached to their writing, the editors of the book manifested a politicised version of the Death of the Author. Those responsible for writing the book's chapters are not individually credited, though their names do appear on a list in the book.

---

[9] Ibid., p. 1.
[10] Ibid., p. 117,. and pp. 121–2.

Radical cultural production and creative writing

Many of the principles which underpinned the community-based writing movement still operate today. The FWWCP was predicated on regular meetings where ordinary people (sometimes with a leader/tutor, sometimes not), with a range of literacy skills, wrote, read and published, poetry, stories and memoir/autobiography. This had an important impact on the relationship between CW and cultural policy, nationally and regionally. Rebecca O'Rourke's ground-breaking book *Creative Writing: Education, Culture and Community*[11] describes this history, discussing its cultural/political implications:

> 'My account reaches outside the carefully planted and tended gardens of the academy into the wild woods of cultural practice. These practices, and the cultural policies they are linked with, include the participative and community arts movement, adult and community education, compulsory education, commercial and state providers . . . (it) situates those who teach, just as much as those who learn, creative writing . . . in a highly contradictory position which I describe as being in and against education.'[12]

O'Rourke's commitment to this work is based on the conviction that 'local cultures of writing can act as forms of resistance to the totalising discourse of the market, but do so only if resistance is consciously and actively pursued', and she applies this to later, more formalised developments of CW.[13] Her inquiry was led by a concept of writing as resistance: 'had late twentieth century campaigns for a more democratic and inclusive approach to writing and literature in British cultural policy and education been successful? They certainly seemed successful. The values and activities of participation had replaced those of appreciation in culture and education; cultural and educational policies now started from an inclusive rather than an elite standpoint. Literature was viewed in the broadest of terms and as an activity that encompassed readers and writers, of all sorts of texts.'[14]

Perhaps in some quarters and for some people it was not only seen this way, but *was* this way. However, there is more to it than just an over-

---

[11] NIACE, 2005.
[12] O'Rourke, pp. 36–7.
[13] Ibid., p. 10.
[14] Ibid., p. 230.

enthusiastic claim that CW is the inheritor of the community arts' principles of the 1970s and 1980s. O'Rourke's trenchant account is a salutary corrective to the 'insularity' of accounts of CW as having developed only from within higher education, and it is certainly the case that the democratising, egalitarian aims of this movement have a specific force in some models of CW pedagogy.

Conclusions

Some important and contradictory phenomena emerged from the counter-culture's flowering of free speech, and from the political movements' insistence on a democratised access to literacy, writing, imaginative expression, publishing and reading. Both were enabled by technological improvements which made publishing and distribution more accessible, more under the control of its producers, and closer to its consumers – creating congruent constituencies on both sides.

In the process, another paradox is revealed: while intellectuals and academics were arguing for a blurring of the distinctions between literary and 'other' texts, and developing systemic (through linguistics and semiology) analyses of literary production, the community movement was asserting the opposite: it was encouraging and celebrating individual authorship, explicitly drawing attention to under-represented social groups.

The two spheres were addressing the text and the author in different ways. Neither the ideals of political collectivism nor an awareness of intertextuality could explain away individual authorship. In fact, individual authorship was being actively encouraged – whether for right-on political reasons, hippie self-expression or academic radicalism. While academics and some politicos were differently arguing for the Death of the Author, the extra-academic and extra-literary worlds were encouraging the emergence of more (and different) individual writers.

7
Textual Politics in English Studies after the Second World War

After the Second World War, the profile of the student population in the UK changed: 'Until the 1960s a small number of universities (twenty-odd) accommodated a bare four per cent of the relevant age-group.'[1] During the 1960s, some fifteen new institutions (sometimes called Plate Glass universities) were built. However, as Isobel Armstrong noted in 1989,[2] even after this expansion, only 8% of school leavers went to university, with a total of 14% going into all forms of higher education, compared with 20% in France, Germany and Holland, and 45% in the US. In 1989 government policy set a target of 30% of school leavers, mature students, women and ethnic groups to be in higher education after the first decade of the next century.

Following the Further and Higher Education Act of 1992, forty-one former polytechnics and colleges were reconfigured as universities, able to award their own academic degrees. In the 1990s, vocational institutions, such as conservatoires and drama colleges, also (with external validation from already existing universities) modified their courses to become degree qualifications. On the surface this implied a democratisation of the status of qualifications across the board. Traditionally, polytechnics had been considered to rank below universities, concentrating more on technical and vocational, than on academic, courses.

---

[1] Ronald Carter, in Martin Dodsworth (ed.), *English Economis'd* (John Murray, 1989), p. 65.
[2] 'English in Higher Education: Justifying the Subject', in Dodsworth, p. 10.

University English

With more students going to university, the numbers of those taking English at A-level (the qualification for university admission) also increased. In 1951, 37,000 school leavers took A-levels in all subjects; by 1985 this had risen to 380,000. Of these, 59,483 took English – 17,738 boys, and 41,745 girls.[3] The gender bias in these figures shows a consistent pattern: 'With a gender ratio that appears to be stuck at 3:1 in favour of women . . . English literature at BA level remains a white, middle class and female subject.'[4]

Current statistics show that numbers wanting to study English at university remain relatively consistent; the University and Colleges Admissions Services (UCAS) figures in 2007 showed English to be the fifth most popular subject, with over 55,000 students in 135 English departments.[5] These figures attest – claims of crises notwithstanding – to the continuing popularity (and importance) of English as an undergraduate degree:

> 'little more than 50 years ago English as a subject in the academic sense had barely begun. Today English might be claimed as one of the most popular of subjects among students, and its specialisations as remarkably numerous. . . . Moreover, with the decline of formerly central subjects such as classics and theology, the study of literature has seemed to offer the student of it some alternative enlightenment concerning the nature of the human condition, and it has also appeared to act as a guide to individual and social values in an ever more estranging universe.'[6]

And yet, while English has retained centrality and popularity, it has also been a constantly contested and debated intellectual site. This is partly because, while it has had the study of literature at its core, it is also always more. It encompasses, and at times elides, the connections between oracy and literacy (speaking and writing), the social and intellectual applications of these two in literature (reading and writing), and the importance of literacy skills in everyday life – communication, relationships and employment. Language can be the most unthinking

---

[3] Lyn Pykett, 'Beyond 'A' Level English: English in the Sixth Form and Universities' in Dodsworth, p. 29).

[4] Ben Knights and Chris Thurgar-Dawson, *Active Reading* (Continuum 2006), p. 15.

[5] English Subject Centre Newsletter, March 2007.

[6] *Contemporary Approaches to English Studies*, ed. Hilda Schiff (Heinemann, 1977), p. 1.

faculty we have, and it can also be the most difficult to understand and theorise: 'In one way language is too familiar to us all; every normal human being has thoroughly mastered one language in childhood without knowing much about the process . . . '[7]

Apart from the increased numbers of universities, and the cultural and political events outlined in the previous chapter, there were also intra-institutional challenges during the 1960s–1980s. According to Peter Widdowson, three radical educational forces were particularly important: 'The Centre for Contemporary Cultural Studies (CCCS) at Birmingham University, the Open University (OU) and the Council for National Academic Awards (CNAA) . . . have contributed more to a radical assessment of English and the teaching of it in the last two decades in Britain than any other institutions. . . . The CNAA, the largest degree-awarding body in Britain, has also fostered interdisciplinarity in many of its colleges and polytechnics, and English has increasingly found itself a component of Humanities courses.'[8]

Art and science

The debates were not merely within the Humanities. In 1959 C. P. Snow gave the Rede Lecture, called 'The Two Cultures and the Scientific Revolution', at Cambridge, based on an article he had written in 1956, which was published in *The New Statesman*. In 1962, F. R. Leavis gave a lecture-riposte, published in the *Spectator*. Letters, articles and books followed: the 'two cultures' debate continued for years, polarising into an argument between art (English) and science, though Snow had first conceived it as a socio-political lecture. Its original title was 'The Rich and the Poor'; this became the title of one of the chapters defending the benefits of industrialisation, arguing that the industrial countries should put the benefits of science at the service of those with less wealth and fewer resources.

With its revised title, it generated passionate debate in and outside the academy. As editor Stefan Collini wrote: 'At the heart of the concept of the "two cultures" is a claim about academic disciplines . . . the divide between two sorts of intellectual enquiry.'[9] The lecture deplored what Snow saw as the philistine gap between the 'literary intellectuals' and the

---

[7] Noel Minnis, in *Linguistics at Large*, ed. Noel Minnis (Paladin, 1972), p. 15.
[8] *Re-Reading English*, ed. Peter Widdowson (Routledge, 1982), pp. 9–10.
[9] C. P. Snow, *The Two Cultures* (Cambridge University Press, 1996), Introduction by Stefan Collini (Part one, the original lecture, first published in 1959, and Part two added in 1964), p. xliii.

'physical scientists', and it was in this wider context that discussion about the role of English in the Humanities took place.

English and Humanities

The interactions between politics, cultural production and the changing demography of higher education affected a range of subjects, traditional and modern. The CCCS and the CNAA were both set up in 1964, a year marked also by Penguin Books' publication of a slim volume, *Crisis in the Humanities*, a collection of essays about intellectual turbulence within the academy, publicised and shared with the wider cultural world.[10] Edited by historian J. H. Plumb, the book addressed nine 'Humanities' subjects, including Classics, History, Philosophy, Divinity, the Fine Arts, Sociology and Economics. Some chapters had appeared in the *Sunday Times* in 1963. The jumping off point, according to Plumb, was a concern about the waning of importance of 'History, Classics, Literature and Divinity . . . [which] were, with Mathematics, the core of the educational system and were believed to have peculiar virtues in producing politicians, civil servants, Imperial administrators and legislators.'[11] He added: 'the humanities are at the cross-roads, at a crisis in their existence: they must either change the image that they present, adapt themselves to the needs of a society dominated by science and technology or retreat into social triviality'.[12]

Graham Hough wrote about 'Crisis in Literary Education': 'The old humanist education was primarily literary, and its ideal was never one for the specialist or the expert. On the contrary, it was an idea of intellect and character combined, an ideal of general personal development. It originated in Greece, was revived at the Renaissance, filtered down through the centuries, and with us reached a late-bourgeois flowering in Victorian England.'[13]

Hough bemoaned the increasing insularity of English study, impervious to the changing cultural mix of the UK's population:

'You can get a degree in English literature but be barely able to read French, and have no living contact with any literature outside English.

---

[10] John Oakley and Elizabeth Owen, '"English" and the Council for National Academic Awards' in Widdowson, p. 105.

[11] Plumb, p. 7.

[12] Plumb, p. 8.

[13] Graham Hough, in Plumb, pp. 97 and 105.

Knowledge of the social and intellectual history that accompanies the literature may be of the slightest. . . . Much English literature has dropped below the horizon because England is no longer the centre of literary creation in the English language, and the English literary tradition is no longer its primary source. For many years now the sheer volume both of creative work and of scholarship in America has far surpassed that in England . . . and there is a growing body of writing in English by Indians, West Indians, and Africans. . . .'[14]

New educational formations: the CCCS and the OU

The Centre for Contemporary Cultural Studies (CCCS) was part of the post-graduate centre at the University of Birmingham. Under the Directorship of Richard Hoggart, then Professor of Modern English Literature, 'The aim was to inaugurate research in the area of contemporary culture and society: cultural forms, practices and institutions, their relation to society and social change.'[15] Its origins as 'the outcrop of an English Department . . . whose premises were largely given by their common foundation in "Left-Leavisism"'[16] are extremely important. Hoggart explicitly linked the work of the CCCS with Raymond Williams' work on the 'culture and society debate', at the same time, identifying a peculiarly British resistance to theory and theorising:

'the peculiar character and strength of the British tradition in literary-cultural thinking . . . has tended to stick close to human beings and to the direct experience of literature; it has been on the whole non-aesthetic and non-abstract, not fond of making intellectual patterns, rather homely, decent and concerned. . . . Thus we have largely undusted assumptions about the nature of elites or minorities, their roles in society, the ways in which their values are transmitted; about the relationships between class and cultivation and power and authority.'[17]

Hoggart's gentle comment about the 'homely' reluctance of British literary culture to deal with abstractions was articulated more frankly a

---

[14] Ibid., p. 99.

[15] Preface to *Culture, Media, Language, Working Papers in Cultural Studies 1972–1979*, ed. Stuart Hall, Dorothy Hobson, Andrew Lower and Paul Willis (Hutchinson, 1980), p. 7.

[16] Michael Green, 'The Centre for Contemporary Cultural Studies', in Widdowson, p. 78.

[17] *Contemporary Criticism*, ed. Malcolm Bradbury and David Palmer (Edward Arnold, 1970), pp. 157–8).

decade later, in 1977, when Hilda Schiff referred to the 'theoretical back-wardness of English studies as compared with other disciplines . . . '.[18] By contrast, Ronald Carter wrote of the new theoretical approaches in the late 1970s and 1980s as 'an openness to new directions in literary theory and a broadening of the parameters of analysis and discussion to include notions of discourse . . . the domains of language and discourse are central to the study of texts and the organisation of texts'.[19]

The Open University (OU), launched in 1969, developed what was previously known as the correspondence course (now called 'distance learning', or, in the US, 'low residency'). Using the resources of BBC radio and television educational broadcasts, the OU attracted all kinds of students onto degree courses structured to fit into the rest of their lives, rather than requiring them to devote a number of years to concentrated study.[20] It too enthusiastically developed multi- and interdisciplinary courses.

The debates: literary criticism and cultural theory

Four significant collections of essays were published between 1970 and 1989, all written from *within* English Studies, by committed teachers and critics concerned about the future of English. All sought to recoup or reposition 'English' in the light of rapidly changing cultural conditions. All argued for the importance of maintaining the centrality of works of literature ('texts') as desired objects of study. Taken together, the books chart a developing debate which accurately tracks the ideological devel-opments within English, starting with 'criticism' in the first; the fourth is emphatic in its address to 'theory'. The terms/categories of 'literature' and 'criticism', which appear unproblematically in the first book, surface as 'text' and 'theory' in the fourth. The age of achieved criticism, opera-tive in the first half of the 1960s, has, by the 1980s, seemingly given way to the age of theory, the 'author' up for question and the 'text', the 'work of literature', both in danger of doing a disappearing act.

That these symposia were not passing occasions is attested by impor-tant, single-authored volumes produced in their wake by many of the contributors. Malcolm Bradbury's *The Social Context of Modern English*

---

[18] Schiff, p. 2.
[19] Ronald Carter, in Dodsworth, p. 50.
[20] Jonathan Rose, *The Intellectual Life of the British Working Classes* (Yale University Press, 2002), p. 297.

Literature[21] was published in 1971; *Structuralist Poetics*, by Jonathan Culler, in 1975;[22] Terry Eagleton's *Literary Theory, an Introduction* appeared in 1983.[23] *Writing in Society*, by Raymond Williams, was also published in 1983,[24] and Catherine Belsey's *Critical Practice*, in 1980.[25] By the 1990s, when theory had become so abstruse that guides were necessary, Jonathan Culler published one of the most useful and succinct of these, *Literary Theory: A Very Short Introduction*, in 1997,[26] and Peter Widdowson traced the complexities of the category 'literature' in his invaluable *Literature* in 1999.[27]

Contemporary Criticism (1970)

In the first collection, published in 1970, Malcolm Bradbury articulated a strong defence of the traditional functions of criticism as a professional training in how to read literature:[28]

> 'New Criticism ... marked the movement of criticism into the academy ... and it encouraged critical democratisation by making appreciation and competence dependent not on the "possession" of taste, but on effective training. ... It marks a change in the social location and function of critical activity. In the past, criticism has normally occurred in an environment reasonably close to that of literary creation.'[29]

While acknowledging an 'increase in speculative theory', Bradbury resisted the tendency of European theory towards 'scholasticism' – that is, discourse-specific, philosophical, logical forms of theory. For Bradbury, the dangers were the '... tendency of criticism, in pursuing its aspirations, to acquire the form of a primary as opposed to a secondary mode of discourse – so that instead of being capable of creating its theory out of texts ... it moves insensibly from description to prescription.'[30]

---

[21] Schocken Books.
[22] Cornell University Press,
[23] Oxford, Blackwell.
[24] Verso.
[25] Methuen.
[26] Oxford.
[27] Routledge.
[28] *Contemporary Criticism*, ed. Malcolm Bradbury and David Palmer (Edward Arnold, 1970).
[29] Ibid., pp. 18–19.
[30] Ibid., pp. 24–6.

Warning that this kind of 'scholasticism' tends 'to move away from matters of value', Bradbury's preference was for the term 'poetics' over 'theory': 'A poetics derived in the first instance from literature itself, rather than from linguistic or cultural theory. It means a poetics that is empirical, in the sense that it is responsive, in a *post facto* way, to the character of any given work to which critical attention is given.'[31]

In his essay in the volume, Richard Hoggart, unusually for the time, used the phrase British 'creative writing'. While acknowledging the wider remits informing cultural studies, his concerns centred round expanded understandings of what 'reading' itself might entail. This involved a combination of ideas about specifically literary 'value', and wider cultural and social values: 'Behind all . . . attempts at cultural reading are a set of major assumptions. . . . Such as: that a society bears values, cannot help bearing values and deciding their relative significance . . . no one individual ever makes a perfect "fit" with the dominant order of values of his culture . . .'.[32]

Of the nine contributors to Bradbury and Palmer's symposium, two argued explicitly for cultural/critical theory-based approaches. Roger Fowler, echoing W. K. Wimsatt and Munroe Beardsby's strictures of the 1940s against the Intentional Fallacy (see Chapter 18), discussed linguistics and the ontology of the literary work – its existence as an autonomous 'text':

> 'A poem is free of an author's intentions and his experiences, and of a reader's responses, because these are variable, irresponsible, undiscoverable, demonstrably erroneous, etc., while the poem remains stable. We cannot locate the poem in the author's state of mind at the moment of creation because this is inaccessible and may be changed by the act of writing . . . we cannot allow the poem to reside in the individual's experience as he [*sic*] reads, because that would be tantamount to saying that there are as many poems as there are occasions of reading, whereas we know very well that there is only one poem.'[33]

Fowler provided a more theoretised formulation of imaginative writing: 'Fictions are language-reinforced conceptualisations. . . . A language is a structured repository of concepts, and every use of language is a particular ordering in a (partly language-dependent)

---

[31] Ibid., pp. 25 and 37.
[32] Ibid., p. 162, p. 161.
[33] Ibid., pp. 178–9.

circumscribed cultural situation. This ought to be a tacit principle for criticism, because it is an inevitable fact of all writing.'[34]

Graham Hough, from the provenance of traditional literary criticism, proved receptive to theory, summarising the critical/theoretical trajectory from Arnold, through Leavis and on to Barthes, without losing sight of the 'object', the literary work itself. Unlike Bradbury, Hough 'cannot think that criticism can continue to live on descriptive techniques and personal responses alone.'[35] He acknowledged the importance of Marxist, materialist approaches to art and literature: 'Criticism so conceived – as a study of literary language – both pays its tribute to the autonomy of literature and defines an area where it can speak with special knowledge. But the autonomy of literature is relative . . . To think on this subject at all requires some application of Marxism. . . . '[36]

Contemporary Approaches to English Studies (1977)

The second collection, *Contemporary Approaches to English Studies*, edited by Hilda Schiff, was published in 1977. It began with a lecture first given to the English Association in 1975.[37] Expressing concerns similar to those of Bradbury and Hough, George Steiner claimed that the reader/critic 'will not . . . discover much in the British [novel] to compare with the visionary compass of the novels of Patrick White or with the probing concentration of Nadine Gordimer . . . little in British polemics, social argument and reportage, certainly after Orwell, is of a class with the craft of Norman Mailer or James Baldwin . . . the current American novel, reaching as it does from the often arcane, narcissistic conceits of Nabokov and John Updike to the classic humanism of Saul Bellow and the experiments, *in extremis*, of Thomas Pychon or Robert Coover, now represents the richest, most complex interplay of intelligence and of style in the language.'[38] Steiner laid this at the door of falling levels of literacy and language use, arguing for a 'central role to the history and usage of the English language'.[39]

---

[34] Ibid., p. 190 and p. 193.
[35] Ibid., p. 54.
[36] Ibid., p. 57.
[37] Heinemann.
[38] 'Why English?' in *Contemporary Approaches to English Studies*, ed. Hilda Schiff (Heinemann, 1977), pp. 11–12.
[39] Ibid., p. 21.

Raymond Williams summarised the etymology of the term 'literature' as a process of relatively narrowing definition. In the Renaissance, the term simply meant a printed book of any kind. With mass book production, the term narrowed to mean 'imaginative' literature (fiction), to carry extra cachet in the nineteenth century. Without using any putative crisis in contemporary fiction as the main argument (as Steiner and Bradbury had), or using the phrase 'creative writing', Williams argued for what he saw as the missing component in contemporary pedagogic practice (the recurring theme of the Missing Subject):

'The extraordinary neglect of the subject of production in modern academic literary thought and in conventional literary thought is attributable to a notion of literature as an object and as existing in the past. . . . I believe that the emphasis on practice is now crucial and that the neglect of practice is a contributory factor to our cultural crisis. . . .'[40]

The final two articles in the Schiff book directly addressed literary and cultural theory. Jonathan Culler argued for structuralism and linguistics to provide 'a poetics which stands to literature as linguistics stands to language . . . one takes linguistics as an analogy which indicates how other cultural artefacts should be studied.'[41] As part of a negotiation between traditional literary criticism and literary theory, Culler insisted that critical/theoretical writing is, in fact, a refinement/development of the activity of reading: 'Interpretations of authors and works are wholly parasitic on the activity of reading literature: the critic who writes about an author is simply producing a more thorough and perhaps more perceptive version of what readers of literature do for themselves.'[42]

Like Bradbury, Culler extended the term 'poetics' to apply, by implication, to literary production and its conventions: 'I should perhaps emphasise that, though it is preferable to talk about reading rather than writing, we are dealing with conventions which are assumed by the writer. He is not just setting words down on paper but writing a poem.'[43]

The final essay, by Terry Eagleton, consisted of a short critical guide to Marxist literary theory. In particular, he pointed to the writings of Pierre Macherey, who 'sees the true domain of criticism as an explanation of

---

[40] Ibid., p. 30.
[41] Ibid., p. 60.
[42] Ibid., p. 61.
[43] Ibid., p. 64.

the *condition of the work's possibility*. . . . For Macherey, the text is . . . always unachieved, "decentred", irregular, dispersed . . . scientific criticism instals itself in the very "incompleteness" of the text.'[44]

Re-Reading English (1982)

The third collection, *Re-Reading English*, edited by Peter Widdowson,[45] published only five years later, in 1982, arrived into a more comfortable theoretical climate: 'In the wake of the past ten years' Marxist–structuralist debate – particularly about Ideology – there developed a body of theory concerned to produce a fully articulated Marxist aesthetics.' Widdowson's symposium was 'an attempt to take stock . . . and to redirect it in response to pressing social and political needs.'[46] Confidently informed by cultural and political theory (including a lone representative of feminism from Wendy Mulford), the book explored ways to take Marxist and post-Marxist theory into the teaching of literature, pivoting round the 'new turn in the 1960s with the work of Raymond Williams and Terry Eagleton.'[47]

John Hoyles singled out 'Williams' sequence of interventions . . . blazing a trail from the cul-de-sac of Left-Leavisism to the high-road of continental Marxism'. Terry Eagleton confidently asserted 'that all imaginative production is social production'.[48] Hoyles drew attention to the Bakhtinian school 'who in the twenties provided the first serious Marxist critique of the Russian formalists and paved the way for a theory and practice of textual politics whereby literary criticism would avoid the twin reductionisms of formalist poetics and vulgar Marxist sociology'.[49]

Peter Brooker linked art with legacies from the 1970s: 'it is vital to develop a socialist pedagogy . . . this demands a challenging and shifting of orthodoxies, a re-articulation of the working ideologies of English as an academic discipline . . .', resulting in 'a materialist criticism', described in terms which are now very familiar:[50]

'If . . . we can appropriate (chiefly from discourse theory and psychoanalysis) the concepts of a decentred human subject, of an internally

---

[44] Ibid., pp. 100–1.
[45] Routledge.
[46] Widdowson, p. 2 and p. 1.
[47] John Hoyles, 'Radical Critical Theory and English', in Widdowson, p. 44.
[48] Ibid., p. 49.
[49] Ibid., pp. 44–5.
[50] 'Post-Structuralism, Reading and the Crisis in English' (ibid.).

riven text, of the intertextuality of discourse, of contradictory and changing subject positions for writers and readers, then we would at once free literary writing from a literary enclosure and question the bulk of written criticism and English courses, founded alike on assumptions of a fixed subject, and strung by distinctions of genre upon single authors and texts in a loose chronology drawn from the received tradition.'[51]

The relationship between theory and practice is, however, rarely smooth. Tony Davies, in his chapter, 'Common Sense and Critical Practice: Teaching Literature', made the salutary point that, despite the avant-garde challenges of theory, 'it is in the humdrum, everyday and generally quite "untheoretical" activity of English teaching that the real effectivity of "Literature" as a practice is to be found'. Within this every-day pedagogical practice, 'the empirical and unreflective character of literature teaching owes something to the strong persistence in English departments of critical notions – realist, reflectionist, intentionalist – whose deconstruction in theory has scarcely damaged their practical effectiveness'.[52] Literary criticism, even while it was being challenged, and sometimes modified and augmented, never disappeared – indeed, still proved to be necessary.

English Economis'd (1989)

The fourth symposium, edited by Martin Dodsworth, *English Economis'd: English and British Higher Education in the Eighties*,[53] appeared shortly after the Education Reform Act of 1988, giving polytechnics and colleges more independence. Additionally, under Margaret Thatcher's Conservative government, tertiary educational remits were changing. In 'English Across the Binary Line: an Institutional View', Daniel Lamont commented: 'The original architects of the polytechnics and colleges apparently saw these institutions as being vocationally oriented and did not consciously intend that they should develop a substantial portfolio of work in the humanities. This differs from the new universities founded in the 1960s which did set out from the beginning to develop work in all areas of knowledge, including the humanities.'[54] Cuts in

---

[51] Ibid., pp. 60–2 and p. 72.
[52] Ibid., p. 34 and pp. 36–7.
[53] John Murray, 1989.
[54] Ibid., p. 78.

funding elicited a prophetic comment from Peter Corbin that 'in the future it is likely that students or their parents, will themselves have to bear an increasing proportion of the cost of their higher education via loans or their private income'.[55]

During the 1980s, a series of reports on English teaching in schools (Kingman in 1988, Cox in 1989) contributed to setting up a National Curriculum 'which will designate the amount of time to be given to different subjects and lay down standards of achievement whereby the performance of students and schools may be judged at virtually every point in a student's career from five to sixteen'.[56] The reports aimed to develop 'a more systematic, linguistically informed basis for a national curriculum for English and for the training of teachers of English'.[57]

Debates about English in higher education, together with the increase in cultural studies/theory, had an impact also on A-level English, as Lyn Pykett observed: 'There are now a number of Alternative syllabuses (at A-level) which encourage a degree of movement away from prescribed book study, and an exclusive concentration on the works of "great" writers.'[58] At the same time, Pykett's research showed that 'the core of the traditional A-level syllabus has changed remarkably little in the last twenty years. . . . I have been struck by just how easy it is to reconstruct, from the central syllabus of each of the A-level boards, almost exactly the same course (even the same texts) which I and my contemporaries followed in the early 1960s: Shakespeare, Chaucer, Milton, Jane Austen, Hardy.'[59]

A cautionary assumption that literary criticism and the canon had simply been swept aside was provided by Martin Dodsworth:

> 'It would be foolish to claim that university departments of English *en bloc* are in the vanguard of a radical redefinition of English studies, but it is equally foolish to argue that they are merely bastions of reaction. . . . The canon, the monolithic literary heritage . . . has, at least in theory, been dismantled, and reassembled or dispersed according to the critical positions adopted by particular practitioners. However, it should be said that the course content and structure endorsed by institutions often lags behind the critical positions held by the groups of individuals who teach in them.'[60]

---

[55] Ibid., p. 43.
[56] Ibid., p. 2.
[57] 'Language and Literature in English Studies' by Ronald Carter (Dodsworth, pp. 53–4).
[58] 'Beyond A-level English: English in the sixth form and universities', in Dodsworth, pp. 33–4.
[59] Ibid., pp. 28–9.
[60] Dodsworth, pp. 35–6.

Textual politics and the disappearing text

Time-lag notwithstanding, the descriptive literary critics (Bradbury et al.), the transitional cultural theorists (Williams, Hoggart et al.) and the new theorists (Eagleton, Culler, et al.), continued to debate the received literary canon and the inevitable value judgements behind it, leading to questions about the stability of the literary text itself:

> The questioning within literary theory of the nature of literature itself, the construction and deconstruction of literary canons and the study of the varying reception of literature relative to social context has led stylisticians to embrace a much wider range of texts as sources of "literariness". It is now not uncommon for jokes, popular fiction and advertising language to be analysed alongside a Shakespearian sonnet or an opening to a novel by Jane Austen, leading to the replacement of literature by the term "text". . . .[61]

Tony Bennett spelled out the implications for the cornerstones of literary criticism, interpretation and evaluation:

> 'This view of the text . . . has been seriously challenged in recent years, mainly by structuralist and semiological schools of criticism. According to these, the text has no within, beneath or behind where hidden meanings might be secreted. Attention is instead focussed exclusively on the process and structures of the text and on the ways in which these produce meanings, positions of intelligibility for the reader or the specific effects of realism, defamiliarisation or whatever. . . . [62]

The intellectual tussle ranged between two extremes: at one theoretical pole, the definition of 'text' was being so expanded as to blur its 'literary' points of demarcation, and thus to imply a relativism to literary judgement, or to deny the function of evaluation altogether. At the other extreme, there was an insistence on allowing the literary work its own ontology, consonant with more traditional definitions of the literary:

> 'There can, of course, be no doubting the *materiality* of the text, its physical existence as a set of written, material notations. Indeed, prop-

---

[61] Carter, in Dodswoth, p. 51.
[62] 'Text and History', in Dodsworth, p. 224.

erly understood, it is this very materiality of the text which disables the view that the text can be fetishised as either the container of a meaning, single and irreducible, or the source of an effect.'[63]

Catherine Belsey offered a convenient way to have both the theoretical and the literary cakes. She suggested that in 'Re-reading the Great Tradition' the 'Leavisite discourse' did not need to be rejected: 'A more constructive strategy is to treat English as a site of struggle, to generate a new critical discourse, to re-read the great tradition not for the sake of valorising it, but in order to release its plurality.'[64]

The elision of 'literature' into 'text' went to the heart of the 'problem' of language. Isobel Armstrong made the conceptual connection: 'English has always had a special place in academic study because it carries out its analyses with the same materials which are its objects of study – it is, as Shelley once said, both the materials of the culture and the tools which cut it – texts written in language analysed through language. ... Language, indeed, is at the heart of our subject, and one could say that the study of the literary text becomes an extension of the study of language.'[65]

Via a rather different route from that of Raymond Williams over a decade earlier, Armstrong also argued for instruction in writing, of all kinds:

'Above all, since language is a cultural practice, students would be practitioners across a wide variety of forms. Just as music students compose in order to understand musical form, creative writing, the composition of rhetoric and metaphor, pastiche, commentary, debate, a variety of dealings with the sign, verbal, aural, visual, would add to the student's work with the formal analysis of the essay. People come into language by using it.'[66]

After the text, writing

From other quarters in higher education came more radically articulated support for imaginative pedagogy. In 1984 Peter Abbs was one of the

---

[63] Widdowson, p. 226.
[64] Ibid., p. 130.
[65] Dodsworth, p. 16.
[66] Ibid., p. 21.

contributors to the twenty-fifth anniversary issue of *Critical Quarterly*.[67] This literary-critical journal was based in Cambridge, and its celebratory publication included the manifesto of the VAA (see Chapter 1). One of the *Quarterly*'s editors, C. B. Cox, had, according to the editorial, been one of the VAA's prime movers, along with Anne Cluysenaar and others. With implicit approval from the *Quarterly* activists, the VAA manifesto announced that 'It is time to return to a more effective and longer-established tradition. English, at all levels, should involve the study and practice of a wide range of modes, written and oral, literary and non-literary.'[68] This was a call for something very akin to CW, but now more concertedly from the inheritors of the Leavisite legacy. By this time, UEA had already set up its MA, and teachers, such as Peter Abbs at Sussex University, Anne Cluysenaar and David Craig at Lancaster University, were already incorporating CW into their teaching.

The theme, if that is the right word, of CW had been present among those working on the *Quarterly* from its first appearance in the spring of 1959. David Holbrook argued that in secondary modern schools pupils 'should spend at least a quarter of their time reading poetry, writing stories, writing plays and poetry, reading novels, having poetry and stories read to them . . . taking part in organised forms of debate, conversation and discussion . . .'.[69]

Critical Quarterly was started to fill the gap since *Scrutiny*'s demise in 1953. The first issue included poetry, creating:

'a split between the editors and some of their *Scrutiny* supporters. Tony and I had both been taught at Cambridge, and for one term had attended F. R. Leavis's practical criticism seminar. During our years at Pembroke College from 1949 onwards we had been typical of many fellow undergraduates reading English in taking little interest in contemporary verse. We read Dylan Thomas, of course, but our attitude towards new poets tended to be one of contempt. We were swayed by Leavis, whose denunciations of contemporary writers such as Auden were naturally popular with youthful, immature audiences. There was a puritanical narrowness of spirit in the Cambridge English school which led us to confine our attention exclusively to Leavis's great tradition, and which left us unresponsive to the pleasures of games with words, or to the small felicities of diction which grace even

---

[67] *Critical Quarterly*, vol. 26, nos 1 and 2 (1984).
[68] Ibid., p. 165.
[69] *Critical Quarterly*, vol. 1, no. 1 (Spring 1959), p. 61.

minor poems. Ted Hughes, also at Pembroke at this time, wisely abandoned the English Tripos after Part One, and transferred his attention
to archaeology and anthropology . . . it is a sign of the Cambridge
atmosphere that I never discovered he was writing poetry.'[70]

In 1986, Colin McCabe wrote an editorial for an issue devoted to
'some of the new work being undertaken in university departments of
English'.[71] Clearly, despite the outpost of UEA's MA in CW, imaginative
writing as a pedagogic component was a contested matter. The Subject
was still Missing:

> 'One aspect of English which is, however, totally missing from this
> collection and which is vital to the future of the subject is the question
> of creative writing and composition. If the cultural tradition is there to
> be interrogated rather than simply transmuted, it is essential that
> students should be able to participate actively in that interrogation.
> Pedagogy cannot be reduced to a question of handing on a critical atti-
> tude – that critical attitude must find form in cultural production. If
> we are to teach our students to read then we must also teach them to
> write. . . . There is no serious tradition of composition within British
> education and little creative writing which is not governed by an ethos
> of free expression; but if English is to become a seriously enabling
> subject, a discipline which can offer its students some real purchase on
> their world then both composition and creative writing must become
> central within the curriculum.'

The next issue of the journal brought fiction to join the poetry, with
Maureen Duffy as Fiction Editor.

Conclusions

The preconditions for CW's arrival in higher education in the UK were
set by the social and political transformations after the Second World
War. This chapter has traced the major intellectual changes which took
place within English itself, in its own responses to these changes, and
within its own configurations. The journey from belletristic description,
through literary criticism (a closer textual process of exegesis, evaluation

---

[70] *Critical Quarterly*, vol. 26, nos 1 and 2, (1984), pp. 7–8.
[71] *Critical Quarterly*, vol. 28, nos 1 and 2 (1986).

and interpretation), was then subject to the socially contextualising discourses of literary and cultural theory.

Throughout the 1970s and 1980s, this enabled a differently inflected return to the sporadic calls for writing instruction in UK higher education, recalling those from earlier in the century. That these calls came from different points along the spectrum of English is especially telling, and perhaps indicates how very difficult it was to establish the importance of CW, within a context of writing instruction. Despite intrepid and determined pioneering by many teachers of, and within, English, the professionalisation of CW developed gradually and unevenly.

8
Creative Writing Professionalised: Summary – the Story So Far

Creative writing's multi-origins constitute a set of variables, each of which has a role to play in influencing its current configuration in the UK. The divide between its two major, and in many ways, conflicting, ideologies, is translated into a set of pedagogic formulations which themselves derive from a number of different social, cultural and educational sources. This is one of the reasons why it is so hard to unpack and discuss. Its putative surface simplicity – as a classroom practice which simple 'teaches' students how to become professional writers – belies the complexity of its historical origins, and of its future possibilities. The following is a summary of the mapping I have so far proposed.

Composition and creative writing in the US

Compared with what happened in the US, CW has been professionalised relatively recently in the UK, with all that that implies: courses, curricula, assessment procedures, pedagogic methodologies and a literature of its own. Despite the immediate influence of the US, explicitly evident in the MA at UEA in 1970, and still a prevalent presence, the preconditions for CW were very different in the UK. This relates initially to a combination of the different configurations of English studies in the two countries, and to the UK's own social and educational histories.

As is clear from D. G. Myers' and Gerald Graff's accounts, in the US, English retained a legacy from Classics and philology in the form of Composition, Rhetoric and Writing courses, which became (and still are) compulsory for undergraduates. Two other developments were also significant: first, the employment of poets such as Robert Frost and others to teach literature at universities in the early twentieth century, and secondly, the influence of the Progressive School movement, which helped to transform approaches to teaching children, incorporating productive, imaginative writing. This latter element will be discussed further in Chapter 9.

Thus, the 'constructivist' elements which were part of Classical studies, re-formed in Composition and Rhetoric in the vernacular (English), and operated as a pedagogic bridge and rationale for instruction in writing; at first this was discursive and later, also imaginative. The *principle* of writing instruction was an integral part of the conceptualisation and pedagogy of university 'English' in the US from the very start.

Cultural intervention

It could also be argued that in part, consciously and unconsciously, the teaching of Composition and Rhetoric, and later CW, operated as contributory factors in the building of a twentieth-century American literature. This was explicitly the case at Iowa, where secular and academic worlds combined in a cultural interventionism, which aimed to encourage new, regional writing. Thus the idea that CW constituted a training for professional writers carried the force of cultural urgency, which partly fed into the incorporation of imaginative writing instruction, initially at postgraduate level.

The UK, the Missing Subject and practical criticism

In the UK, the break with Classics and philology was more decisive. While some legacies from philology remained in the teaching of early English language, the 'modern' schools of university English concentrated on literature, with no writing instruction equivalent to Composition and Rhetoric. Maverick campaigning individuals, such as Quiller-Couch in the second decade of the twentieth century, and Stephen Potter in the 1930s, called for pedagogic attention to discursive and imaginative writing, with Potter describing it as the 'Missing Subject'. The very fact of English studies' greater radicalism in the UK was ironically partly responsible for jettisoning what might have become a basis for developing some form of curricular-centred writing instruction.

Scholarly concentration, in the literary and university spheres, was on rehabilitating and preparing texts for publication and study. Finally, the exciting and complex demands of Modernist literature in the early twentieth century added to the pressures to develop new thinking, methods of study and exegesis. Codified through the work of I. A. Richards and the Leavises, this resulted in a critical language, which led to practical criticism in the UK, and New Criticism in the US.

There was, therefore, no significant formal writing instruction at university level in the UK (apart from some courses in journalism) until well after the Second World War, despite occasional individual arguments for such courses.

Autodidacticism and cultural politics

This is not, however, to suggest that writing instruction was completely absent from educational history in the UK, but rather to stress that it was incorporated in a different historical trajectory. The connections between campaigns for literacy, access to education for all children and the UK's long-term powerful nineteenth and twentieth century autodidactic and adult education traditions infused extra-academic writing activities, which in two significant periods in the twentieth century represented serious attempts to 'think' the relationship between politics and literature. The national- and cultural-political movements of the 1930s encouraged grassroots artistic activity, and the community arts movements in the 1970s and 1980s influenced writing groups by stressing the democratic right of all to have a 'voice', to write their experiences in imaginative and discursive forms. These were boosted by new technologies and the counter-cultural developments during the 1960s and 1970s: in theatre, poetry, literature, voices 'hidden from history' generated literature which situated itself outside both literary and university worlds.

Universities and new intellectual spaces

Expansion in the provision of higher education in the 1960s combined with intellectual radicalism in the 1960s and 1970s affected university English, and its wider academic contexts. The combination of inter- and multidisciplinary study, along with new intellectual and cultural interests, pushed at subject boundaries; not only in the creation of new discplines, such as Cultural Studies, but within the configuration of English itself. Literary criticism became, in some areas, a contested site, with the Arnold–Richards–Leavis axis, its canon and claims for moral centrality, under pressure, but by no means dismissed. Socio-cultural analyses, linguistics and literary theory challenged and made demands, to some stimulating, but to others threatening.

The combination of expansionism, greater disciplinary flexibility in universities, as well as ideological challenge from within, combined to create fissures and disciplinary spaces into which CW could move – though not without opposition. The important, but relatively short-lived, Verbal Arts Movement in the 1980s in the UK reached into all the parts of the subject cluster: literature, language, basic writing skills and imaginative writing. Expressing regret that the compositional aspect of Classical studies (Rhetoric) had not survived into English studies, the VAA called for a revolution in attitudes to writing instruction – discursive, skill-based and applied, and imaginative.

As in the first half of the twentieth century, other writers joined their voices to the call for writing instruction: from different vantage points, in and outside the universities, Raymond Williams, George Steiner, Colin McCabe, Jonathan Culler and Isobel Armstrong all saw the need for literary studies to contain productive textual elements, as well as interpretive/critical exegesis. Some came to their conclusions precisely because of the issues opened up by socio-political and cultural analysis – which came out of work in and about literary theory.

It was from within this last area of intellectual work that one of the most magnetic cultural aphorisms of our time has come: the Death of the Author, the phrase which has lent this book part of its title. It appears paradoxical that just as the existence of the author and the autonomy of the text are being denied, via the debate between literary criticism and literary theory, the notion of the 'text' as a productive practice begins to enter the academy in the form of CW.

The irony was that the conditions which enabled the arrival of CW in the academy in the UK, also contributed to what I shall argue are some irresolvable contradictions within the main ideas which inform CW and have shaped its pedagogy and practice. While literary theory did not address itself primarily to imaginative writing as a pedagogic practice, its contentious questioning of what constituted a 'literary' text, and its focus on process, through the development of linguistics, enabled such a pedagogy to begin to be 'thought' of as possible. This is profoundly ironic, given how vigorously, on the whole, CW spurns theory, or opposes its 'practice' (right-brain) to theory's intellectualism (left-brain).

Creative writing since the 1960s

The time lag of two decades, between the first MA at UEA in 1970, and the first full undergraduate degree at Middlesex University in 1990–1, bracketed the legacies from English and extra-university cultural developments outlined in previous chapters. It also introduced new elements and principles, some derived from US CW practice, and some from the UK's indigenous cultural and educational history. While the MA explicitly pursued an aim of cultural intervention at the 'top', as it were – in terms of the training of high-art writers who would boost the contemporary canon – other, more generic, traces were also evident.

Writing instruction based on the principles of democratising access to producing 'literature' was divided between its development as a skills-based training in US Composition, and a more highly politicised movement in the UK. From these two diverse sources, along with the cultural interventionism at the 'top' (i.e., academic training to produce professional writers), came the claims to pedagogic uniqueness for CW, in the form of the workshop. While it would seem that the calls of such as Quiller-Couch, Potter, the VAA, McCabe and many others have finally been answered in glorious variety, the present is no less complex than the past, and has produced new isses and contradictions.

Developments in CW in the US since the Second World War helped to consolidate the CW pedagogy which currently drives its expansion, as well as its varied, and often contradictory aims – those summarised in the Introduction. These will be examined, analysed and evaluated in the following chapters. Underpinning the post-1960s development of CW is one more important element, which has both a historical and a contemporary dimension: creativity and play.

9
Play and Pedagogy: Creativity and Creative Writing

Progressive education

D. G. Myers attributed the first serious use of the phrase 'creative writing' to a course of study dating from the mid-1920s, and the work of Hughes Mearns. The latter's book *Creative Youth* was an enthusiastic and prose-lytising anthology collected from five years' work with American high school pupils, between 1920 and 1925.[1]

Mearns assured his readers that 'We are not primarily interested in making poets or even in making writers.'[2] Despite this, he insisted that his teaching produced 'quality' writing: 'Judges have assured us that the poems in this volume had merit.'[3] While there is no doubt at all that Mearns was serious about the democratising potential of creativity for all pupils, part of his account of teaching presages some of the contradictory features of university CW. While teachers did not dictate to the pupils what and how they should write, corrective 'criticism' was pedagogically inbuilt: 'We never praised outright until we found the superior thing, be it an idea, a line, or a completed verse.'[4] One girl was told her poem was 'bad', making her quite miserable; whereupon she went off and wrote a better poem.[5] The ends apparently justified the means. Along with fun and parties and reading aloud, there was 'the bitter struggle of writing and rewriting'.[6]

---

[1] Doubleday, 1930, p. ix (first published in 1925).
[2] Ibid., p. 2.
[3] Ibid.
[4] Ibid., p. 26.
[5] Ibid., pp. 13–14.
[6] Ibid., p. 28.

Bedales, Dartington and Summerhill

By the 1920s there were also a number of progressive/experimental schools in the UK, including Dartington Hall in Devon and Summerhill in Suffolk. These independent, fee-paying schools were preceded by Bedales, set up in 1893 by John Haden Bradley. He, his wife and other like-minded teachers believed passionately in co-education, though it took five years before girls joined the boys at the school. Social and lifestyle radicalism marked the Badleys' approach, particularly in their connections with the Fellowship of the New Life, started in 1883 with 'a cherished purpose to establish self-supporting communities based on manual work, the eventual purpose of which was to show how society would be reconstructed'.[7]

Bedales' historians, Wake and Denton, claimed that 'Bedales was perhaps the first important independent school to appoint someone to think out and develop in practice, a whole programme for the school, that was to include speech and drama.'[8] Arnold Dolmetsch, the indefatigable enthusiast for the revival of 'early music' (from the medieval to the 'classical' era), was a regular visitor. Dolmetsch made reproduction early instruments, helped to introduce the recorder into schools, and conducted an orchestra at Bedales well into the 1920s. A healthy outdoor life was promoted, along with woodwork, metalwork, bookbinding and weaving. Poets W. B. Yeats and Walter de la Mare came to read their work to the pupils.

Mrs Badley took responsibility for the girls' education: 'Girls were to wear a loose blouse, cloth knickers and skirt (no stays of course) and for active exercise a "gymnastic" costume. Mrs Badley saw all girls before they left and, over a delightful tea, urged them to work ceaselessly for women's rights, not to marry the first man who asked them and never to wear corsets.'[9] The school developed methods of classroom teaching based on allowing children to learn, each at their individual pace.

The Elmhirsts took over Dartington Hall, in Devon, with two aims: the first was to revive the fortunes of the Dartington Estate, after the erosion of agricultural labour before 1914, by establishing farming, horticulture, textiles and cider as viable economic enterprises. The second plan was to start a co-educational boarding school, which opened for business in 1926.

---

[7] Roy Wake and Pennie Denton, *Bedales School: The First Hundred Years* (Haggerston Press, 1993), p. 34.

[8] Ibid., p. 82.

[9] Ibid., p. 47.

With so many enterprises, children could participate in all kinds of practical work. In the spirit of the Arts and Crafts Movement, 'the arts were recognised, from the beginning, as the most powerful and universal of all forces in education. Chiefly there was the belief that everyone should be given an opportunity and help to appreciate and participate in the arts, *whatever their social and intellectual understanding.* . . . Members of the Estate were early encouraged to attend the local evening institute in Totnes, Workers' Education Association lectures. . . .'[10] In its early years, drama was the foregrounded art form encouraged at the school, with plays produced by teachers, helped by professional puppeteers, dancers, painters, actors and musicians. Bernard Leach, the potter, joined the staff in 1932.

Summerhill, founded by A. S. Neill in 1921, in Germany, settled at Leiston, in Suffolk, in 1927. Like Bedales and Dartington, Summerhill taught conventional school subjects alongside craft – pottery, woodwork and metalwork, as well as art, music and drama; pupils attended lessons voluntarily. Pupils wrote and produced the plays, and made costumes and sets. The school was/is still run on self-government lines, with weekly School Meetings, each person (pupil and staff) having one vote: 'Education should produce children who are at once individuals and community persons, and self-government without doubt does this.'[11] In its early days the press called Summerhill a 'Go-as-you-please' school. Its basic principle was 'to make the school fit the child',[12] rather than the other way round.

All three independent (private) boarding schools combined degrees of self-government with child-centred education; this in turn combined the arts and sciences with practical work, in a wider idealism of creating more responsible citizens for the future, following the devastations of the First World War. Play and self-discovery through creativity as a means to learning were an integral part of this process. Where 'creative writing' as such had a place, it was strictly in relation to drama, and group performance.

The play's the thing

H. Caldwell Cook, teacher at the Perse School (where both E. M. W. Tillyard and F. R. Leavis studied), took a more explicit writing-centred

---

10 Victor Bonham-Carter, with William Burnlee Curry, *Dartington Hall: the Formative Years 1925–1975* by (The Exmoor Press, 1970), p. 53. First published 1958
11 *Summerhill* by A. S. Neill (Penguin, 1972), p. 11. First published in 1962.
12 Ibid., p. 20.

approach. His book *The Play-Way: An Essay in Educational Method*,[13] developed articles he had written in 1914, and published in *The New Age* magazine. Cook formulated a theory of learning based on play. Observing the way children negotiated their way through infanthood, Cook took up ideas being developed on the continent and in the US: 'The natural means of study in youth is play. . . . A natural education is by practice, by doing things, and not by instruction. . . . And telling can only be the servant of trying, not its substitute.'[14]

Completed during the First World War, *The Play Way* included Cook's strong convictions about the kind of citizen this method could produce for the future: 'A social revolution of some kind will be necessary in England after the declaration of peace on the continent; for, even supposing some fair principle established by force of arms, it has still to be wrought into a living practice by right education and good government.'[15] Cook was reacting against regimented structures of education, as well as military-style training in some boys' semi-monastic public schools. He wrote that the classroom belongs to the boys; it is not 'a sanctum nor a penitentiary'.[16]

Fitting the school to the child, according to Cook, resulted in an enthusiasm for play (and learning), shared between teacher and pupil, and realised through original writing: 'the boys must themselves come forth as poets'.[17] His focus on learning through 'doing' was full of conviction: 'As a playmaster I know it is more practical to start the whole miracle with the one word "Make". You must fall straight away upon the actual work, and you will find out what you are doing as you go along. More and more you feel what you ought to do, and now and then, if you are lucky, you manage to do it.'[18]

Learning through making (play), doing it oneself, rather than studying what others have done, was the informing principle. There were, however, some unresolved pedagogic contradictions. Early in the book he exploded: 'Why this everlasting slavery to books?'[19] While he recommended reading Shakespeare out loud, and using Grimm's fairy tales and English ballads, this was only as spurs for the boys' writing. He published a number of volumes of children's prose, poetry and drama, called the

---

[13] Heinemann, 1917.
[14] Ibid., p. 1.
[15] Ibid., p. viii.
[16] Ibid., p. 23.
[17] Ibid., p. 16.
[18] Ibid., p. 20.
[19] Ibid., p. 8.

'Perse Playbooks', to demonstrate the proof of the creative pudding. Cook taught in an all-boys school – cautioning: 'I cannot safely include girls in any statement I make, for I have had no experience of teaching them.'[20]

Marjorie Hourd, on the other hand, asserted that her approach in all-girls' schools, was just as valid for boys.[21] For purely pragmatic reasons, she wrote, she used 'the feminine pronoun' almost throughout her book – making her an unwitting precursor of feminist critiques of the ubiquitous male pronoun. Her book was published in 1949, after the Second World War. In her teaching the activity (the verb) of playing became the object (the noun) of the play, the staged and performed drama. She routinely included 'dramatic play, play-writing and play-acting'.[22]

Her account of teaching was full of enthusiasm, and conviction (unlike Cook), that books were, indeed, the way to productive writing-play: 'At the age of eight or nine children are ready to explore the world of books and they need a great deal of material.'[23] She used the *Iliad*, the legends of King Arthur, *King Lear*, and lots of Shakespeare, consciously combining literary stimuli for the children, with a grounding for literary understanding:

'If . . . we put Shakespeare into the hands of children under fourteen, we shall be disappointed if we expect them to explain his meaning to us . . . it is for this reason that it is more profitable at this stage for the child to become the playwright than the critic – the active participant in a creative process than the passive recipient of meanings interpreted directly by the teacher.'[24]

For Hourd too there were larger aims: the purpose of arts-based teaching, she wrote, is to help produce 'better persons and better societies' (a quotation taken from Herbert Read's influential book *Education Through Art*).[25] She was convinced that 'learning through doing' produced knowledge. This involved a progressive process of 'knowing and not knowing, knowing that you know or do not know, and lastly being able to explain the knowledge or lack of it'.[26]

---

[20] Ibid., p. 13.

[21] *The Education of the Poetic Spirit* (Heinemann, 1962, first published in 1949).

[22] Ibid., p. 23.

[23] Ibid., p. 28.

[24] Ibid., p. 62.

[25] Faber, 1943.

[26] Hourd, p. 111.

Cook and Hourd were self-conscious campaigners; their books designed to encourage other teachers. By recouping the idea of 'play' as more than mere childish behaviour, as embodying ways in which children explore and come to know more about their relationship with the world, teachers could develop and incorporate forms of play, elevating them to a pedagogic principle.

These ideas infused primary school teaching after the Second World War, where young children were inducted into the formalities of learning via organised and guided extensions of 'play'. However, during the 1960s and 1970s, notions of 'play' and 'creativity' took on more politicised and adult lifestyle resonances.

Play power

During the 1960s, the 'hippie' movement politicised the idea of play in rather different, and sometimes transgressive, ways. Playful adults doing serious things playfully became a self-conscious lifestyle protest; celebrating play as opposed to work, pitching 'The sober, violent, puritan, Left extremists, versus the laughing, loving, lazy, fun-powder plotters'.[27] Richard Neville's book *Play Power* was an account of an idealist (and idealistic) notion of childplay adopted by young adults.

Neville's book opened with a poem by D. H. Lawrence, the first line of which is 'If you make a revolution, make it for fun'. Such serious play came up against the law, when it championed free expression in print and argued for the drug laws to be repealed. The magazine which Neville co-edited, *Oz*, was the subject of one of the show trials of that era, in 1971, 'the longest obscenity trial in history', according to its chronicler, Tony Palmer.[28]

Thus, while the post-war educational politics of creativity were channelled into state primary schools, the adult politics of play demonstrated – however briefly – that they could be a radical and disruptive cultural force.

Lifestyle creativity

At the personal, individual level, the notion of playful creativity became part of self-help literature. Tony Buzan claimed that 'it now seems we use even less than one percent of our brain capacity', arguing that we all

---

[27] Richard Neville, *Play Power* (Granada, 1973), p. 207 (first published 1970).
[28] *The Trials of Oz* (Blond & Briggs, 1971).

have untapped potential. Drawing on research into the supposed neuro-physical bases of thought activity, he concluded that: 'The creative brain is generally left out of education. Any activity which involves imagination, colour, rhythm or form has been traditionally frowned upon as less intelligent.'[29] While Buzan wrote about the importance of linking 'right brain' activities – images, rhythm, colour, day dreaming – with 'left brain' activities – words, numbers, logic analysis – his campaigning stress was very largely on the former. He recommended developing creativity with a 'Mind Map', eschewing the organisation of thoughts into sentence or list form. The argument was that if we break with the normative rules of pedagogy and utilise right-brain features (rhythm, colour, etc.), we not only learn better (i.e. observe the rules), but we enhance our mind's potential, and come within reach of happiness.

Ironically, however, while Buzan appeared to celebrate a generic creativity within everyone's reach, his argument was 'proven' by an appeal to the exceptional, rather than the ordinary, achievement. Einstein apparently 'discovered' the theory of relativity on a summer hillside. By privileging this one moment in Einstein's life (right-brain revelation) over the fact that he spent years in the laboratory/library (left-brain labour), the carrot of democratised creativity was 'proven'. The genius with exceptional individual achievement, privileged the mysterious and unpredictable. It's the so-called 'right brain' which carries off the prizes. This is seductive, while simultaneously putting the goal out of reach: there can only be one Einstein. Left-brain activity (thinking and logic) are diminished; discursive uses of language inferiorised.

The glimpses of ambiguity in this argument echo the contradiction within part of Mearns' democratising philosophy: 'Poetry, an outward expression of instinctive insight, must be summoned from the vasty deep of our mysterious selves. Therefore, it cannot be taught; indeed, it cannot even be summoned; it may only be permitted.'[30] These conceptual ambiguities are carried through into CW, via the vexed and over-determined notions which underlie creativity.

Creativity: from extraordinary to ordinary

Creative writing may now be the proud title of the newest arts discipline in the academy. However, creativity, the faculty which enables the

---

[29] *Make the Most of Your Mind* (Pan, 1988), p. 121.
[30] Mearns, p. 28.

particular (literary) form of the discipline, has also become one of the most catch-all terms of our time, covering both ends of the artistic/productive spectrum. In his introduction to a collection of interviews with arts practitioners, John Tusa commented wryly that '"Creative", "creation", "creativity" are some of the most overused and ultimately debased words in the language. Stripped of any significance by a generation of bureaucrats, civil servants, managers and politicians, lazily used as political margarine to spread approvingly and inclusively over any activity with a non-material element to it, the word "creative" has become almost unusable.'[31]

Raymond Williams' potted history of the word 'Creative' traced its theological roots, from God as the prime Creator, through into the sixteenth century to mean 'present or future making'; in the eighteenth century, 'create' and 'creation . . . acquired a conscious association with art, which was itself changing in a complementary direction'. The term 'creative' as applied at first just to art, became in the twentieth century 'a general name for the faculty' to which it refers.[32] Williams concluded:

> 'This is clearly an important and significant history, and in its emphasis on human capacity, the term has become steadily more important. But there is an obvious difficulty. The word puts a necessary stress on originality and innovation, and . . . we can see that these are not trivial claims. Indeed, we try to clarify this by distinguishing between innovation and novelty, though novelty has both serious and trivial senses. The difficulty arises when a word once intended, and often still intended, to embody a high and serious claim, becomes so conventional, as a description of certain general kinds of activity, that it is applied to practices for which, in the absence of the convention, nobody would think of making such claims. Thus any imitative or stereotyped literary work can be called, by convention creative writing, and advertising copywriters officially describe themselves as creative.'[33]

As the twentieth century came to an end, this more functional use of the term became the emblem of activities far beyond those of the arts, as Rob Pope observed: 'Creativity is needed, it is insisted, to meet the challenge of accelerating changes of an unprecedented magnitude; and the

---

[31] John Tusa, in *John Tusa on Creativity* (Methuen), pp. 5–6.

[32] *Keywords* (Picador, 1976), p. 73.

[33] Ibid., pp. 73–4.

key areas of both change and challenge are those of scientific discovery, technical invention, commercial competition and military rivalry.'[34]

Conclusions: bracketing creativity

Today's buzzword use of 'creativity' cloaks its important history, particularly in its journey into primary-school teaching, via the Progressive Schools movement, here and in the US. In the UK, original writing by the children, largely channelled into drama, became embedded as part of changing philosophies of education. 'Creativity' was an epistemological instrument. In its appropriation as a generic mental faculty in everyday life, creativity became the means whereby right-brain activities were privileged above left-brain activities as the means to self-fulfilment, and even happiness. Child-centred learning, which privileged 'play' and activities associated with the arts, was transformed into a post-1960s radical force which often denied the attributes commonly associated with so-called left-brain activities: logical, discursive intellectual, 'grown-up' processes.

As we shall see, these developments are reasserted within CW itself: the uneasy balance between creativity as the exceptional, or as the ordinary, potential in all of us. The constant slippage between the two poles becomes institutionally significant in the ways it is incorporated into the fundamental principles of CW pedagogy, and its literatures.

---

[34] *Creativity: Theory, History and Practice* (Routledge, 2005), p. 19.

10
Creative Writing: a Literature of its Own

Like all branches of knowledge and intellectual endeavour, CW has a literature of its own. Of course, there have been many texts about writers and writings, 'poetics' texts, providing models and rubrics of what is considered proper to literature at the time. However, the modern CW text has emerged specifically in relation to its appearance as a subject in the academy, the texts functioning also as self-help books for those outside academia. These texts, consciously and immanently, provide the clearest source for the theorisation of CW's underlying principles.

The professional writer

The creative writing 'how-to' handbook dates back to the turn of the twentieth century, the arrival of the professional writer and the need for texts for writing instruction in English: 'The census returns for 1881 listed some 3,400 authors, editors and journalists. In 1891 there were nearly 6,000; in 1901, around 11,000; in 1911, nearly 14,000. At the same time there was an equally rapid increase in the number of new outlets available to writers. Magazines and periodicals sprouted up as never before in the 1880s and 1890s, while by the end of the century the London Directory contained the names of over four hundred separate publishing houses.'[1]

The idea of literature as a profession challenged the construct of the gentleman–scholar–writer. While such belles-lettristes were widely

---

[1] *The Rise and Fall of the Man of Letters* by John Gross (Penguin Books, 1973), p. 220. First published in 1969.

respected, their semi-amateur status was a defining condition of their work. As John Gross observed, journalism could be a career, but literature was still seen as a vocation. The idea that writing fiction or poetry might be respectable and earn money, was shocking. Walter Besant, writer and campaigner, gave a lecture at the Royal Institution in 1884, pointing out that 'the claim that a great novelist should be considered to occupy the same level as a great musician, a great painter, or a great poet, would appear at first a thing ludicrous and even painful'.[2] However, in defence of the professional writer, he argued that 'It is now well known that a respectable man of letters may command an income and a position quite equal to those of the average lawyer or doctor. It is also well known that one who rises to the top may enjoy as much social consideration as a Bishop and as good an income.'[3]

The Society of Authors and writers' rights

Walter Besant was one of the founders of the Society of Authors in 1884; its first President was Lord Tennyson. Besant was Chairman of the (Management) Committee for the first four years, and edited the Society's publication, *Author*, for the first seven years. In 1899 the Society had 1500 members; it now has over 8000 members. The Writers' Guild of Great Britain, the other major professional organisation for writers in the UK, was founded in 1958–9, incorporating members of the Screenwriters' Association, formed in 1937. The Royal Society of Literature was founded in 1820 by George IV to 'reward literary merit and excite literary talent', and the worldwide association of writers, International PEN, was set up in 1921. The National Union of Journalists (NUJ) was established in 1907, the same year that John Churton Collins' School of Journalism at Birmingham began. The NUJ currently has around 35,000 members.

Copyright

With the professionalisation of the writer, copyright law was modified. The Royal Licensing Act of 1662 had been the first serious attempt to regulate the book trade – not in defence of writers, but to protect print-

---

[2] Walter Besant and Henry James, *The Art of Fiction* (Algonquin Press, 1900), p. 5.
[3] Walter Besant, *The Pen and the Book* (Thomas Burleigh, 1899), pp. vi–vii.

ers against piracy (i.e. anyone printing/publishing any written text they wanted). According to G. H. Thring, the Secretary of the Society of Authors, 'This Act . . . was brought in as a restraint on free trade, and, with this end in view, it forbade the printing of any book unless first licensed and entered in the register of Stationers' Company. It forbade the printing of books contrary to the doctrine of the Church or opposed to the established government. . . . The Act finally forbade any person from printing or importing, without the consent of the owner, any book which any person had the sole right to print by virtue of letters patent or entry on the register of Stationers' Company.'[4]

The first Copyright Act to validate the author's claim to copyright in, and control over, his/her published work became an Act of Parliament in 1709–10, and is known as the Statute of Anne. This was a fixed term of protection (initially 14 years) for published work. Later, this extended to 50 years after the author's death, and is now 70 years after the death (physical, and neither figurative nor Barthesian) of the author, or 50 years for posthumous publications.

Internationally, things were more anarchic. From the mid-1870s, measures were taken to rationalise international copyright. This culminated in the International Copyright Act of 1886–7, which followed the Berne Convention for the Protection of Literary and Artistic Works. In 1891 the American Copyright Bill became law, so that UK authors could retain copyright in work published in the US. The UK Copyright Act of 1911 incorporated sound recordings, and the Copyright Act of 1956 (note the proximity of this date in relation to the founding of the Writers' Guild) brought new technological developments, such as film and broadcast material, under the copyright umbrella.

Walter Besant and Henry James

Besant's fiery treatise *The Pen and the Book* was published in the rapidly changing literary climate at the turn of the twentieth century. It was 'written for the instruction and the guidance of those young persons, of whom there are now many thousands, who are thinking of the Literary Life',[5] and prompted by a recent event: 'In the summer of this year (1898) the Committee of the Publishers' Association issued a set of draft

---

[4] Ibid., 1899, p. 273.
[5] Ibid., p. v.

agreements in which it was clearly shown that they intended to claim the whole of literary property for themselves as their pretended right.'[6]

Besant's advice was grounded in a determination to demystify the publishing process, so that would-be (and already) professional writers could protect their rights to earnings, and be armed with information to defend themselves against predatory publishers: 'the fact remains that if any body of men, rich or poor, are allowed the power of cheating, cooking accounts, overstating charges, or of inventing charges with impunity, they will cheat, cook accounts, overstate charges, and invent charges. That is, most of them will. . . . They know, and they must know, that they are THIEVING.'[7] (Besant's capitals.)

The book explains the concept of 'literary property', advocating fairer contracts between writers and publishers, and advising any writers unsure of their ground to consult one of the new breed of professional mediators, literary agents. Besant provided details of the costs of setting up type, binding, corrections, advertising; he recommended a graduated royalty system, and warned against rapacious publishers who tried to get the writer to pay some – if not all – of these costs.

The rest of the book consists of writerly comment and advice, warning at the outset, with what becomes one of the delimiting cornerstones of CW pedagogy, that 'In treating of Imaginative Literature one thing is most certain that, without the gift, it cannot be taught.'[8] This appeal to the still-current notion of the Romantic talent/genius, is balanced by the assertion that writing is hard work:

> 'It is a life of study: a life of imagination: a life of meditation: a life of observation: a life of research: in every case accompanied by, and carried on for, the production of Literature. . . . The popular idea is that poems, plays, essays, Romances, stories are the gifts of Fortune, and come by chance without any effort on the part of the writer. That is a common belief and a common error. . . . Prepare for serious work . . . you must be prepared to write and to rewrite, if necessary, with patience, until you have produced your effect.'[9]

Much of his practical advice could easily find a place in today's 'how-to' books: he advocated writing something every day, taking notes 'upon

---

[6] Ibid., p. 191.
[7] Ibid., p. 201.
[8] Ibid., p. 73.
[9] Ibid., pp. 39–40.

returning home after a walk',[10] presenting a relatively simple notion of fiction as mimesis/realism, and advocating personal experience as the key: 'everything in Fiction which is invented and is not the result of personal experience and observation is worthless . . . the characters must be real, and such as might be met with in actual life, or, at least, the natural developments of such people as any of us might meet; their actions must be natural and consistent; the conditions of place, of manners, and of thought must be drawn from personal observation'.[11]

Besant's Royal Institution lecture was published in *The Art of Fiction* in 1900, together with a riposte by Henry James.[12] Despite the Romantic caveat, Besant was strongly in favour of teaching imaginative writing: 'How can that be an art, they might ask, which has no lecturers or teachers, no school or college or academy, no recognised rules, no text-books, and is not taught in any University. . . . Clearly, therefore, they would go on to argue, such art as is required for the making and telling of a story can and must be mastered without study, because no materials exist for the student's use . . . .anyone, they think, can write a novel; therefore, why not sit down and write one?'[13] He argued for literature to be put on a par with the other arts, claiming it as 'an art in every way worthy to be called the sister and the equal of the arts of Painting, Sculpture, Music and Poetry . . . an art which, like them, is governed and directed by general laws; and that these laws may be laid down and taught with as much precision and exactness as the laws of harmony, perspective and proportion'.[14]

Henry James's response was courteous and elegant, with a more sophisticated conceptual (nay, theoretical, even) approach. He challenged the idea that there is any simple one-to-one mimetic relationship between life and literature: 'The only reason for the existence of a novel is that it *does* compete with life.' It is '. . . excellent and inconclusive to say that one must write from experience; to our supositious aspirant such a declaration might savour of mockery. What kind of experience is intended, and where does it begin and end? Experience is never limited and it is never complete. . . . The power to guess the unseen, from the seen, to trace the implication of things, to judge the whole piece by the pattern, the condition of feeling life, in general, so completely that you are well on your way to knowing any particular corner of it. . . .'[15]

---

[10] Ibid., p. 63.
[11] Ibid., p. 87.
[12] The Algonquin Press, 1900.
[13] Ibid., p. 8.
[14] Ibid., p. 3.
[15] Ibid., p. 54 and pp. 64–5.

James elaborated further on the constructedness of the fictional 'world', countering the idea that 'character' could be equated with 'real people': 'What is character but the determination of incident? What is incident but the illustration of character?'[16] Unlike Besant, James was not convinced that writing could be taught: the writer's 'manner is his secret, not necessarily a deliberate one. He cannot disclose it, as a general thing, if he would; he would be at a loss to teach it to others.'[17]

Writing and the university: Quiller-Couch and criticism

In 1913–14 Sir Arthur Quiller-Couch gave twelve lectures, which were first published in 1916, as *On the Art of Writing*.[18] Between 1916 and 1921, the book was reprinted five times, with six further printings, in a pocket edition, between 1923 and 1933. The lectures inaugurated Quiller-Couch's post as King Edward VII Professor of English Literature, and were given even before Cambridge made its decision to establish the English Tripos in 1917 (the first examinations were taken in 1919).

The lectures are enthusiastic and scholarly; packed with literary knowledge, extensive quotations, close and detailed textual reading.

The Preface to the published lectures was decisive:

'Literature is not a mere Science, to be studied; but an ART, to be practised. . . . I propose to you that, English Literature being (as we agreed) an art, with a living and therefore improvable language for its vehicle, a part – and in no small part – of our business is to *practise it*. Yes, I seriously propose to you that here in Cambridge we *practise writing*: that we practise it not only for our own improvement, but to make, or at least to try to make, appropriate perspicuous, accurate, persuasive writing a recognisable hall-mark of anything turned out by our English School. By all means let us study the great writers of the past for their own sakes; but let us study them for our guidance; that we, in our turn, having (it is to be hoped) something to say in our span of time, say it worthily.'[19]

So confident was he, that he predicted, with boundless optimism, that 'this our neglect to practise good writing as the constant auxiliary

---

[16] Ibid., p. 69.
[17] Ibid., p. 61.
[18] Cambridge University Press.
[19] Ibid., p. 2.

of an Englishman's education, would be amazing to you seated here today as it will be starkly incredible to the future historian of our times'.[20]

Quiller-Couch argued that in modern languages, Greek and Latin, and in painting, students were expected to compose/produce as an intrinsic part of learning. This argument had a functional urgency, since as universities increasingly adopted English as the *lingua franca* in all disciplines, science students were no longer required to write up their work in Latin, and needed competence in written English.

In the fourth lecture Quiller-Couch argued for a cross-genre approach: 'trying to discover what this or that form of it accomplishes with ease and what with difficulty, and why verse can do one thing and prose another . . .'.[21] He took a block of instructions from the students' handbook, split the lines up and re-wrote the paragraph as a poem (anticipating experiments by Stanley Fish and others). Over-ambitiously, perhaps, he enthused that it was possible to re-enter the author's original compositional procedures: 'I want us to be seeking all the time *how it is done*; to hunt out the principles on which the great artists wrought; to face, to rationalise the difficulties by which they were confronted, and learn how they overcame the particular obstacle.'[22]

Quiller-Couch went beyond polemic, to codify craft-specific advice, for what he considered consensus on 'good' writing, avoiding jargon, cliché and metonymy:

'to write Jargon is to be perpetually shuffling around in the fog and cotton-wool of abstract terms. . . . The first virtue, the touchstone of a masculine style [*sic*], is its use of the active verb and the concrete noun . . . take Shakespeare. I wager you that no writer of English so constantly chooses the concrete word, in phrase after phrase, forcing you to touch and see. No writer so insistently teaches the general through the particular.'[23]

Apart from the persuasive appeal to Shakespeare as a model, Quiller-Couch elaborated a qualified theory of mimesis, along with an acknowledgement of ways in which language is both a representation of thought, and itself structures thought:

---

[20] Ibid., p. 3.
[21] Ibid., p. 15.
[22] Ibid., p. 23.
[23] Ibid., p. 27.

'So long as you prefer abstract words, which express other men's summarised concepts of things, to concrete ones which lie as near as can be reached to things themselves and are the first-hand material for your thoughts, you will remain, at the best, writers at second-hand. If your language be Jargon, your intellect, if not your whole character, will almost certainly correspond. Where your mind should go straight, it will dodge. . . .

We laid down certain rules to help us in the way of straight Prose:
(1) *always always prefer the concrete word to the abstract.*
(2) *almost always prefer the direct word to the circumlocution.*
(3) *Generally, use transitive verbs, that strike their object; and use them in the active voice, eschewing the stationary passive, with its little auxiliary* its *and* was's, *and its participles getting into the light of your adjectives, which should be few. For, as a rough law, by his use of the straight verb and by his economy of adjectives you can tell a man's style if it be masculine or neuter, writing or 'composition'.*
(4) *Prefer the short word to the long.*
(5) *Prefer the Saxon word to the Romance.*[24] (His italics.)

It was not merely because he was so ahead of his time that Quiller-Couch's advocacy of teaching writing was not seen through. E. M. W. Tillyard commented that

'the chief sin of the Cambridge English School is that it has never insisted on a high enough standard in the writing of English.'[25]

However, Quiller-Couch's fervour was not entirely wasted. Tillyard referred intriguingly to

'the optional original composition that has been a part of the English tripos since its beginning'.[26]

In fact, from its very beginnings the breadth and range of the English Tripos was quite extraordinary. From 1919, when the subject was first examined, there were questions every year about the position and representation of women in literature and questions on living poets. In the papers on early English literature, students were expected to answer questions on architecture, city planning, monasteries, Elizabethan song-

---

[24] Ibid., p. 38.
[25] E. M. W. Tillyard, *The Muse Unchained* (Bowes & Bowes, 1958), pp. 91–2.
[26] Ibid., p. 96.

books and the history of printing. Both Part I and Part II papers from 1929 onwards (when it was possible to take English as a single honours degree) occasionally included essay questions demanding an imaginative take. In 1926 students could write an imaginary, additional chapter of Aristotle's *Poetics*, on the use of comic relief. In 1930 students could choose to write an imaginary dialogue between Wordsworth and Johnson on poetic diction, or a dialogue debating Browning's comments on genius.

Early handbooks in America: Adele Bildersee

Writing instruction books were initially generated in the US as textbooks for Composition and Rhetoric. From the mid-1920s and through the 1930s CW handbooks began appearing, many by women, who were still often excluded from official university teaching.

In 1927, Adele Bildersee published *Imaginative Writing*.[27] She distinguished between Composition and imaginative writing, beginning (predictably) with the unteachable: 'the art of writing cannot be taught; it can only be learned . . . accordingly the book has as its center, not in the subject matter to be taught, but in the students to be reached'.[28] Like Besant, she asserted that all writing is hard work: 'Is it not true of every other art? Is it not true of every form of skill in whatever field it is displayed?'[29]

Like Besant, she gave advice about taking notes, developing observation, thinking about perceptions based on the senses, eschewing the abstract in favour of the concrete, avoiding cliché and using active verbs. Bildersee's method is highly systematic; the book worked through the process of writing a story, building each element chapter by chapter. The influence of Composition was reflected in sections on building sentences, and various ways in which paragraphs can be linked – dovetailing language-structuring skills with imaginative tasks and issues. As illustration of the variety of ways fiction was constructed, she offered careful analyses of passages of fiction. She discussed figurative language, provided a structural analysis of narrative movement, and it is not till over half way through the book that she suggested that the student should now begin to write his/her own story.

---

[27] D. C. Heath & Co.
[28] Ibid., p. ix.
[29] Ibid., p. 3

'How-to' books after the Second World War: R. V. Cassill

The tone and attitude of CW books in the expansionist climate after the Second World War changed significantly. It confirms some of the 'principles' floated earlier in the century, codifying them in a series of more contemporary tenets (mantras, one might even call them). This new tone was presaged in the 1930s, in the US, by Dorothea Brande, whose influential book *Becoming a Writer* is discussed in more detail in the next chapter. In 1962, *Writing Fiction*, by R. V. Cassill, was published.[30] Cassill was a graduate of the Iowa Writers' Workshop and one of the founders of the American Association of Writing Programs in 1967. Apart from the 'talent can't be taught' mantra, his book has recognisable precepts on offer: show, don't tell; reading as a writer; the 'self' and personal experience as the first and best sources of a writer's material. Such precepts are not offered for the first time, but they are 'naturalised' explicitly and implicitly in pretty well all the British and American CW texts of subsequent decades. Here, we find, alongside the above precepts, is a resistance to knowledge acquired outside the 'self', a questionable attitude to reading, and continuous stress on self-expression. Literature may be an imitation of life, but it is, above all, an imitation or representation of the self:

> 'as soon as we have learned something about our craft we are tempted to turn from concentration on our own experiences to the public world of great events – to write about spies and congressmen. But the first commandment is to go back stubbornly to our own field. . . . In the long run the reward for this may only be that the writer will discover who he truly is.'[31]

Cassill appears to acknowledge the complexity of the writing process: 'Of course language is all there is in a story. Language is the material that is arranged and fitted into the author's design. . . . It should never be assumed that the voice in any first person story is the author's own voice.'[32] However, he still pins the imperative of writing the 'self' to a mimetic goal: 'we want to – in the final analysis we have to – imitate life'.[33]

---

[30] Pocket Books, 1962.
[31] Ibid., p. 23.
[32] Ibid., pp. 215–16.
[33] Ibid., pp. 203–4.

Inevitably, this leads to uncertainty about the self, and a concomitant fear of the blank page – 'But begin you must',[34] while writing about oneself brings dangers: 'the choice of becoming a writer is the choice to face some fears, including the fear of being a hollow person, a dull person with nothing to say'.[35]

Cassill advocates reading, but only to a limited extent: 'If he has time and opportunity, a young writer ought to supplement his writing program with classes in the analysis of contemporary fiction.'[36] As a gesture towards this, after the first sixty pages, nearly all the rest of the book is taken up by six complete exemplary stories for students to read and use as models, although how this is to be done is not explained. This inclusion of *soi-disant* model exemplars is a more consistent feature of today's American CW books than those of the UK. Quite how they are meant to operate as models for writing is unclear; it might be mimetic – i.e. how to write like Raymond Carver – but the complexity of this is not developed.

Conclusions

The professionalisation of the literary industries at the end of the nine-teenth century produced the modern professional writer, in the UK and in the US. In combination with the arrival of English as an acknowl-edged subject, some attention was given to teaching/learning writing. In the UK, apart from Besant, James and Quiller-Couch, there was Oscar Wilde's *The Critic as Artist* (1891), a witty Socratic night-time dialogue between two gentlemen, and Arnold Bennett's *The Author's Craft* (1914). These were directed to the would-be 'gentleman' writer, not to the university student.

Running as an unquestioned motif through all the books is the firm conviction that to write fiction at all, it is necessary to have talent, a gift, perhaps even genius. This is seen as simply 'there', in thrall to the Romantic notion that it is given, bestowed, mysterious, with (in a sense) the writer as little more than scribe. This, of course, creates problems when it comes to *whether* imaginative writing can be taught at all (except to those with talent); Besant and Bildersee believe it can be taught; the former because it is an art like other arts, and with its own 'laws';

---

[34] Ibid., p. 17.
[35] Ibid., p. 15.
[36] Ibid., p. 7.

Bildersee, because she is part of the new tradition of writing instruction in Composition. For them, as with Quiller-Couch, writing is an art, which can be learned and practised. For Quiller-Couch it is also a skill that crosses disciplinary boundaries.

However, *what* can be and is taught is in danger of being delimited (unteachable, or only marginally teachable), and this is a motif which is writ larger in later CW literature. The concept of 'craft' or 'skill' is offered as the possibly teachable, but on the clear understanding that it is secondary to the real thing. The terror of the blank page described by Cassill as a necessary component of CW represents the absence, or fear of absence, of talent/genius, and this too is more forcefully articulated in post-1960s CW literature. The assertion that writing is hard work, stressed in all these early CW books, becomes puzzling; as a counter to the Romantic assertion that the talent is either 'there' or not, it raises further questions about the content of this 'hard work', where it comes from, and what exactly it is that is being 'worked' or practised.

Besant and Cassill take the line which later becomes most dominant: that the best, if not the only, source of imaginative writing is personal experience and the 'self'. Henry James's questioning of this is strong, but his lone desire for complexity is somewhat undermined by the fact that he believes (a) that no writer can explain how s/he does it, and (b) that imaginative writing is, in any case, unteachable. In other words, from whatever their position, the enthusiasm for teaching CW is, even in its early stages, hedged in with bewilderment at the 'invisibility' of its primary source – there is nothing 'out there' which can be grasped; there is only the personal experience of the writer – whatever that may be – and the elusiveness of talent.

In the Besant/James discussion two opposing positions are put: for Besant, imaginative writing is based on personal experience, as expression of the self, as fundamentally mimetic (an indirect argument for realism as the desired form), taught as a professional skill, but with talent as the inaccessible imponderable. This is set against James's pre-theory assertions that literature 'competes' with, rather than reflects life, that there is an indissoluble symbiosis between character and incident, and that the essentially 'private' (i.e. inner) nature of the writer results in a questionable ability to articulate the process satisfactorily, and (effectively) the futility of trying to teach 'it'.

Quiller-Couch, however, argued for writing as a generic skill, taught to all students, spanning discursive and imaginative literature, centred on a mimetic theory of literature, and setting out a set of stylistic rubrics which have continued to operate as guidelines through the high decades of literary criticism, and into the arrival of CW. However, there is a tension between the generic benefits of writing instruction (embedded in Quiller-Couch's arguments) and the foregrounded specialness of the creative, which depends on talent, if not genius.

11
The Literature: Household Tips and Recipe Books

The term 'literature', applied to CW 'textbooks' carries a nice irony: these are metatexts about creating texts, using language to guide the construction of linguistically-determined conventions. There is a considerable body of genre-specific 'how to' books – poetry, fiction, drama, screenwriting, detective stories, science fiction, as well as journalism and autobiography (sometimes called 'life' writing in the UK, and part of Creative Non-Fiction in the US). More recently, CW compendia, called coursebooks, or workbooks, have been published.[1] These may be marketed as 'textbooks' in the conventional sense – recommended by teachers, whether or not they are used by them in the classroom, and also explicitly written for use outside courses, directly addressed to the individual reader – 'you'.

Magazines such as *Writer's News* (note the singular) and *Mslexia* aim explicitly at the aspiring professional writer. *Mslexia* was founded in 1999 in Newcastle, with funding from the National Lottery and Northern Arts, and styles itself as a 'national magazine for woman [*sic*] writers'. Both journals include news about competitions, courses, festivals, publishing opportunities, and lots of 'tips' from established (or, at the very least, published) writers. The magazines imply strongly that publication could be within anyone's reach. The term 'amateur' is rarely used in any CW publication; this is consonant with the virtually

---

[1] See *The Writer's Workbook* (note the singular possessive), ed. Jenny Newman, Edmund Cusick and Aileen La Tourette (Edward Arnold, 2000); *The Creative Writing Handbook*, ed. John Singleton and Mary Luckhurst (Macmillan, 2000); *The Road to Somewhere*, ed. Robert Graham, Helen Newall, Heather Leach and John Singleton (Palgrave Macmillan, 2005).

ubiquitous promise (caveats nothwithstanding) or lure of professional success. The thriving fields of amateur dramatics, painting and music in the UK, where people are passionately serious and enthusiastic, and may even have professional aspirations, are less fastidious about using the term 'amateur', as a technical marker of their status.

Writing as self-expression

Becoming a Writer, by Dorothea Brande, belongs chronologically in the previous chapter, but, as we shall see, it belongs ideologically with today's tradition of CW 'how-to' books. First published in 1934, it was reprinted in the 1980s, graced with an introduction by Malcolm Bradbury. Its presence on many CW reading lists gives it the status of a classic, flagging the central tenet which hovers behind virtually *all* CW teaching: 'that only part of the business of writing can ever be consciously taught. Most has to be discovered, from within.'[2] For Brande, while genius cannot be taught, there is something called 'writer's magic' which is 'teachable'.[3] Brande's book, wrote Bradbury, 'was written in Freudian times, and rightly assumes that writing is a psychological matter: at once a conscious activity and an unconscious one'.[4]

This re-rationalises the Romantic concept of genius, or its synonyms – inspiration, mystery, magic, the secret, the muse – with the post-Freudian unconscious – the invisible, the unpredictable, perhaps even the dangerous. The James/Besant divide – imaginative writing as art versus self-expression – is rearticulated in the Health Warning with which so many contemporary CW books begin. The crucial element which makes the great writer is unteachable. You either have 'it' (genius, talent, a gift) or you haven't. The ineffably desirable genius/talent continues to be intimately bound up with the individual self, and takes the form of repeated exhortations to 'write what you know', asserting that all writing comes from 'personal experience'. If this is done properly, it is implied, a route may be found to the elusive 'genius' (the writer's 'magic', as Brande put it) which might be lurking within.

Dorothea Brande remarked: 'It is a commonplace that every writer must turn to himself [*sic*] to find most of his material.'[5] Paul Magrs reit-

---

[2] Dorothea Brande, *Becoming a Writer* (Macmillan, 1983), p. 13.
[3] Ibid., p. 22.
[4] Ibid., pp. 12–13.
[5] Ibid., p. 111.

erated this some decades later by suggesting 'that it's always best if you "write about what you know"'.[6] Elsewhere he advised: 'Think about the stories you already tell about your life' as sources for fiction.[7]

Taken to its logical conclusion, this denies the potential of anything defined as outside immediate 'personal' (i.e. autobiographical) experience. According to Trevor Pateman, 'If we have never experienced profound depression . . . either in ourselves or in another, I find it hard to see how . . . we could do much more than mimic it in an artistic work, rather than express it fully.'[8] The idea that Shakespeare must have poisoned a king to write *Hamlet*, or that Agatha Christie must have been a detective and a murderer, is clearly ridiculous.

This approach is enshrined in writing exercises in the 'how-to' books, which encourage the 'beginner' to generate writing by drawing on personal, real-life experiences they have had – memories, people they know, traumatic events they have experienced, dreams and fears. Such an approach appears unproblematic – after all, this is material to which each of us has personal and unique access; the difficulty is that it over-privileges the personal and fetishes the autobiographical. Additionally, it actively *invites* the student/reader to trawl their emotions, in order to uncover and work on, and with, the most vulnerable. This makes it virtually impossible to discuss in any rational way the relationship between the 'personal' (in the sense of real events in which we have been involved), the 'inner' world of the imagination (the 'invented' rather than the experienced), and the articulation of these through the use of language in fictional conventions. Such over-individualisation of the sources denies the relationship between modes of imaginative thought and their materiality.

Underlying this is the assumption (explicit or implicit) that all fiction writing, not just autobiography, life-writing or memoir, is some form of 'confessional', or (in effect) a kind of gossip. Much reviewing, even in serious newspapers and magazines, takes this approach, 'reading' fiction as thinly disguised autobiography. Much (valid and interesting) academic scholarship meshes biographical research with a writer's fiction, in order to try and claim which real-life person or event 'inspired' the relevant fiction. In all these instances, the virtually unspoken conclusion is that the 'great' writer must be writing about a great self, privileged with unusual experiences, leaving the rest (of us) to

---

[6] *The Creative Writing Coursebook*, ed. Julia Bell and Paul Magrs (Macmillan, 2001), p. 65.

[7] Ibid., p. 41.

[8] Celia Hunt and Fiona Sampson, *The Self on the Page: Theory and Practice of Creative Writing in Personal Development* (Jessica Kingsley, 2002), p. 158.

expiate their (our) lesser life experiences through the fiction, poetry or drama of others. The quest is for the writer beneath the work, not the work itself.

There are occasional, momentarily dissenting, voices in the literature. In the Bell/Magrs volume, Nell Dunn wrote: 'It is said that all fiction is an autobiography. What we write about has to be felt and therefore experienced, but it can be experienced in the imagination and needn't be necessarily lived experience.'[9]

The self and its way of life

Such overwhelming stress on personal experience necessarily entails a focus on the individual and his/her way of life. As Brande put it, 'becoming a writer is mainly a matter of cultivating a writer's temperament'.[10] Writing, according to Julia Cameron in *The Artist's Way*, another widely recommended book, '. . . is a spiritual journey, a pilgrimage home to the self'.[11] Although there are a few practical writing exercises at the end of each of her twelve chapters, her real interest is a functional deployment of CW, as an expression of Creativity. For her, this means a vague pantheism combined with hippie mystical overtones: 'Creativity is God energy flowing through us, shaped by us, the light flowing through a crystal prism.'[12]

For Cameron there is a proto-medical dimension: 'artist brain is our creative, holistic brain . . .'.[13] We are all, to some extent, she claims, 'creatively blocked' and must 'engage in creative recovery'.[14] 'Recovery' is her key word. It is round this that the book and its 'philosophy' revolve: there are *twenty-five* index entries for different kinds of 'creative recovery', versions of which appear on *176 out of a total of just over 200 pages* (my deliberate, horrified italics).

The implication is that life is an illness or an addiction from which one must recover into and through creativity (i.e. writing) and thus be 'healed'. The book is steeped in the language of addiction recovery, with a seasoning of the Biblical/evangelical and apocaplyptic: 'In January 1978 I stopped drinking. . . . I fell upon the thorns of prose. I bled . . . I

---

[9] Bell & Magrs, op. cit., p. 79.
[10] Brande, op. cit., p. 34.
[11] *The Artist's Way: A Spiritual Path to Higher Creativity* (Pan books, 1994), p. 203.
[12] Ibid., p. 163.
[13] Ibid., p. 13.
[14] Ibid., p. xiii.

have seen blocked painters paint, broken poets speak in tongues, halt and lame and maimed writers racing through drafts.'[15] All that's missing is the 'Hallelujah' chorus. Such pretentious stuff (however genuine and traumatic the originating experience) is the kind of thing which, quite justifiably, gives CW pedagogy a bad name, presenting it as a proto-therapeutic experience, rather than a set of pedagogical imperatives.

Such weight on the individual life means that the *practice* of writing is collapsed into the 'way of life': 'Being a writer is . . . a way of seeing, thinking, being . . .'[16] According to Brande, this entails a major feat of self-development, if not maturity: 'If you can discover what you are like, if you can discover what you truly believe about most of the major matters of life, you will be able to write a story which is honest and original and unique.'[17] The logic is that if you are not able to write such a story, then you have not discovered what you are like and what you believe.

Inevitably, it is a matter of cultivating the appropriate lifestyle: 'Most writers flourish greatly,' wrote Dorothea Brande, 'on a simple healthy routine with occasional time off for gaiety.'[18] 'Creativity flourishes when we have a sense of safety and self-acceptance,' wrote Cameron.[19] 'We have to accept ourselves in order to write,' claimed Goldberg.[20] 'Let's get back to the sweetheart, that person we're going to develop and give form to inside us, whose only job is positive thought.'[21]

Cameron's book is a life-conduct manual, teaching ways to be a 'better' person, living a life of meditation and solitude. Its principles are diametrically opposed to the idea of the mad, bad, wild and suffering Romantic artist, out of control, whose genius and direct contact with an unconscious, even anti-social side of him/herself, are the precondition for great art. The uncontrolled imagination – (Dylan Thomas drunk in New York, Edith Piaf down and out on the streets of Paris; writing deriving from misery or despair) yields now to the monk or the nun, the morally pure, ascetic citizen. In this curious and convoluted way, CW manages to hold onto the unpredictability of the Muse, while offering the healing reconciliations of psychotherapy; an impossible conceptual contradiction. The gurus give and the gurus take away.

---

15 Ibid., p. xii.
16 Natalie Goldberg, *Wild Mind* (Bantam, 1990), p. xiv.
17 Brande, p. 114.
18 Ibid., p. 89.
19 Cameron, p. 42.
20 Natalie Goldberg, p. 53.
21 Ibid., p. 56.

The terror of the blank page

Such obsession with getting the right kind of self, to provide the precondition for the Muse's visit, leaves the student with the ultimate possibility that they may not possess talent or genius, and can therefore do little more than face the 'blank page' (or screen) with 'terror' – a word repeated so often in CW literature that it takes on the force of a precondition for writing. If s/he can't think of anything to put down on the page, then the self must be wanting – there must be no 'self' to 'express'. It is the self which is being judged, not the work or the working process.

To read or not to read

Again and again CW literature tells people to read, offering the revelation that to be a 'good' writer, one has to be a good reader. Natalie Goldberg coaxes, as if addressing a child who won't eat his/her greens: 'Read books. They are good for us.'[22] More acerbically (and accurately) Sara Maitland has commented that 'It is as though people who come to writing classes are escaping from, rather than moving into, reading.'[23]

That is precisely the point. With the overwhelming stress on personal experience as the source of material for imaginative writing, reading does, indeed, loom as superfluous. It is memory and emotion which are the exclusive spurs, not intellectual interest, curiosity, and the many resources (books among them) for acquiring new knowledges. In this context, the respected and respectable academic term 'research' becomes a threat to the delicate pleasures of conjuring up some personal experience, which can then, with the minimum of effort, be captured in Booker-prizeworthy cadences.

It is not enough to collapse the CW problem into the more general one that many students read too little. The corrective exhortation is treated as a special (almost religious) revelation, rather than a pedagogic necessity, as it is in other academic disciplines. In its separation of writing from reading, CW makes a claim for its individuated specialness, with CW students somehow accorded specialness above all other students of all other disciplines. While none of the literature is explicit about a return to the Arnold/Leavis trajectory, preaching the saving power of literature, it would not be too much to suggest that this is strongly implied.

---

22 Ibid., p. 43.
23 Ibid., p. 55.

CW reading lists tend to be short, used as 'background' reading, and only to a limited extent relevant to the teaching process. It is sometimes argued that reading lists should be constructed to suit each individual student; an idiosyncratic procedure, which, while it might have some specialist justification, also serves to atomise the idea of reading, and reduce the possibility of any programme of reading shared between all. Reading lists in course literature (postgraduate as well as undergraduate) rarely include literary history, criticism, theory, aesthetics. Reading is not part of the *required* work. If students don't read, one can hardly blame them. Why should they, if they have been told again and again that all writing must come from personal experience? Despite the repeated exhortations in CW books, writing is thus pedagogically separated from reading. Despite the mantra that all good writers read a lot, reading has now effectively become the new Missing Subject.

Behind this hovers the over-privileging of right-brain activity, in the interests of exercising 'creativity'. By contrast, thinking about, analysis, left-brain rationality, the excitements of intellectual inquiry, are ruled out of court. This is confirmed by the way in which non-fiction elements in assignments tend to consist of self-reflective 'commentary', rather than discursive essays/discussion of other people's writing. The 'non-creative' generally garners a small percentage of the final mark. This is problematic for a number of reasons, and will be discussed in more detail in Chapter 14.

Writing as work and rewriting

With great disingenuousness, the CW literature takes the lid off another apparently little-known fact: that all completed writing involves preparation, taking notes, writing rough, perhaps fragmented versions, re-writing, producing drafts, revising, editing, proof-reading. While it may be appropriate to explain this principle to a child acquiring literacy, when addressed to adults it is patronising; did anyone ever *really* think that a novel/poem/play appeared complete and perfectly formed in its final published version? If anyone did seriously believe that, it can only be from the force of the conviction that the Muse brings the words fully formed, with the student or writer merely a stenographer, taking dictation from voices off, powerless, submissive, at the mercy of larger forces.

The stress on writing as 'work' (i.e. something which must be 'worked') has become more than a hangover from Besant's need to justify writing as a profession (i.e. labour which earns someone a living). It has, paradoxically, become something which opposes 'work' to the magic and the mystery desired by all, and unattainable by most. It fetishises even more the idea that 'real' writers are born or Muse-blessed.

The writing memoir

One of the primary models offered for CW's pedagogy is the master *(sic)*-apprentice, or guru-acolyte: the expert teaching their art/craft. Therefore the writing memoir, autobiographical words of wisdom, interviews, aphorisms by famous, successful, money-earning writers, are considered as valuable pedagogic resources. Despite their fascination and readability, these are not pedagogic aids. They may be anecdotal, be interesting as artistic memoirs, recounting the way work, the imagination and the life may inter-relate. The books may be 'inspiring', in the sense that they convey what has been done and what might be possible, but they are strictly ancillary to any serious pedagogic process.

Margaret Atwood's thoughtful book *Negotiating with the Dead: A Writer on Writing* was based on the series of six Empson Lectures she gave at Cambridge University.[24] Recounting her childhood, education and early writing, Atwood punctuates the book with observations about the practice of writing and comments on other writers. Stephen King's marvellous book *On Writing* is a forceful, compelling page-turner, driven by his superb narrative skills, with a personal catastrophe (a road accident) as its turning point.[25]

John Gardner's *The Art of Fiction*, subtitled 'Notes on Craft for Young Writers', is a robust, no-nonsense approach to writing, based on years of university CW teaching.[26] Ray Bradbury's *Zen in the Art of Writing* is a chatty series of essays threaded with anecdotes and metaphorical sweeps as he tries to capture and define the Muse.[27] Jorge Luis Borges's *This Craft of Verse* contains the Charles Eliot Norton lectures, given at Harvard College, 1967–8; a mixture of autobiographical snippets and scholarly and learned disquisition.[28]

As one might expect from these professional writers, all the books are grippingly readable. Again and again they stress that writing is work (i.e. it is how they earn their living), and that it is hard work. That it is labour.

---

[24] Cambridge University Press, 2002.
[25] Pocket Books, 2002 (first published 2000).
[26] Vintage Books, 1991 (first published 1983).
[27] Bantam Books, 1992 (first published 1990).
[28] Harvard University Press, 2000.

That it produces something which enters the marketplace. That it does not spring fully formed onto the page. As with other jobs/occupations, some moments are amazing and satisfying, and much of it is tedious, unending administration. The actual writing is work, hard work. Very hard work. Just like any other freelance job. Very insecure. All very obvious, but the constraint to assert the obvious again and again is only there because of the power of the assumption, or the desire, that it is already just 'there', in waiting, a mysterious gift.

Writing the invisible

In the case both of the Romantic Muse and of the therapeutised-self-through-writing, something profound and *invisible* is being broached. Whether the 'source' of the writing comes from 'inspiration' or from the expressing 'self', that source cannot be seen. Writing does not involve any manipulation of pre-existing materials, beyond paper/screen, and pen/fingers. There is no musical instrument, no clay, no paint and canvas/paper, no marble. It is not structurally dependent on organised group activity: a choir or orchestra with a conductor, a drama group with a script and a director. It is stringently individuated, with its materials (source, as in the brain/mind; language as the means and mode) all *invisible* until words are put on paper. It is an imaginative mode of thought until organised in and through written language.

Therefore, *what* is taught also appears to be invisible. One cannot 'see' people imagining or thinking. No wonder that the blank page and its concomitant supposed 'terror' are so fetishised as to appear inevitable. No wonder the concept of 'writer's block' is so regularly adduced: if the Muse is absent and the self is inadequate, there can be no words for the page. The 'inner mystery' of learning CW is reaffirmed, along with the impossibility (*pace* Brande and others) of really learning it at all. That is what is really meant by the cliché that CW cannot be taught, that it can only be 'learned' – a very odd formulation which merely serves to let the teacher off the hook of responsibility. These mutually exclusive concepts are contained within the impossible conundrum of the uncontrollable Muse cohabiting with the calm, therapeutised writing self. This is not a pedagogically viable model.

Paradoxically, this problematises access to language, imbuing language itself with an almost superstitious gloss, as if it is magical and unteachable, rather than cultural, acquired and applied through practical knowledge of its forms and written conventions. CW books commonly contain what are called writing 'exercises', a term which harks back to school-use on the one hand, and on the other to the idea that 'exercises' are generally seen as secondary to the 'real thing': an infantilised introduction to the ungraspable. 'Exercises' are also seen as lesser, because they come from the teacher or the book, and are therefore not about the student's (or reader's) personal experience. Even though some exercises may raise important writerly issues (narrative voice, or focalisation, for example), they can only make cumulative pedagogic sense in a context where they are structured and discussed.

Writing as therapy

The concept of imaginative writing as art has been partially eclipsed in contemporary CW literature by the concept of imaginative writing as self-expression and proto-therapy. However, even as writing-as-therapy is the foregrounded ideology, it rests on a retained concept of the Romantic, and irrational genius as the desired achievement.

It is important to stress that this is an entirely different matter from the valuable work done by people using the arts in clearly demarcated therapeutic contexts. Celia Hunt and Fiona Sampson have written informatively about the '. . . the growing interest in the practice of autobiography and creative writing as a means of gaining insight into oneself, of coping with difficult emotional or psychological problems, or as a way of dealing with difficult life experiences such as emotional traumas, illnesses, ageing and death.'[29] This may be a perfectly valid activity and fascinating in its own right, but it is using CW as part of self-development in a way which abuts far more on a fundamentally therapeutic, rather than a literary-productive, remit.

Conclusions: infantilising creative writing

In today's 'how-to' CW books, there is an uncomfortable slide from the unteachable genius to the teaching of imaginative writing as – in effect – a form of therapy. The tone of many books is uncomfortably patronising, using a form of address which is very similar to registers appropriate for talking to very young children. Consider the following:

---

[29] Ibid., p. 10.

'Whatever you write is right. *You can't write the wrong thing!* It doesn't even have to be in *proper* English. Write when and where you feel like it; day or night, in bed, in a café (difficult on a bike). Write only two lines, or lots – in a notebook, on scraps of paper, perhaps in a folder.

1   Scribble whatever comes into your head for 6 minutes – don't stop to think!

It might be a list, or odd words or phrases – spelling and proper sentences don't matter!

2   *Either:* Carry on.
     Or: Write about: a dream, a memory, a time of loss.
     Or: Make a list of all the important people in your life. It doesn't matter if they are alive or dead now. Choose one to describe. What did they say? Write a letter as if you were talking to them.'

Recognisable is the simple vocabulary, the user-friendly tone ('you'), reassurance, encouragement, suggestions to write when you 'feel' like it, an exhortation not to think (!), a little joke to help you along (difficult on a bike), a statement that grammar, spelling and punctuation don't matter, and a strong emphasis on the personal experience: write about a dream, about a time of loss and one of the important people in your own, personal life, from your own, personal history.

There are 'tips' about starting writing, and the familiar assumption that writing is a frightening and/or very personal experience. But you could imagine, couldn't you, that you might be saying all or some of the above to a child, or a young person? You'd be soothing them, telling them not to be frightened, that you aren't going to judge them, asking them just to write about something they know very well. This would suggest that you know and understand how absolutely shit-terrifying (though you would not use that word to a child, would you?) it is to write anything at all, and because you know this, you are able to take their hand (not the one with which they are writing, of course) and guide them through the dark and dangerous places of their imagination, their psyche, even their unconscious.

For most CW teachers, the tone and content of the above is probably not at all problematic. However, this does not come from a CW text-book. It is taken from a patient leaflet in a GP surgery, used to help with 'anxious or depressed' patients.[30] In that context it may be couched in

---

[30] Gillie Bolton, 'Writing or Pills' in *The Self on the Page*, ed. Celia Hunt and Fiona Sampson (Jessica Kingsley, 2002; first published 1998), p. 83.

the most productive way, but the fact that it is indistinguishable from CW advice should give us all pause. This extract leads into the heart of CW methodology, which is suspended in uncomfortable contradiction along the Romantic/therapy axis. The next chapter analyses how this is realised in the workshop and its pedagogy.

12
The Workshop and the Emperor's Clothes

The creative writing workshop exists in two senses: the 'Workshop', referring to the institutional distinctiveness of CW as an academic discipline, and the verb 'to workshop', referring to the practices and methodologies of CW pedagogy. Student writing is 'workshopped'. In 'Creative Writing: a Good Practice Guide', Dr Siobhan Holland described the 'distinctive attributes of Creative Writing as an academic discipline ... as a practice-based rather than a vocational or service-based discipline.'[1] The workshop thus also becomes the *sine qua non* for creative writing itself, together with the privileged space (some would say, unique and challenging) in which the practice comes into meaningful pedagogic being.

Early workshop history

The dominant model for the CW workshop is the structure developed at the University of Iowa. Iowa's first taught course in 'Verse Making' in the spring of 1897 set a precedent which helped to pave the way for 'creative' work to be submitted as part of the requirements of postgraduate Masters [*sic*] degrees in the 1920s.[2] Stephen Wilbers, historian of *The Iowa Writers' Workshop*, suggested that the protocols of the CW workshop originated in local writers' clubs: 'Their purpose was to improve the participants' skills as writers by allowing each member to have a turn reading his or her original work, after which the group would respond

---

[1] English Subject Centre, Report Series No 6, February 2003.
[2] *Seven Decades of the Iowa Workshop*, ed. Tom Grimes (Hyperion, 1999).

with suggestions and literary criticism. . . . Accordingly, the method (later to be called the "workshop" approach) was adopted by the University when it offered its first course in creative writing.'[3]

Norman Foerster, director of the School of Letters (1930–44), succeeded in getting the creative dissertation accepted for the PhD degree in the early 1930s, and in 1939, the title 'Writers' Workshops' was officially used for the first time. In 1949 the Iowa English Department incorporated CW into its undergraduate English Major. The consolidation of Iowa's achievements in the 1940s and 1950s, under director Paul Engle (1942–66), led to the Iowa Writers' Workshop becoming, in effect, the prototype for CW courses in the US during the 1960s, often founded and run by Iowa Workshop graduates.

Janet Burroway, an American writer who studied at Barnard University during the 1950s, highlighted the differences between attitudes to CW in the US and in the UK: 'At the Poetry Center of the Young Men's Hebrew Association (in New York) I made coffee and onion dip for the Young Writers' Reading Series (Truman Capote . . . etc.). . . . In the 1960s, which I spent mostly in England, I often found myself defending the notion of creative writing as a university subject and also often critiquing a Sussex student's fiction or poetry – occasionally at the same time. . . . By the time I returned from Sussex to teach in Florida State University in 1971, creative writing was the hottest subject in the English department – "the boom trade of the English bizz" as one not entirely approving colleague put it. . . . Student demand was high. . . .'[4]

The tutorial precedent

In academic terms, the 'workshop' is another word for the 'seminar': small-group teaching which aims to maximise student participation. As we saw in Chapter 2, the origins of the tutorial come from both ends of the educational class spectrum. In the nineteenth century, principles of self-government were reflected in classes in the Co-operative and adult education movements. The 'tutorial class', developed by the University Extension movement, took its teaching model from the oldest-established universities of Oxford and Cambridge, making a distinction between mass lectures and the small group.

---

[3] Stephen Wilbers, *The Iowa Writers' Workshop* (Iowa University Press, 1980), p. 20.
[4] *Teaching Creative Writing*, ed. Moira Monteith and Robert Miles (Open University Press, 1992), pp. 60–1.

Toynbee Hall, founded in London in 1883, 'expressed in a different way the new spirit which was stirring in the older universities . . . men from the colleges in Oxford to engage in social and educational work in the heart of London and to plant the idea of a people's university based on a fellowship of teaching and learning . . . (the tutorial class) . . . will provide far more thorough and systematic teaching than is possible in a course of lectures . . . ever since the first university tutorial classes were established, stress has been laid upon the importance of discussion as a method of adult education. . . . the successful class is one in which all the members, and not merely one or two of the more vocal, are contributing actively to the common effort.'[5]

Groups and structure: writing and educational

While formal CW took longer to arrive in the UK, informal writers' groups were not unknown. In 'The Teaching of Creative Writing', Philip Hobsbaum reminisced back to the early 1950s. As a Cambridge under-graduate at Downing College, Cambridge, where F. R. Leavis taught, Hobsbaum organised a writing group in 1952, typing out copies of poems and stories and sending them round beforehand for members to read. In 1955 he started a similar group in London, and subsequently 'managed' (as he put it) others in Belfast and Glasgow. He described part of his role: 'I usually let the discussion polarise to some extent before intervening . . . it was a matter of avoiding closure.'[6]

DUET

The seminar, or small-group pedagogy, was explored during the 1970s, combining political democratisation, community-based creativity and radical work in psychotherapy. A university-based organisation called DUET (Developing University English Teaching) was founded in 1979 by Professor John Broadbent: 'In the later 1960s at Cambridge I was tiring of one-to-one tutorials, so I began holding seminars. Then I moved to the University of East Anglia where the basic teaching unit was the seminar . . . people came late to classes or not at all, hadn't read the books, did not participate or talked demotically. . . . In an effort to get

---

[5] Robert Peers, *Adult Education* (Routledge, 1959, 1972), p. 46 and p. 230.
[6] Monteith and Miles, p. 30.

out of this, I regressed to techniques used in primary schools – thematic topics, dramatic improvisation . . . '[7] Broadbent and his colleagues set up conferences and workshops, to explore group dynamics. The experience was described by Susan Bassnett, on DUET's twenty-fifth anniversary:

'DUET was born at the height of the Great theory Wars, the crisis point in literary studies, before the advent of post-colonial thinking, when we were trying to come to terms with wave after wave of new ideas – feminism, post-structuralism, deconstruction, post-modernism, to name but four. Those of us trained in the Leavisite mode, or like myself in the more philological methods of close reading deriving from Empson and the Russian Formalists were literally at the epicentre of the critical revolution. We were teaching courses that belonged to one era, reading late into the night books and essays that were changing our view of the subject and of the world. . . . What made DUET special was its unique combination of the scholarly and the personal: alongside rigorously prepared academic sessions, all participants were assigned to a creative writing group and, most controversially, to a group run on Tavistock principles, close to the old idea of encounter groups that had come into prominence in the 1970s and early 1980s. . . . I remember tears, arguments, confrontations, extraordinary moments of revelation, and a resulting shift of perception that has never left me.'[8]

Authority

Authority, leadership and democratic participation were the socio-political issues at the heart of these small group activities. Feminism placed particular importance on leaderlessness, on equal participation by every member of the group, on the democracy of experience and voice. This was in part a response to the experiences of many women in groups where men were always dominant. The small group provided a different model from the idea that women's experiences were secondary, not-heard, in public and in private.

The idea of 'consciousness-raising' expressed this principle; each individual woman could discover how her personal, individual experience

---

[7] John Broadbent, '"Forms of Life": How the DUET Project Began', in *Developing University English Teaching*, ed. Colin Evans (Edwin Mellen Press, 1995), p. 18.

[8] English Subject Centre, *Newsletter*, 9 November 2005, p. 25.

was not just isolated, but interwoven with larger social and ideological structures shaping society. Feminism appropriated a slogan first widely used by the Situationists, French radical students in the late 1960s, that 'the personal is political'. At the centre of this was an encompassing idea that private life, the thoughts and imaginations of individuals, were structurally bound up with social organisation; the role of the state and its relationships with the individual and the family.

The equation of leaderlessness with democracy was shared by many cultural groups. There was often exhilaration, empowerment and achievement, but there were also often competing differences which were ignored or covered over. Each individual brought their own histories and agendas (class, culture, ethnicity, expectations, needs) into the process. It was clearly not enough just to declare that power-relations could be easily put aside.

The supposed 'structurelessness' of such groups was analysed in an American feminist magazine, 'the second wave', in 1972: 'Any group of people of whatever nature that comes together for any length of time for any purpose will inevitably structure itself in some fashion . . . to strive for a structureless group is as useful, and as deceptive as to aim at "objective" news story, "value-free" social science or a "free" economy . . . the idea of "structurelessness" does not prevent the formation of informal structures, only formal ones. . . . As long as the structure of the group is informal, the rules of how decisions are made are known only to a few and awareness of power is limited to those who know the rules. . . . The rules of decision-making must be open and available to everyone, and this can happen only if they are formalised.'[9]

The continuing influence of this egalitarian ideology has a significant place in the pedagogic tenets behind the models for CW teaching.

Pedagogic models in the workshop: peer review

There are a number of models appealed to, for the specialness of the CW workshop. These are derived from different cultural traditions, and different pedagogic practices. First, workshop practice has been compared with the academic practice of peer-reviewing (in journals and publishing). In a report on the 'Proceedings of the Creative Writing Conference' (Sheffield Hallam University, 1999), Patricia Wooldridge

---

[9] By Joreen, vol. 2, no. 1 (1972), pp. 20–1.

wrote: 'I believe that the use of peer assessment provides a vital support in the development of undergraduates' writing.'[10] In 'Professional Judgement in the Assessment of Creative Writing', Danny Broderick observed that 'Peer group assessment is a key element of current teaching methodologies.'[11]

Professional friendship: publisher/writer

George Marsh presented a similar egalitarian professional model: 'At the heart of tutoring literary writing is a relationship that is ideally like that between two writer friends, when one asks the other to advise on a manuscript before submitting it for publication.'[12] However, Marsh's friendships merge with a rather grander, more professionalised division of labour, which is not based primarily on either peer or friendship equality: 'The tutor's role should be like that of a publisher's editor or agent.'[13]

This last has proved a popular model, because it offers the cachet of literary professionalism. Paul Engle, Director of the Iowa Writers' Workshop for twenty-four years, reinforced the publisher model in a letter to Stephen Wilbers in 1961. He 'likened the teaching that can be done in a workshop to the function of an editor like Maxwell Perkins, who shaped and pared into presentable form the massive manuscripts of Thomas Wolfe'. This model was also suggested by Robert Miles: 'In effect, the seminar reduplicates, in miniature, publishing.'[14] The model of the workshop process as mirroring the publishing/editorial process served in a different political context for the FWWCP; there was: 'a commitment to using the group as the first readership or audience for work, and as the body that decides about editing, shaping, public reading or publication.'[15]

Master/guru/apprentice/disciple

In Chapter 1, we saw how John Moat likened the relationship established at the Arvon Foundation, to that of guru and disciple. Along the

---

[10] Sheffield Hallam, p. 119.

[11] *Writing in Education* (National Association of Writers in Education (NAWE), Autumn 1998).

[12] 'A Commentary on Aims and Assessments in the Teaching of Literary Writing', in Monteith and Miles, p. 45.

[13] Ibid., p. 46.

[14] Monteith and Miles.

[15] *The Republic of Letters*, ed. Dave Morley and Ken Worpole (Minority Press, Group Series No. 6, 1982), p. 5.

same lines, Engle compared 'the student enrolling in a workshop and the artist seeking instruction by a master'.[16]

Conflictual authority models

These are overlapping, but also conflicting models. Peer review and friendship models imply parity between those concerned, mixing professional with personal parity. The publisher–writer relationship is a professional relationship, where the writer has entered the market-place; the book/text is now a commodity which goes into production, and the (ideal) editor is a knowledgable close reader, passing on advice to improve the completed text, to make it publishable (the product). There is structured dependence, here, with power ultimately in the hands of the publisher/editor. The master–apprentice–guru–acolyte model, regularly presented in the literature, implies heavily directed guidance and advice, in which the receiver (student) accedes to and follows the knowledge and wisdom of the leader. The power-relation here is very clear: from expert to novice. The concept of the 'master class' derives from the master–apprentice model, and will be discussed later (see Chapter 13).

Workshop practice and power-relations

Pivotal to workshop protocol, whatever its model, and seen as constituting its distinctive professional practice, is a special form of 'criticism', or critiquing. This applies to under- and postgraduate workshops. As Danny Broderick described, in the 'seminar/workshop . . . students' own work in progress is reviewed and revised through critical discussion. . . . This cooperative critiquing of work by peers . . . places emphasis on the analysis of the text as literary artefact. . . . Students are asked to make value judgements on their own and each others' texts as part of the process of arriving at the artefact.'[17] In the process of 'workshopping', therefore, the CW seminar is driven by procedures of *re-writing*, rather than writing.

There is a missing element in this account: in the seminar the tutor is present, and s/he makes the final judgement in assessing and marking students' work at the end of the course. This inevitably creates an inbuilt tension between the theoretically egalitarian responses of the

---

[16] Wilbers, p. 84.
[17] Danny Broderick, NAWE website, 1999.

peer–friendship group, and that of the tutor, which might be quite different. Siobhan Holland reported from a CW conference at Bath Spa University in 2001 that some delegates thought 'It is not fair to students to find their work praised in workshops and criticised in assessment feedback.'[18]

The publisher/editor analogy is equally flawed. The larger part of workshop time (and the foregrounded activity) is reserved for discussing student writing, material produced outside class. Even if the student thinks it is 'complete', the fact that it is then subject to group 'criticism' renders it conceptually, and actually, incomplete. No publisher's editor (especially these days!) will spend large amounts of time reading and commenting on any manuscript in detail unless it is already commissioned or bought, and therefore en route to publication. Publication is not what happens in the classroom (some argue that reading aloud is a form of 'publication'; it is only so in a marginal sense). Student work is doubly 'work-in-progress', because individual pieces of writing are technically incomplete, and because each class is part of a course-long process.

Criticism and value judgement

If the main pedagogic activity in the workshop is supposed to be the application of 'criticism', there must be value judgements of some kind at stake. In the workshop, such value judgements are inevitably concealed, because not taught and shared. The CW literature does not theorise or discuss its critical values. The fact that the workshop devotes the majority of its time to unfinished student writing, operating a methodology via 'feedback' or 'critiquing', underlies the special claim of CW to focus on 'process' rather than 'product'. Its rubrics are relatively straightforward, based on students' responses to the texts of others, via the process of feedback or critiquing.

'Feedback' can mean favourable or adverse opinion (this is 'good' or 'bad'). 'Criticism' or 'critiquing' can be (often is) used in the colloquial sense of put-down, disapproval. The solution of 'constructive' or 'positive' criticism means saying nice things first, pointing out what you 'like', what you think is 'good'. This contrasts with its opposite, 'negative' criticism, which involves pointing out what is 'wrong' or what

---

[18] 'Creative Writing Structures and Trends' (English Subject Centre, Working Paper, no. 5).

doesn't 'work'. The mooted ideal is to find some form of 'constructive criticism', which is meant to 'help' the student re-write their work, if they want to.

The ideological confusion returns to the Romantic/therapy axis, and to the varied, and sometimes contradictory aims of CW. If CW is training professional writers (those who already have 'talent'), then the great-writers approach privileges the text over the writer; if students are taught that CW expresses the self (writing as therapy), then the person is privileged over the writing. The first overvalues the art, the second overvalues the person, and together they confuse the object of the work and its objectives. They cannot be simultaneously contained within the same pedagogic model.

The workshop as a House of Correction

Tom Grimes, in *Seven Decades of the Iowa Workshop*, was explicit about the internal dynamics of the workshop experience: 'Nearly every participant has sensed and reacted with some apprehension to a spirit of competition in the Workshop setting. But many writers view the ordeal of measuring their talent against the talent of others as a necessary crisis in their artistic development. Paul Engle believes that the intensity of this experience contributes to the writer's growth.'[19]

Robert Graham, who visited the Iowa Workshop in 2001, reported on one of Frank Conroy's classes: 'A fellow student describes what he calls his "ordeal", and someone else likens the workshop process to an autopsy. Conroy's comments on the workshop included comments such as: "We . . . spend 95% of our time finding out what is wrong." A student noted that "Conroy believes he isn't doing his job unless the occasional student bursts into tears or faints." One teacher describes his own classroom role as ". . . traffic cop. I make sure things aren't getting out of control". After a particularly gruelling session, a woman tutor comes in, "like a den mother", with a basket of sweets for everyone.'[20]

Tom Grimes elaborated: 'Then come the Workshop discussions. The line edits that pick apart the imagined integrity of your story before the end of the first sentence. The declaration by others of utter mystification when it came to being able to say what your story was about. The lancing comparisons of your pale imitation to the work of obviously influential

---

[19] Grimes, p. 131.
[20] NAWE website, Autumn 2001.

masters. . . .' He concluded, unsurprisingly, that 'What the Workshop has done, strangely enough, is taught us what not to do. . . .'[21] An appropriate slogan, suggested Grimes, for the Workshop, might be 'Abandon all Hope, all ye who enter here'.[22]

If these are examples of the primary model of peer-reviewing, or the master/apprentice relationship, then something is seriously wrong. The patronising of individual vulnerability alongside a method which cannot fail but be discouraging and educationally disempowering is not a context in which genuine teaching and learning can take place. Such workshops are sado-masochistic Houses of Correction on a Victorian scale. The workshop principles alternate hard-cop/soft-cop methodologies. Training great writers entails toughening them up to 'take criticism', to survive baptisms of fire. In writing-as-therapy, the emphasis is on avoiding hurting people's feelings (after all, if the writing is thought to be expressing the 'self', then the 'self' will be vulnerable). 'Supportive criticism' finds ways to say something is rubbish without upsetting or patronising the writer by saying 'well done for trying'.

The problems are only occasionally acknowledged. Siobhan Holland wrote of 'The need for robust support structures for students who may well draw on traumatic experiences in the processes of reading and writing.'[23] According to Liz Almond, the workshop 'should provide a safe environment whereby you can get to know and respect other people through their work and begin to develop an ability to offer constructive criticism.'[24] 'It takes time,' she explains, 'to develop a critical vocabulary if you're not used to responding to other people's work.'[25] Yes; it's called doing an English degree.

Rob Mimpriss is one of the very few CW students who have publicly (if cautiously) questioned the received wisdom of the workshop: 'I have been moving towards the conclusion that the workshop has little to offer the writer, and may at times do harm. . . . Not everyone will feel willing to speak, and what they say will be influenced by the group dynamic as they learn how hard it is to be the only dissenting voice, to be cruel when others have been kind, or to damn one student's work after praising another's.'[26] Occasionally, a teacher has articulated reservations. Ali

---

[21] Grimes, pp. 7–8.

[22] Ibid., p. 3.

[23] Holland, p.6.

[24] 'The Workshop Way', in *The Creative Writing Handbook*, by John Singleton and Mary Luckhurst (Macmillan, 1996, 2000), p. 18.

[25] Ibid., p. 22.

[26] 'Rewriting the Individual; a Critical Study of the Creative Writing Workshop', in *Writing in Education*, no. 26 (2002).

Smith admitted that: 'Teaching creative writing workshops gives me irritable bowel syndrome.'[27] Alan Maher commented that 'Offering criticism of another's writing can be a precarious affair; listening to criticism can be downright disastrous.'[28]

From her 1992 research project into community writing groups, Rebecca O'Rourke concluded that 'People are working with cobbled together models of constructive criticism drawn from school – criticism as negative, unpleasant and fault finding – and from the market – criticism as a selective judgement. I found few models drawn from the writing process – criticism as a means to extend, clarify and challenge the writer. . . .'[29]

She reported concerns about 'feedback' and 'criticism': 'A contradiction began to emerge. People went to writing groups in order to get feedback on their work and yet were almost always unhappy with the feedback they received. The issue was partly a question of whose responsibility criticism was seen to be: did it belong to the writer, the group or its leader/tutor. . . . Some . . . felt encouragement was incompatible with criticising work.'[30] These comments were not voiced within the workshops, but away from it, to her, as someone safely outside the group: 'The language which people used to describe feedback was distinctive and it was at odds with the actual process I observed. The language was violent and aggressive. Phrases such as "rip it to pieces", "pull it part", "pull no punches", "give it the once over" and "brutally honest". . . . It conjured up a process in which the writing and the writer's feelings were literally taken apart.'[31]

Students wanted more guidelines from the tutors: 'Tension surrounding feedback and criticism was a constant theme in the life of the creative writing groups and courses. It was cited as the most important aspect of the activity, and the one people wanted most to change.'[32] Students were aware that peer comments came (inevitably) from inadequately informed responses – 'many students do not trust the judgement of their peers'.[33] Students, quite rightly, wanted tutors to take responsibility – 'to deal in absolutes – what was right and what was wrong, good or bad – and to offer definite opinions'.[34]

---

[27] Julia Bell and Paul Magrs (eds), *The Creative Writing Coursebook* (Macmillan, 2001), p. 24.

[28] 'Collective Works: Tindal Street Fiction Group', in Bell and Magrs, p. 311.

[29] *Writing in Education* (NAWE, Autumn 1994).

[30] Ibid..

[31] *Creative Writing: Education, Culture and Community* (NIACE, 2005), p. 211.

[32] Ibid., p. 206.

[33] Ibid., p. 133.

[34] Ibid., p. 156.

O'Rourke's conclusion was that 'Central to the problem are issues of power and authority within courses/groups.' This is very clear indeed, both from the conflictual pedagogic models into which CW is constrained to fit, and from the frankly brutal process to which students are subjected.

Celia Hunt and Fiona Sampson have suggested that: 'CW classes may become, on occasion, arenas where deep feelings and emotions are unearthed and expressed, and teachers and group leaders may sometimes find themselves in the position of counsellor or therapist, without the appropriate skills to act as such.'[35] Teachers need 'to be aware of the importance of creating in the classroom a "holding environment", to use Winnicott's term, within which participants can feel safe enough to engage more closely with their inner worlds. This can be done by organising peer support within the writing group itself, or through the availability of individual consultations with the tutor, or by having available counselling or psychotherapeutic backup which can be used when necessary.'[36] This is very clearly to conflate pedagogic and therapeutic structures and procedures, and gives CW teachers an impossible – if not emotionally dangerous – responsibility.

Conclusions

This chapter has elaborated on the pedagogical implications of the irreconcilable conflict at the heart of the Romantic/therapy axis. The conflictual models are shoe-horned into a pedagogic practice which renders the workshop as a House of Correction, built round *re-writing*, rather than *writing*. Untheorised (or, at best, very under-theorised) principles of 'criticism' are translated into by turns brutal and patronising exchanges. This devolves the conceptual oppositions into the centre of the student–teacher relationship. In addition, this denies CW's relationship to its own histories, which are those embedded in the history of English: literature, literary criticism and literary theory. The apparent sanctuary within which creativity is supposed to flourish turns out to be a repository for a set of Emperor's clothes which do not fit; piecemeal pragmatic assumptions about rewriting drive the hard-cop/soft-cop process, in the interests of the irreconcileable Romantic/therapy axis.

---

[35] *The Self on the Page*, ed. Celia Hunt and Fiona Sampson (Jessica Kingsley, 1998, 2002), p. 12.
[36] Hunt and Sampson, p. 33.

13

Comparative Approaches in Other Art Forms: Art School and Conservatoire

Because CW addresses imaginative writing as a process which is related to producing an art form (literature), the workshop has also been compared with other art forms with longer pedagogical histories. Peter Abbs argued that CW pedagogy 'is suggested more by the workshop where actors and actresses prepare for rehearsals, than by the academic seminar or the ordinary classroom'.[1]

Books about the history of training in fine art and music are thin on the ground; the two discussed here are rare examples of other arts' practice pedagogy, which, like CW, remain un- or under-theorised.

The fine arts and the academies

'Artists were not trained within the medieval university system at all. They went directly from grammar school into workshops, or from their parents' homes straight into workshops. Students spent two or three years as apprentices, often "graduating" from one master to another, and then joined the local painter's guild and began to work for a master as a "journeyman-apprentice".'[2]

Italian Renaissance Academies were initially composed of cultural and intellectual gatherings of courtly aristocrats. Here more formal ways of teaching fine art developed. In these Academies, anatomy (based on

---

[1] *A is for Aesthetic* (Falmer Press, 1989), p. 72.
[2] James Elkins, *Why Art Cannot be Taught* (University of Illinois Press, 2001), p. 7.

human dissection), life drawing, natural philosophy and architecture were all part of the curriculum. At the Florentine Academy of Design (1560) 'students learned mathematics, including perspective, proportion, harmony and plane and solid Euclidean geometry. The idea was to get away from the empirical, haphazard kind of learning that artists had faced in workshops, and to substitute theories.'[3]

During the seventeenth and eighteenth centuries, the Baroque Academies widened their training. The French Academy was founded in 1655, the London Royal Academy of the Arts in 1768. The early nineteenth century saw a rejection of the older academies, in favour of the Romantic notion that 'the subjective, individual vision of each artist is more important than any sequence of classes or standardised theory'.[4]

Music and the conservatoire

Musical training was initially in the hands of the church (in the West), for devotional purposes: 'The first use of the term *conservatorio* is found ... in Naples in the sixteenth century, where the first *conservatorio* for boys was founded in 1537 and singing was part of the boys' duties. By the early eighteenth century the famous Venetian *ospedali*, which were similar institutions for girls, flourished. . . .'[5]

The Royal Academy of Music was founded in 1822, and the Guildhall School of Music in 1880. Until the late 1980s, universities and conservatoires tended to have an educational division of labour, with the latter concentrating on training musical performers, and the former on theoretical and historical studies, though also including some practical training. Music teachers working in schools need, at the very least, to be able to play the piano and sing. Since the polytechnic/university changes in the early 1990s, conservatoire, art and drama schools have conferred degree qualifications, though still with a greater bias towards practical and performance studies.

I have direct experience of being in a conservatoire: as a mature (in age, anyway) student, I took a four-year Performers' course in a department of Renaissance and Baroque Music at a London conservatoire in

---

3 Ibid., p. 10.
4 Ibid., p. 27.
5 George Odam in *The Reflective Conservatoire*, ed. George Odam and Nicholas Bannan (Ashgate, 2005), p. 15.

the early 1990s, followed by an MMus in 'Performance and Related Studies'. On the Performers' course (effectively an undergraduate degree), there was no essay writing and little musical history; students taking the BMus did have history lectures, and were required to write essays, and were schooled in (for example) Schenkerian analysis, while also receiving intensive aural musicianship training. At MMus level work did include essays, a final dissertation, and a written examination. At both under- and postgraduate level, the centre of all the instrumental and vocal training was, and still is, the weekly one-to-one lesson: in 'private', unobserved, on the basis of which, in examined recitals, individual students are graded. There is ensemble work, but it is not assessed. As Helena Gaunt commented in *The Reflective Conservatoire*:

> 'The personal nature of one-to-one teaching and learning relationships was a striking theme. The intensity and privacy of the engagement resembled the intimacy of personal or therapeutic relationships more than the conventional teaching/learning relationships; on the other hand, there were none of the structures of training or supervision here, which professionalise therapy. . . . The combination of artistic identity and one-to-one relationships suggests that both teacher and student may be bound up in highly complex interactions, thereby making accountability for the success of any relationship difficult to pin down, especially without clear structures of support and critical evaluation.'[6]

Gaunt was particularly concerned about the unequal emotional power-relationship. The 'ethical boundaries' are unmarked, and 'seemed to be largely in the control of the teacher, so highlighting the distribution of power in the relationship'.[7] The problem comes down to a conflict between pedagogic means and ends: 'Dominant themes . . . were establishing students as independent learners, and equipping them with a professional toolbox. It was not always clear, however, how the teaching techniques and approaches supported these aims.'[8] The effectively private interaction generates an ongoing, implicit competition: each teacher instructs many students, but for each student there is only one teacher/guru. Developing technical skills and musical 'expressiveness', or 'interpretation' are at the heart of the teaching.

---

[6] Ibid., p. 268.
[7] Ibid., p. 265.
[8] Ibid., p. 267.

Professional standing is a prerequisite for teachers: 'Most, if not all . . . teachers need, by definition to be working musicians at the top of their careers.'[9] The musician-teacher may prefer to think of him/herself primarily as a performer, even where, in practice, the major part of their income may come from teaching, providing a resonance with many CW teachers who want to see themselves as 'writers', even though their income may come from academia, and their literary publications are few.

Music and the guru

The models of guru–disciple, master–apprentice survive most directly in the conservatoire; as Gaunt has noted, 'This is the apprenticeship model that was the foundation of artisan and industrial practice in western Europe right up to the industrial revolution.'[10] Within other musical cultures, 'Traditionally each guru has a personal style (mostly formed by their own guru, handed down and assimilated into a new personal style variation in a form of apostolic succession) and information is transmitted only through doing in imitation.'[11] In the Indian and Scottish folk traditions, for example, learning by ear is privileged over learning to read music, and the foundation of the individual style of performance is based on accurate imitation of an already established style, as executed by the individual guru (who, by definition, encompasses both the bedrock of the tradition, and the achievement of distinctive excellence).

In this historical paradigm, there is no necessary contradiction between learning the fundamental technical *and* traditional skills, and the *potential*, achieved or not, of the qualities culturally declared to be worthy of guru status – the elements of individual expressivity in performance. However, within the post-Romantic conservatoire tradition, while technical and physical athletic-type training are absolutely fundamental, the privileging of originality and individuality becomes a far stronger motivator and shaper of the teacher–student relationship. Clearly, each teacher coaches in the style which characterises his or her own performative interpretation, while at the same time encouraging 'originality'. After years of study with the same teacher, the 'success' of the student in their final examined recital depends on the teacher's 'approval' – a highly personalised inflection of a professional interaction.

---

[9] Ibid., p. 221.
[10] Ibid., p. 181.
[11] Ibid., p. 181.

Within the privacy of this one-to-one relationship, everything is heightened; it is not too extravagant to point out that there is an erotic charge built into such a pedagogic relationship, enhanced by close contact with the 'genius', the charismatic Svengali whose gifts might rub off (as it were) on the novice by virtue of proximity. In such a hot-house atmosphere, there are 'Intense expectations of the one-to-one relationship', sometimes leading to friendship, sometimes to difficulties, and sometimes leading to the need for counselling: 'There were, however, no structures clarified for assisting in dealing with problematic relationships.'[12]

The masterclass – reality

The CW literature sometimes compares CW teaching to the 'masterclass', 'the only context in which performance teaching is made public'.[13] However, the model for this is the one-off masterclass display, generally a showcase through which eminent musician/teachers 'perform' teaching: their one-off display of expertise is matched by the student's display of obedience. Watching other people absorbed in rehearsal is riveting; not just because this is a private-made-public, shop-window display, but because it demonstrates the excitement, the detail, the rewarding difficulties of such work. The fact that there is an audience present defines the relationship within the constraints of timed performance. The masterclass is a spectator sport, not a pedagogic model.

Implicitly, through the one-to-one musical teaching norm, each student is being trained to be a soloist – or, at the very least, to be 'as if' a soloist. This is one way of encouraging excellence and individual achievement; but it is paradoxical; after all, even soloists work within ensembles. In conservatoires, while orchestras and chamber music are compulsory, such work is low down on the scale of importance. Orchestral and choir work are not assessed, even though, realistically, this is where most graduates might conceivably be employed. The hierarchy within conservatoire training is heavily biased towards individual achievement.

Orchestras and choirs entail a different set of pedagogic priorities. In parallel with drama schools, ensemble work enables students to learn a repertoire, and to develop specific performance skills. Anecdotal

---

[12]   Gaunt, in Odhan and Bannan, pp. 262–3.
[13]   Ibid., p. 181.

accounts of musical conductors and theatre directors construct them as working in a variety of ways, from strict and authoritarian (the bully, performance as a baptism of fire – *cf* the CW workshop), or the encouraging and inspiring, justified by their artistic 'vision' and the creative rewards reaped by the participants. However, because the ensemble (musical or dramatic) must, in effect, perform as one, in co-operation with each other, there is never any serious question about the conductor/director abdicating either their power or their authority, though they may carry out their responsibility in different ways. In neither individual nor ensemble work, does the conservatoire teacher abdicate their authority, or pretend to any simplistic egalitarianism.

The art school and criticism

In fine art, the use of 'criticism' as a punitive pedagogic tool bears similarities to CW. In the US, the final assessment of a student's work takes the form of a 'Critique'. A panel of examiners/assessors spends between 20 and 45 minutes, according to James Elkins, discussing the student's final portfolio. The student is generally present, and might engage in discussion with the assessors, though not in a formally structured 'viva voce'.

'Critiques,' declared Elkins, 'epitomise the problems of teaching art, and they condense the issues I have been exploring into an agglomeration of nearly intractable difficulty.'[14] Where critiques were once a radical move 'from the Romantic master classes . . . whose purpose was to avoid the unexplained rankings that were the norm throughout the baroque',[15] they now highlight an endemic problem in fine art education: 'we do not know how we teach art, and so we cannot claim to teach it or to know what teaching it might be like . . .'[16] The criteria for value judgements listed by Elkins, on which he claims final critiques are based, depend on a list of typical descriptors, some of which may be all too familiar: 'interesting, moving, inventive, powerful, authentic, compelling, strong, original, difficult, gorgeous, innovative, stimulating, wonderful, beautiful, excellent'. He adds: 'they are neither professional, ethical, theological, metaphysical, scientific, nor teleological. . . . They are *rhetorical* criteria, strategies to help students get noticed.'[17] Because teachers do not make their principles explicit, there is no shared vocab-

---

[14] Elkins, op. cit., p. 110.
[15] Ibid., p. 111.
[16] Ibid., p. 92.
[17] Ibid., pp. 113–14.

ulary of understanding between teacher and student: 'The fact that there is no good theory about art critiques does not bode well for the possibility of understanding what actually happens in art classes.'[18]

Elkins has made some interesting comments about early twentieth-century Bauhaus teaching. First-year courses at the Bauhaus used exercises developed by Friedrich Froebel, the inventor of the kindergarten system. Froebel gave children woollen balls, blocks, laths, paper and hoops, and encouraged them 'to draw, to compare sizes, make patterns, investigate texture and colour, weave and model clay'. The rationale was that learning takes place best in nonutilitarian interaction with materials. Like the Bauhaus instructors (and those involved in the Progressive Education movement), Froebel held that theory – what he called 'mind' – 'need not, or cannot, develop before activity'.[19]

While this may be appropriate for young children, it does not, as Elkins put it, necessarily 'correspond with artmaking that is done in later years'.[20] The grown-up ideology which corresponds to this nursery-school philosophy is (like CW) justified by familiar Romantic notions: 'We sometimes say that art teaching is not amenable to rational analysis since it is fundamentally a matter of inspiration.'[21]

Elkins offers some telling metaphors for the mystery ingredient of inspiration: 'Ultimately, the best image for this theory is infection, since it stems from Plato's original definition of *mania*. Inspiration is infectious. If you are around someone who is enthusiastic, you are at high risk: you may catch the passions that animate that person, even if they may not be good for you . . . teachers nourish their students . . . or feed them like bacteria, or infect them like Typhoid Mary.'[22]

In comparison with other ways of teaching, this demonstrates – at the very least – some shortfall: 'Say, for example, that a university physics professor likes to give lectures by improvising a kind of stream-of-consciousness monologue, moving freely among loosely associated topics, mixing material from freshman and graduate-level courses, adding personal reminiscences, fables, mottoes, digressions . . . a first-year physics student would need to listen very carefully; she would understand a few equations, but some would be over her head, others would be irrelevant, and a few would be too simple.'[23] Basic physics

---

[18] Ibid., p. 119.
[19] Ibid., p. 37.
[20] Ibid., p. 37.
[21] Ibid., p. 93.
[22] Ibid., p. 99.
[23] Ibid., p. 93.

can't be learned this way, and, by extension, nor, ultimately, can, or should, the arts.

Elkins' arguments are powerful, but he is profoundly pessimistic about any possibilities for reform: 'As I see it, art teaching is already a mess, and any attempt to change it is very likely to change it for the worse.'[24] Only two modifications are thinkable for him. The first is dubbed 'intentionality', which means that teachers should 'intend' to teach, taking conscious responsibility for what they do: 'no matter what else teaching is, it is not a comprehensible activity unless the teacher sets out to teach.'[25] The second is to provide tactics to enable students to resist and survive the horrors of the critiquing process.

Conclusions

It should be clear, even from this brief survey, that models superficially drawn from other arts' teaching are not appropriate for CW – if only because they reproduce the same problems. The seductiveness of the masterclass idea is belied by the fact that it is performance and not pedagogy; the privacy of the guru–disciple analogy is, in our culture, too emotionally and powerfully loaded.

The temptation to characterise CW as a 'studio-based' art is implied by the fact that new things are 'made' as a result of the pedagogic process, and derives also from the insistence that literature is an art, and not merely an object for scholarly study. By suggesting that CW has more in common with the other arts than with English, further contradictions are revealed: between CW as a practice-based pedagogy, and the rubrics which inform its practice in the workshop and in the framing of its pedagogic procedures.

---

[24] Ibid., p. 110.
[25] Ibid., p. 92.

14
Literary Criticism: Value Judgements and Creative Writing

The workshop process, based on feedback, or critiquing, depends on the application of some form of criticism within the pedagogic process itself. It is this, in part, which leads to a widespread assumption that the workshop itself 'teaches' criticism. This constructs a difficult relationship between the practice of literary criticism in traditional English teaching, where the exegesis addresses texts in the public domain, and the practice of 'criticism' in the workshop context, applied – to use a temporary shorthand – to work in progress. The discussion of the underlying criteria for the latter process emerges in the literature in discussions about assessment and marking.

In 'Analysing the Aesthetic', in 2000, Ann Atkinson, Liz Cashdan, Livi Michael and Ian Pople offered criteria for marking undergaduate CW coursework. Under 'Language', the following was suggested for a First Class mark: 'Language fully controlled: fully particularised use of language that shows complete control of selectivity, originality and editing of language at all stages of the text.' Under 'Structure': 'Fully explores creative possibilities and economies of structure.'[1]

In 2004, Amanda Boulter reviewed a number of CW assessment criteria from various universities. From these she selected a number of recurring criteria, including vividness, particularised detail, power, persuasiveness, writing that is moving, originality, authenticity.[2] These generalities, like those deduced by Elkins, provide a great deal of leeway for interpretation, relying often on an unspoken consensus.

---

[1] *Writing in Education* (NAWE, no. 21, December 2000).
[2] 'Assessing the Criteria: an Argument for Creative Writing Theory', in *New Writing*, ed. Graeme Harper and Richard Kerridge, vol. 1: 2 (2004), pp. 134–5.

The fact that this is un- or undertheorised speaks to the difficulty of distilling the principles which underlie all arts' criticism – the values which are culturally defined by aesthetics. CW is not the only art that needs such clarification. However, whatever its problems, insofar as CW workshop and assessment criteria have a history, it is located in literary criticism. The appropriation of a methodology from one practice to another is more problematic than it might appear, raising and re-raising questions about the relationship between criticism and theory, as well as that between reading and writing.

Criticism and theory: Leavis and Wellek

The relationship between literary criticism and literary theory is one of long-standing contestation, as well as mutual benefit. In 1937 there was a courteous, but vigorous exchange between F. R. Leavis and Rene Wellek in *Scrutiny*, a reminder that concerns about the relationship between methodology and theory are not just special to our 'post-theory' age. The epistolary dialogue began with Wellek's admiration of Leavis's critical revaluations/evaluations, followed by a request for Leavis to articulate his 'theory'. From Leavis's book *Revaluation*, Wellek compiled a usefully succinct list of stylistic features which he thought constituted Leavis's immanent 'theory':

> 'your poetry must be in serious relation to actuality, it must have a firm grasp of the actual, of the object, it must be in relation to life, it must not be cut off from direct vulgar living, it should not be personal in the sense of indulging in personal dreams and fantasies, there should be no emotion for its own sake in it, no afflatus, no mere generous emotion-ality, but a sharp, concrete realisation, a sensuous particularity . . . the only question I would ask you is to defend this position more abstractly and to become conscious that large ethical, philosophical, and, of course, ultimately, also aesthetic *choices* are involved.'[3]

Wellek added: 'Your insistence on a firm grasp on the actual predis-poses you in the direction of a realist philosophy and makes you unap-preciative of a whole phase of human thought: idealism as it comes down from Plato.'[4]

---

[3] 'Literary Criticism and Philosophy', in *The Importance of Scrutiny*, ed. Eric Bentley (Grove Press, 1948), p. 23.
[4] Ibid., p. 24.

Leavis declined to spell out any underlying 'assumptions', because 'I myself am not a philosopher, and that I doubt whether in any case I could elaborate a theory that he [i.e. Wellek] would find satisfactory. . . . Literary criticism and philosophy seem to me to be quite distinct and different kinds of disciplines. . . . This is not to suggest that a literary critic might not, as such, be the better for a philosophic training, but if he were, the advantage, I believe, would manifest itself partly in a surer realisation that literary criticism is not philosophy. . . . I believe that any approach involves limitations, and that it is by recognising them and working within them that one may hope to get something done.'[5] He suggested that it is, nevertheless, possible for work which is not itself consciously theorised, to aid theory: 'There is, I hope, a chance that I may in this way have advanced theory, even if I haven't done the theorising.'[6]

In the 1950s Northrop Frye wrote of literary criticism that it was (still) 'restricted to ritual, Masonic gestures, to raised eyebrows and cryptic comments and other signs of an understanding too occult for syntax'.[7] While this occultism may have been (still be) somewhat obscure, it is still active as a cultural consensus, in the literary and academic worlds. Book reviews in the serious newspapers, literary journals, arts review programmes on radio and television all draw on traditional formal literary principles, as evaluative criteria. As Stanley Fish pointed out in 1980, 'the fact of agreement, rather than being a proof of the stability of objects, is a testimony to the power of an interpretive community to constitute the objects upon which its members . . . can . . . agree'.[8]

As Wellek had done earlier, Frye suggested the evaluative underpinnings of literary criticism: 'in value assumptions: that the concrete is better than the abstract, the active better than the passive, the dynamic better than the static, the unified better than the multiple, the simple better than the complex'.[9]

While most literary historians date the codification of practical criticism from the Cambridge of the 1920s and 1930s, many of these still widely-accepted stylistic rubrics had already been formulated. Quiller-Couch's list of 'rules' for 'good' writing, could easily pass today. It is worth repeating them, to show the continuum through Leavis in the

---

[5] Ibid., p. 30, p. 31, p. 34.
[6] Ibid., p. 34.
[7] *Anatomy of Criticism* (Princeton, 1957, 1990), p. 4.
[8] *Is There a Text in this Class?* (Harvard University Press, 1990, 2003), p. 338.
[9] Frye, 336.

1920s and 1930s, to stylistic choices which are still rehearsed in a great deal of CW literature:

'We laid down certain rules to help us in the way of straight Prose:

(1) *always always prefer the concrete word to the abstract.*
(2) *almost always prefer the direct word to the circumlocution.*
(3) *Generally, use transitive verbs, that strike their object; and use them in the active voice, eschewing the stationary passive, with its little auxiliary its and was's, and its participles getting into the light of your adjectives, which should be few. For, as a rough law, by his use of the straight verb and by his economy of adjectives you can tell a man's style if it be masculine or neuter, writing or "composition".*
(4) *Prefer the short word to the long.*
(5) *Prefer the Saxon word to the Romance.'* [10]

Evaluation and literary value

Within literary studies, evaluation of some kind, at the level of language, text and organisation, is inevitable. As Rene Wellek emphasised: 'the task of evaluation is unavoidable as all students of literature do judge, whether they select their text by tradition and reputation or whether they do it in an individual act of sympathy or enthusiasm. . . . Choices, explicit and implicit, are everywhere involved. What to exclude . . . what to single out . . . and what, inevitably, to appreciate and value.' [406] One must study something, and any oppositional critique must still identify its object.

Literary theory, even in its most anti-canonical moments, has not been, and could not be, free of value judgements, even where it claimed to be non-evaluative. As far as the canon is concerned, the value-base of the traditional literary system has submitted to occasional expansion, rather than being decisively toppled. I opened (literally at random) Catherine Belsey's important book *Critical Practice* on p. 79, to find, within three pages, poems by Donne and Wordsworth, and a speech from Shakespeare.[12] Another key text, *The Semiotics of Theatre and Drama*, by Keir Elam, opened at p. 145, uses a passage from Samuel

---

[10] Arthur Quiller-Couch, *On the Art of Writing* (Cambridge University Press, 1916), p. 38.
[11] *The Attack on Literature* (Harvester Press, 1982), pp. 48–9.
[12] Routledge, 2003 (first published 1980).

Beckett's *Endgame*. All canonical texts. The issue can never be *whether* to evaluate, but to think about, and to make explicit, what evaluative criteria are being applied, and on what they are based, in whatever context.

Criticism, philosophy and mimesis

Leavis's riposte that Wellek was asking him to think as a philosopher is highly pertinent. The stress on the 'concrete' and the 'particular', which Wellek connected to 'a realist philosophy', has other implications, particularly in relation to language's 'two interdependent aspects, a power to denote and a power to connote, that is, a power *to refer* and *to express* a feeling about that which is referred to'.[13]

Jonathan Culler's theoretical formulation has further pinpointed an important relationship between literary criteria, philosophy and form:

'traditionally, Western philosophy has distinguished "reality" from "appearance", things themselves from representations of them, and thought from signs that express it. Signs of representations, in this view, are but a way to get at reality, truth or ideas, and they should be as transparent as possible; they should not get in the way, should not affect or infect the thought or truth they represent. In this framework, speech has seemed the immediate manifestation or presence of thought, while writing, which operates in the absence of the speaker, has been treated as an artificial and derivative representation of speech, a potentially misleading sign of a sign.'[14]

CW criteria built round ideas of plausibility, convincingness, believability, often imply a mimetic 'theory' of literature (i.e. as 'imitation of life'). Wolfgang Iser elaborated the way in which this rests on cultural consensus: 'If . . . we praise a novel because its characters are realistic, we are endowing a verifiable criterion with a subjective assessment, whose claim to validity lies at best in a consensus. Objective evidence for subjective preferences does not make the value judgement itself objective, but merely objectifies its preferences.'[15] The formal features of a

---

[13] Peter Abbs, *English within the Arts* (Hodder & Stoughton, 1982), p. 13.
[14] Jonathan Culler, *Literary Theory: A Very Short Introduction* (Oxford, 1997, 2000), p. 9.
[15] *The Act of Reading* (Johns Hopkins University Press, 1978), p. 25.

piece of writing, given high value, cannot be seen as merely neutral categories.

If imaginative writing as an 'imitation of life' is vaunted in the workshop, it is relatively easy to see why the CW fiction workshop has tended to produce variants on realism – a concern of CW in the US (see Chapter 15). The idea that language and reality, words and their referents, can be easily correlated, is very different from the Saussurean notion that 'Language is not a "nomenclature" that provides labels for pre-existing categories; it generates its own categories.'[16] To point out this contradiction is not to dispense with referentiality (see Chapter 20). Nor is to take sides in any diversionary discussion about whether realism is, *per se,* good or bad, reactionary or progressive.

The creative–critical

The appropriation of terminologies deriving from traditional literary criticism into workshop practice, ignoring historical debates between theory and criticism, and leap-frogging over contemporary literary theory, is one sign of the often uneasy relationship between English and CW. CW has not only developed its own methodologies, but also its own 'solutions' to the convention of the academic essay. This is sometimes asserted as a reconciliation between the creative–critical, since the CW community is generally at best suspicious of, at worst downright hostile to, any kind of discursive, or proto-discursive writing.

CW's solution to this has been to develop, for both undergraduate and postgraduate students, what is variously called commentary, self-reflective writing, a critical essay, a writing journal, an exegesis, ficto-criticism, or the supplementary discourse. This accompanies the 'creative' work proper – the fiction, poetry or drama. This development is an acknowledgement of the symbiotic link between discursive criticism in literary studies, and at the same time a statement of autonomy, which serves to reinforce CW's assertion that imaginative writing is self-expression, located in the field of right-brain 'creativity', which is counterposed to logic, the structuring of argument, and the acknowledgement of its own histories.

However, the solution, which might appear to hybridise the relationship between the creative and the critical, or even transcend their differences, raises more questions and problems. The development of

---

[16] Ibid., p. 59.

self-reflective commentary bears an important relationship to the explicit incorporation of subjectivity into what is often considered an otherwise 'impersonal' pedagogic process. The narrative of these alternative forms of commentary heavily features the first-person pronoun – foregrounding the student's own report, or point of view, on the pedagogic process in which they have participated. The main problem with this is that it actually returns the *ersatz* left-brain activity (otherwise represented by the discursive essay) to the sphere of therapy. The reading and assessment of these documents in the end hinges on the way in which the teacher 'reads' the student self, and believes what the student 'tells' about his/her thinking. In a field where 'show, don't tell' is often trotted out as golden advice, this is more than a little ironic. Again, it is the self, rather than the work, which is being assessed.

CW criticism as a theory of reading

Paul Dawson has argued that the 'pedagogical practice of the workshop is fundamentally one of critical reading',[17] rather than one based on a theory of writing. This suggests a) that the heritage of literary criticism is unproblematic, and b) that theories of reading and theories of writing are interchangeable, or even one and the same thing. For Dawson, what enables the workshop is 'a theory of reading. . . .'[18]

Dawson has claimed (and he is not the only one) that the workshop actually 'teaches' criticism, co-opting Percy Lubbock's definition of literary criticism in *The Craft of Fiction*, published in 1921,[19] to validate workshop practice:

> 'The qualms that Lubbock experiences in the face of a canonised text are not felt when his method is transferred to the student manuscript. For workshopping does not just ask how a finished work might have been improved, but how a work in progress might be coaxed towards becoming a finished piece.'[20]

This is an odd appropriation of traditional literary criticism which, in whatever form, does not have as its project the matter of how a finished

---

17 Ibid., p. 60.
18 Ibid., p. 88.
19 Jonathan Cape, 1966.
20 Dawson, p. 98.

work 'might be improved', but addresses the 'complete' work in its published form. Any Machereyan 'gaps' or 'absences' derive from the process of critical reading/interpretation and exegesis, and have as their object a hermeneutical outcome, not one of changing or literally re-writing the original object.

The Lubbock-Dawson equation of critical-reading with writing-criticism may be seductive as a justification of CW methodology, but it is conceptually flawed. Reading and writing entail different actions and processes, applied to different 'objects' at different moments, with quite different outcomes. Even where they may take place within the same procedure, they are analytically distinct. Reader-response and reception theory have developed precisely out of this understanding.

The proposition that CW is based on a theory of reading returns us to the vexed question of intentionality, and the idea that authorial intent can be captured through reading. Lubbock idealistically believed that through criticism, 'The hours of the author's labour are lived again by the reader, the pleasure of creation is renewed.'[21] This same trope is repeated for CW students in R. V. Cassill's *Writing Fiction* (1962): 'rather than trying to understand a finished work as critical observers, students must attempt to recreate the process of composition as if they were the writer'.[22] Applied to workshop practice, this assumes that the student's 'intention' can somehow be discovered, through a combination of retrospective clairvoyance and mind-reading – second-guessing what might improve the text, and what its author may have had 'in mind'. To build a pedagogical set of principles on 'reading' the impossible, the invisible, is to reaffirm the unteachability of the most highly desired and elusive element of CW: talent, and genius.

Dawson has justified CW pedagogy as a 'theory of reading' by reversing its perspective: in the workshop, he suggested, this becomes '*reading from the inside*; the practice of writing as a means of developing literary appreciation and critical skills' (his italics).[23] This amounts to a colonisation of what has traditionally been the province of literary studies; the CW workshop now teaches criticism, 'from the inside', but without any attempt to relate such criticism to the history of literature and its varied traditions of commentary, let alone investigate and question the principles of such criticism. To claim that CW is based on a theory of reading

---

[21] Lubbock, p. 24.
[22] R. V. Cassill, *Writing Fiction* (Pocket Books, 1962), p. 94.
[23] Ibid., p. 71.

is additionally ironic, when reading itself has, to judge by the frustration and exhortation of CW's teachers, become the new Missing Subject.

Conclusions: from description to prescription

In 1992, Malcolm Bradbury wrote that CW 'has generated very little in the way of self-analysis or theoretical publication. . . . It could also be argued that literary criticism itself provides us with the theory that can profitably surround the subject.'[25] Pointing out that the evaluative criteria for literary criticism were developed *post hoc*, as descriptive categories adduced from published literary work, he argued that 'the only effective kind of critical theory is one that is empirically descriptive rather than prescriptive; one which tolerates the variety of literature's variation and innovation and is accordingly *post facto*.'[26]

This raises a crucially important point: if a significant cultural tradition is based on *post facto* analysis, the template cannot simply be transferred from product to process, without, to put it simply, transforming description to prescription. Of course, all pedagogy is, to some extent prescriptive. However, the judgement of product (the complete text) prematurely forecloses the pedagogic process, leaving no time or space for the investigation and understanding of its 'raw' materials – language, conventions, and, in the end, the nature of the individual, socially contexted, imagination. The workshop is thus driven by a series of piecemeal pragmatic assumptions about *rewriting*, not reading or writing.

---

[25] Malcolm Bradbury, *Times Literary Supplement, 7* January 1992.
[26] Bradbury and Palmer, pp. 24–6.

15
Composition and Creative Writing: US Critiques

The analyses and reservations about CW pedagogy in previous chapters have already been aired. Because of the longer history of CW, and the linked presence of Composition, academic and public literary discussion have occurred and recurred during the past three decades. In most cases CW and Composition are all part of English departments; however, the professional organisations which match these are separate: CW has its own organisation in the Association of Writing Programs, and English belongs with the Modern Languages Association.

A creative writing manifesto

In 2000, David Fenza, Executive Director of the Associated Writing Programs (AWP) in the US, wrote a long riposte to pieces written by various academics and writers during the 1980s and 1990s, called 'Creative Writing and its Discontents'. Fenza answered a number of criticisms of CW, and presented a thirteen-point manifesto for the subject.[1]

Counterposing the benefits of CW as against theory, Fenza drew on his own experience in graduate school: 'for a brief, regrettable while, I fell under the spell of certain literary theories. I deposited critiques in workshops that were so deeply informed by the latest philosophical, linguistic, psychological, and political discourse that even I had no idea what I was saying . . .'.[2]

---

[1] Published in *The Writer's Chronicle*, March/April 2000, and reprinted in *Writing in Education*, issue no. 20 (Summer 2000).
[2] Ibid., p. 21.

Locating the main reform of CW as a 'shift in literary culture from one that was mainly retrospective to one that was both retrospective and prospective, both historical and creative,'[3] Fenza made considerable claims for CW, some of which will already be familiar: 'Classes in creative writing are an excellent means of introducing students to a wider range of intellectual inquiry and humane virtues . . . to teach students critical reading skills, the elements of fiction and verse, general persuasive writing skills, and an appreciation of literary works of the present and past.'[4] More grandly, he claimed that a programme in CW 'Fosters a study of literature that marries theory and practice, aesthetics and scholarship, literary conservation and innovation. . . . Advances the ideals of a liberal and humane education by inspiring, exercising, and strengthening the efficacy of the human will to do good, to make a meaningful difference in art and in society.'[5]

The claims are ambitious, and even if they were sustained by the realities of CW pedagogy, would be more than somewhat overwheening; effectively, CW sounds as though it can and does usurp all the functions of an English department, as well as bringing back into focus the (in some quarters) discredited aims of Arnold, the Leavises et al. The idea that this particular kind of exercise of creativity, through harnessing the imagination in education, produces a more desirable citizen, also echoes the ambitions of many of those involved in the Progressive Education movement; these are important claims, which go well beyond those of limited educational reform.

Fenza was not the only one to claim great cultural importance for CW in its impact on the literary world. In 'Theory, Creative Writing and the Impertinence of History', R. M. Berry wrote in 1994 that: 'One could persuasively argue that in America the most influential theory of literature since World War II has been creative writing. John Barth estimated that by 1984 CW programs had produced over 75,000 literary practitioners . . . [with] the likelihood that CW programs exert a more direct influence than any other part of the American academy on the non academic production, distribution and consumption of literature.'[6]

---

[3] Ibid., p. 16.
[4] Ibid., p.18.
[5] Ibid., p. 19.
[6] *Colors of a Different Horse*, ed. Wendy Bishop and Hans Ostrom (National Council of Teachers of English, US, 1994), p. 57.

Criticisms of CW

As a consequence, perhaps, commentators kept a close eye on CW. Joseph Epstein took the line that workshops contributed to a dumbing down of poetry, in 'Who Killed Poetry?'[7], and Dana Gioia argued that poetry had become cliquey and esoteric in 'Can Poetry Matter?'[8] Positioning their critiques more politically, in 1988 Donald Morton and Mas'ud Zavarzadeh suggested an opportunistic reason for changes in attitudes to CW in English departments:

> 'Humanist scholar-critics who not so long ago were contemptuous of creative writing programs because they degraded literary scholarship, have come today to rely on the institutional power of creative writers (realists who are on the bestseller lists and are therefore popular/powerful in universities) to help rescue them from the onslaught of theory.'[9]

CW, they argued, helped the 'humanists' to counter assumptions challenged by postmodern theory, including 'the idea of the free "subject", the integrity of "experience", the sharp separation of "reading" from "writing", the individual "voice", the "authority" of the author, uniqueness of "style", the obedience of the reader, "originality" and "intuition"'.[10] As a result, the workshop process, they argued, regressively aimed to recover intentionality: 'the meaning that is located in the text by its ordinary agent, the author'.[11]

The emphasis in the workshop on a 'pluralistic' individualism, led by notions of self-expression, 'exposes the fact that the very concept of pluralism itself' (i.e. the notion that there is 'equality' in difference) reproduces 'the relations of exploitation in (capitalist) society'.[12] Far from encouraging egalitarianism (at undergraduate level, at any rate), as Fenza claimed, CW's principles and methodologies produced the opposite.

---

[7] *Commentary*, August 1988.
[8] *Can Poetry Matter?* (Graywolf Press, 1992).
[9] 'Cultural Politics of the Fiction Workshop', in *Cultural Critique*, no. 11 (Winter 1988–9), p. 168.
[10] Ibid., p. 155.
[11] Ibid., p. 158.
[12] Ibid., p. 167.

English – composition – creative writing

A symposium published in 1989, edited by Joseph M. Moxley, is still regularly referenced in CW discussions in the US.[13] All the contributors were CW teachers, many also trained and skilled in teaching Composition. A few contributors suggested that the traditional CW workshop was flawed and needed some 'alternatives'. Moxley rehearsed the familiar trio of criticisms levelled at CW: that it was insufficiently 'rigorous', that students were ignorant about literature and reluctant to read, and that 'standards' were low.

Before the 1970s, wrote Eve Shelnutt, in 'Notes from a Cell: Creative Writing Programs in Isolation', 'creative writers in the university were men of letters . . . whose relationship to imaginative writing was profoundly linked with the study of literature as an indicator of a society's well-being. . . . MFA students are largely separated from the broader intellectual life of the university . . . not the fault of writing students but a result of the structure of English departments that contain literature, composition and writing programs.'[14] Now CW itself was seeking isolation.

In a feisty and controversial article in 1999, 'Creative Writing in the Academy',[15] David Radavich acknowledged the institutional strengths of CW: 'Today, creative writing represents one of the three major "power blocs" in our department, along with literature and composition, competing for courses, positions and funding support.'[16] However, he too targeted CW's isolationism and the anti-intellectual consequences:

'Courses that teach poetry, fiction and drama writing can offer students valuable insights and experience on today's college campuses. But only if creative writing classes are brought into deeper and wider relationship with other courses in the curriculum; only if such programs maintain a pedagogy not geared toward packaging for the marketplace but instead emphasising reading skills, critical thinking, language awareness, and historical consciousness, qualities and abilities that will prove useful in many walks of life; and only if such programs can be made to foster more understanding of public concerns and social responsibility.'[17]

---

[13] Joseph M. Moxley (ed.), *Creative Writing in America: Theory and Pedagogy* (National Council of Teachers of English, 1989).

[14] Ibid., p. 7 and p. 9.

[15] *Profession* (Modern Language Association, 1999).

[16] Ibid., pp. 4–5 (of typescript sent to author).

[17] Ibid., p. 10.

In the three-way structure of US English departments (English, Composition and Creative Writing) this isolationism, according to Eve Shelnutt, explained why 'There are no theorists of the teaching of creative writing equal to the theorists of literature and composition.'[18] Donald M. Murray pointed out that the emphasis in the workshop on 'criticism' and revising assumed that students already knew how to 'write'. George Garrett wrote that 'the writing *workshop* is not the only, or, indeed, always the best workable model for teachers of creative writing. We are going to have to consider other kinds and forms of class-work in addition to the workshop.'[19] One of the concepts drawn from composition pedagogy pointed to what is called 'pre-writing'; which, while not an entirely comfortable concept, at least shifts the focus from workshop-based re-writing to the process of writing itself: thinking, taking notes, writing drafts. In the US these – what we would call study skills – are more firmly located in Composition courses.

In her second essay, Eve Shelnutt went further. On the grounds that students needed 'protection' from the workshop, her teaching included a range of other work: memorising exercises, reading and discussing professional writers' memoirs, occasional theoretical texts, before students wrote their own stories. Shelnutt is forceful in asking students NOT to reveal any possible 'personal' sources for their fiction. Precisely because she recognises that there may be deep feelings and even 'trauma' behind some writing, she excludes them from class discussion. They are private.

This highlights what is a profoundly ethical matter, very rarely acknowledged as such; what writing-as-therapy encourages in personal revelation from students, whether in their writing or in classroom discussion, is actually, however carefully buttressed, intrusive. The stress on memory, difficult emotional experiences, dreams, personal relation-ships becomes coercive when it is the required basis of the pedagogic practice itself. When CW commentators write about needing to bring therapeutic mechanisms into the classroom, they are describing a situation of their own making. While all of the above 'personal' elements may form part of the panoply of resources students bring to their writing, it is, to put it crudely, for them to know and think about, not for teachers to coerce into public display. Volunteering information is one thing, but coercing personal revelations is frankly unethical. Anna Leahy took a forthright line on this: 'Frankly, I don't want to know personally

---

[18] Shelnutt, p. 15.
[19] Moxley, p. 61.

about students' heartbreaks, their family tragedies, or their enlightening experiences at raves. . . .'[20]

Composition, literature and the CW workshop

The debate about CW reforms is interestingly informed by Composition teachers who also teach CW. In 1994, Hans Ostrom commented that CW teachers 'fall back on the workshop in its simplest form: "going over" poems and stories in a big circle, holding forth from time to time, pretending to have read the material carefully, breaking up squabbles like a hall monitor, marking time.'[21] Katharine Haake echoed this: 'What could it take, after all, to sit around in a circle and explain to my students how to make their stories better?'[22]

This recalls Gerald Graff's comment on the importance of the New Criticism as a necessary support for unschooled teachers:

'It was perhaps the instructors who needed the New Criticism most. . . . From my own experience . . . in a stepped up Ph.D program of the early sixties, I can testify that usually I was lucky to be one evening ahead of my undergraduate classes. I remember the relief I experienced as a beginning assistant professor when I realized that by concentrating on the text itself I could get a good discussion going about almost any literary work without having to know anything about its author, its circumstances of composition, or the history of its reception. Furthermore, as long as the teaching situation was reduced to a decontextualised encounter with a work, it made no difference that I did not know how much the students knew or what I could assume about their high school or other college work – just as it made no difference that they had no more basis for inferring anything about me than I had about them. Given the vast unknowns on both sides of the lectern, "the work itself" was indeed our salvation.'[23]

---

[20] In *Power and Identity in the Creative Writing Classroom: The Authority Project*, ed. Anna Leahy (Multilingual Matters, 2005), p. 21.

[21] *Colors of a Different Horse*, ed. Wendy Bishop and Hans Ostrom (National Council of Teachers of English, US, 1994, p. xiv).

[22] 'Teaching Creative Writing if the Shoe Fits', in Bishop and Ostrom, p. 77.

[23] *Professing Literature: An Institutional History* (University of Chicago Press, 1987), pp. 178–9.

Hard-cop, soft-cop criticism

In 2005, Mary Swander described 'the abusive basketball-coach method to teach writing workshops. . . . We were to learn through trial by fire, through negativity, through humiliation, through hearing what we and others had done wrong. In any other skill-building class, from forming language to driver's education, students were asked to practice the basic steps of the craft, carefully mastering one chunk of knowledge before adding another. Why was the teaching of creative writing so different?'[24] Interestingly, she compared part of this approach to pre-Progressive Education approaches, where a punitive and harsh pedagogy allowed adults to find easy ways to control children; and also to a hangover from militarism during the period following the Second World War expansion: 'Many of the workshop students of that period were on the GI bill, returning vets who were familiar with this philosophy. And the workshop was mostly male.'[25]

Questions or answers

A common trope in the relatively small number of texts which have reservations about CW pedagogy is the the use of *questions*, rather than argued disquisition. This is in keeping with soft-cop 'constructive criticism', which has produced a reservation about asserting alternatives too directly, as well as a reluctance for debate. It is also congruent with CW's hostility to the 'left-brain' pursuit of logical argument, through discursive writing. Hans Ostrom asked: 'What might be gained by dismantling the workshop model altogether and starting from scratch?'[26] The implied answer to this can only be 'a great deal'; otherwise the question would not be asked in a rhetorical form.

Katharine Haake, one of the very few who discuss gender in CW pedagogy, produced an extremely provocative, and fundamental, series of questions: 'If the workshop is of questionable, or limited, value, what alternative methodologies can we conceive for our pedagogy? What might be appropriate goals for our classes? How might we learn from current composition theory to shift our emphasis away from the product

---

[24] 'Duck, Duck, Turkey: Using Encouragement to Structure Workshop Assignments', in Leahy, p. 167.
[25] Ibid., p. 168.
[26] Bishop and Ostrom, p. xx.

to the process of writing? What might constitute an effective creative writing curriculum at the undergraduate and graduate level? How can creative writing be most productively situated within English studies? What are the ideological assumptions of our enterprise? Finally, what is it we want our students to learn?'[27]

She, at least, answered some of her questions. CW teaches, she wrote, 'that writing proceeds from language, which is itself a system of signs governed by rules and conventions, and not a transparent medium through which we reflect on the world' – in other words, linguistic and poststructural theory are vital to any approach to teaching CW. However, when she presented such approaches to her classes, she found that 'the vast majority [of students] was clearly disinterested in the critical framework I'd provided. Half were in the class because they wanted to "express themselves"; another half were there for easy credit.'[28]

Reform

However, even in the US, real intra-disciplinary reform has remained an intractable matter. Peter Vandenberg, writing in 2004, commented that there is little serious co-operation between composition and CW, and pulls from both to separate from English: 'While compositionists often assume to be directing the movement toward advanced undergraduate study "in" writing, academic creative writers have a deeply entrenched sense of ownership over the term and a curriculum deeply embedded in most English departments. Compositionists seeking to institutionalise writing majors in their own terms face a formidable ideological resistance from creative writers unable to share their discourse.'[29]

One of the main reasons for this was articulated by Wendy Bishop: 'Seldom discussed are the basic commonalities of writing a poem and writing an essay. . . . Literature with a capital L is primarily a canonised set while writing literature with a small l may be thought of as writing in order to understand genre conventions, writers' choices, readers' responses. . . .'[30] This creative–critical hierarchy is more clearly articu-

---

[27] *What Our Speech Disrupts: Feminism and Creative Writing Studies* (National Council of Teachers of English, 2000), pp. 80–1.

[28] Ibid., pp. 77–8.

[29] 'Integrated Writing Programmes in American Universities: Whither Creative Writing?', *New Writing*, vol. 1: 1 (2004), p. 10.

[30] 'Crossing the Line: on Creative Composition and Composing Creative Writing', in ibid., pp. 190–1.

lated in the US, where the conceptual gulf between the genius-produc-ing-Literature and the workhorses teaching basic writing skills is partly reproduced in the CW–Composition pedagogic divide.

The CW teacher

Under the so-called egalitarianism bruited by workshop protocols is the actuality of the pedagogic relationship between teacher and students. In 2001 Kelly Ritter's trenchant piece, 'Professional Writers/Writing Professionals: Revamping Teacher training in Creative Writing PhD Programs', addressed the difficulties facing new/young teachers of CW.[31] Ritter was teaching composition and CW, first-year courses often taught by PhD assistants. Ritter pulled no punches: these young teachers '. . . have stumbled along, without formal, professional training or guid-ance'.[32]

While other doctoral disciplines provided a 'regular theoretical peda-gogical training',[33] CW teachers were expected to 'pick up' approaches to teaching by osmosis, from their own workshop experiences. Ritter highlighted the way CW deliberately distanced itself from other academic practices: 'They are *writers*, not teachers. They are *artists*, not academic professionals.'[34] Professional writers brought in to teach simi-larly resist the reality of their academic position: 'Purists in writing programs often reject the notion that a writer who succeeds as a writer by trade need be trained in any formal, academic sense.'[35] Thus, while '. . . undertaking a degree that in general stands as an intellectual, schol-arly terminal degree in the English studies community . . . they are doing so in the service of a historically anti-intellectual, sometimes anti-schol-arly field, creative writing'.[36]

The teacher as authority

The desire for career-academic teachers of CW to be identified as 'writers' is a reinforcement of the hierarchy of the creative–critical divide. When

---

[31] *College English*, vol. 64, no. 2 (November 2001).
[32] Ibid., p. 210.
[33] Ibid., p. 210.
[34] Ibid., p. 210.
[35] Ibid., p. 215.
[36] Ibid., p. 209.

CW students are also referred to as 'writers', a spurious egalitarianism is adduced, along with yet another implied claim for the specialness of CW. In her article 'The Resurrected Author: Creative Writers in 21st-century Higher Education', Jeri Kroll, an American teaching in Australia, used a number of terms for CW students: 'authors', 'apprentice writers', 'young writer', 'acolyte', 'creative writing student', 'writer', 'postgraduate author'.[37]

If both teacher and student are referred to as 'writers', the distinction between them (hierarchical and/or functional) is screened in favour of a terminological egalitarianism which belies the reality. The teacher is a professional, whose job in the classroom is to teach, and the student is there to learn what s/he does not yet know. There is nothing demeaning about this. The best classroom experiences in any subject can be wonderful precisely *because* they are based on this division of labour.

The relationship between gender and authority (touched on in Chapter 12) was articulated by Anna Leahy in 'Who Cares – and How: the Value and Cost of Nurturing': 'Creative writing itself is deemed feminine in relation to literary studies or literary theory and based on notions of creativity as a right-brain, intuitive, spontaneous, emotional process.'[38] This follows the gender tussle for authority within CW itself, which mirrors that in literature. Quiller-Couch's desire to assert the 'masculinity' of literary style represented a conflation of respectability for the new subject of English, with male authority; within CW, with its higher percentage of female than male students, the gender tussle is still present. For male teachers, the appropriation of the 'feminine', as still associated with literature (art, emotion, intuition), is balanced against the more technical, 'scientific' features of Composition. Indeed, Leahy suggested that the approaches of compositionists can be adapted for CW, to counteract the assumption that 'creative writing professors can best learn through osmosis, individual trial and error, and reinvention of wheels without yet knowing very much about the vehicle from the driver's seat'.[39]

Conclusions

There are conclusions to be drawn, which can be extrapolated to apply to the CW situation in the UK. The family trio of composition, literature

---

[37] 'New Writing', vol. 2, 2004, pp. 89–102.
[38] Leahy, op. cit., p. 15.
[39] Ibid., p. xii.

and creative writing in the US highlights one of the central tussles in CW's aims: between that of training professional *writers* and the wider remit of teaching imaginative *writing* as such, raising fundamental questions about methodology and pedagogical procedure. The isolationism of CW, with its colonising desires and suspicion/hostility to the intellectual/theory aspects of literary study, as well as the experiences of composition have not made any integrated rapport in the USA any easier, even where the strands co-exist in the same department.

There is more than a passing awareness of the ethics of exposing personal experience in the workshop. Despite reservations about the emotional 'health' of students, the assumption still prevails that difficult, or even traumatic emotions are to be forced or brought into the classroom (or, at the very least, are licensed), resulting in a call for procedures more appropriate for a therapy group than a university seminar.

Because of the differences in teacher-training in the US, the inadequacy of CW training (for the UK, read 'virtual absence of') contrasts with the more concerted preparation of PhD students for English and composition teaching. Seemingly, along with the Muse to help the putative great writer, comes teaching expertise as a gift, or by osmosis from the workshop experience.

Questions are regularly raised about the need for reform, if not radical change in CW pedagogy; while there is clearly a logic about calling for greater liaison between English–Composition–CW, the barriers against such contact are constructed by a number of factors: there is a struggle as to hierarchy, with English literature and CW jostling for supremacy, and Composition as the humble support. In particular, there is CW's own wilful isolationism, its claim of supreme specialness, which leads to its refusal to look at its own history, the history of the discipline which gives it its criteria (literary criticism), and to take on board the complex and important legacies of literary theory. And here Theory itself must carry some responsibility, for did it not proclaim the Death of the Author? And does not CW, in its own claims, and in the vocabulary of its literature, entirely depend on the presence of the Author? Read on for answers.

16
Reconceiving Creative Writing: The Author is Not Dead, Merely in Some Other Text

The death of the Author

The Death of the Author was a glorious conceit. Roland Barthes' seven-page essay, first published in 1967, loosed a phrase which has become a cultural cliché. If the Author is Dead, how did s/he die? Was it natural causes, was it an accident or was it murder? If the first, was it slow or sudden; if the second, how did it happen? If the last, what was the motive and whodunit? The answers are not only important as an extension of work in theory, but because the presence of CW in the academy supposedly counters the finality of the claim of the Author's death. According to CW, the author is returned to the centre of discussions about literature, along with the text, subjectivity and intentionality.

Ownership and authority conceptualised

In his brilliant exegesis of postmodern concepts of authorship, Sean Burke has pointed out the central contradiction in Barthes' thesis: 'One must, at base, be deeply *auteurist* to call for the Death of the Author.'[1] In other words, the Author not only never went away, but her/his necessary presence was reaffirmed by the very theory which sought to abolish him/her. Explaining the impetus which prompted his book, Burke wrote:

---

[1] *The Death and Return of the Author* (Edinburgh University Press, 2004), p. 27.

'When one (also) takes into account the sheer incomprehensibility of "the death of the author" to even the finest minds outside the institution, it is clear that the concept functioned to keep the non-academic at bay. . . . It was from an impatience with this insularity that *The Death and Return of the Author* emerged.'[2]

Burke dissected texts by Barthes, Derrida and Foucault, focusing on those which are key to postmodern cultural philosophy. Like all textual scholars, Burke's analyses are based on close reading: 'What is proposed here . . . is a close reading of anti-authorial discourses, an inquiry into how authorial absence is elaborated as a point of theory, and how it is put into practice as a guiding principle of interpretation and critical histories.'[3] Secondly, by 'reading' gaps in the theorisation and analysing the circularity of the arguments, he has vitally cleared a space within which the concept of the 'Author' can be clearly seen as always present, in some form, and indeed, ultimately regenerated by the very theory which sought to overthrow it.

Individual and systemic authorship

Burke distinguished between three kinds of authorship, two of which are conceptual. First, there is empirical individual authorship (singular, named, responsibility for the production of a text); second, there is the contribution of an individual authorial responsibility in founding (writing) named systems of thought – where 'Aristotle is, in a sense, the author of Aristotelianism, Euclid the author of geometry', effectively involved in the 'founding of a discursivity'.[4] The third systemic kind of authorship is linked with the second – a concept of authorship encapsulated within cinema's 'auteur' theory – and refers to the inter-relationship between individual responsibility (the division of labour) and the collaborative authoring entailed in producing a coherent, identifiable, singular work.

While there are clear conceptual distinctions between the first and the second kinds of authorship, there is also a contradiction embedded in the very distinction:

'Barthes's corpus is as alive and as well as that of any post-war writer, as is his biography. The theorist of the author's death became a

---

[2] Ibid., p. ix.
[3] Ibid., p. 18.
[4] Ibid., pp. 91–2.

celebrity in France, an enthusiastic interviewee on television, the radio, for newspapers; he went on to write two confidently autobiographical works, texts which were not autobiographies but autobiographical, books of feeling, impressions, of the self; he talked, we know, of writing a novel . . . might we not venture that the birth of the reader is not achieved at the cost of the death of the author, but rather at that of showing how the critic *too* becomes an author?'[5]

The irony continues: the theorists '*created* oeuvres of great resonance, scope and variety . . . a vast body of secondary literature has grown up around their work, one which . . . has re-enacted precisely the predominance of source over supplement, master over disciple, primary over secondary. They have been accorded all the privileges traditionally bestowed upon the great author. No contemporary author can lay claim to anything approaching the authority that their texts have enjoyed over the critical establishment in the last twenty years or so. Indeed, were we in search of the most flagrant abuses of critical *auteurism* in recent times then we need look no further than the secondary literature on Barthes, Foucault and Derrida. . . .'[6] Thus 'criticism itself has become a primary discourse'.[7] Malcolm Bradbury's fear that criticism (or theory itself) was in danger of becoming a primary discourse seems to have been fulfilled.

Auteur and performance theory

Auteur theory developed in France, where 'Truffaut argued that French cinema should move away from the prevailing model of the 1950s, in which film was seen as subordinate to an original "literary" text.'[8] As the director took/was given over-arching credit for film (its *auteur*, its 'author'), the initiating script's writer 'is conventionally seen as a minor player in the hierarchy of film production'.[9]

Equally, performance theory, which applies semiological analysis to the many functions contributing to the creation of meanings in stage performance, has also, effectively, diminished or even dismissed the role of the writer, through the idea that the written script is merely a 'blue-

---

[5] Ibid., p. 61.
[6] Ibid., p. 178.
[7] Ibid., p. 177.
[8] Andrew Bennett, *The Author* by (Routledge, 2005), p. 104.
[9] Ibid., p. 103.

print' for the 'real thing' – the meaning-creating moment of perform-ance. See Chapter 21 for further discussion of this.

Usurpation and authority

Burke suggests that in these discussions of the multiple manifestations and implications of authorship, there is a tension, amounting to a conceptual power struggle between usurpation and authority: 'the death of the author is promulgated . . . in the form of usurpation . . . insepara-ble from a strong act of rewriting by all these critics: Barthes rewriting Balzac, Foucault making literally what he will of four hundred years of philosophical thought, Derrida rewriting Rousseau. The seizure from the author, of the right to produce the text is the motivating thrust behind all these extirpations. . . . Having rewritten the canonical text, the critic goes on to produce texts of his own.'[10]

One could not put the case more clearly; the term 'usurpation' is apt. Just as the theoretical journey to annihilate Author and Text leaves the critic/academic-reader intact, so here the covert attack is identified as a process of usurpation. If it is inaccurate to use the term 'author' to cover the production of individual texts, what is it that the theorists them-selves do when they write and publish? If their status (economic and ideological) as academics/critics necessitates their identification as authors (i.e. they may proclaim the death of authorship but they cannot help but be authors), then a further act of concealment becomes neces-sary.

This has taken the form of a metaphor. Theorists have appropriated the term 'writing' as a metaphor for reading, and consequent critical exegesis/interpretation. Even Burke uses the word in this way: he refers to 'a strong act of rewriting', to the 'act of rewriting'. The use of writing as metaphor becomes a covert way for the critical mode to assert its primacy over the 'creative' mode, while appearing to privilege the latter by giving it critical attention. As Burke noted:

'The decision as to whether we read a text with or without an author remains an act of critical choice governed by the protocols of a certain way of reading rather than any "truth of writing". Which is to say that authorial absence can never be a cognitive statement about literature and discourse in general, but only an intra-critical statement and one

---

[10] Burke, p. 177.

which has little to say about authors themselves except in so far as the idea of authorship reflects on the activity and status of the critic.'[11]

In other words, the concept of the death of the author is about critical procedures which really concern the scholar/critic's relationship to the text, displaced onto a putative discussion about the author. Such discussion is convenient because it slides phonetically from author to authority, and thus to the idea that there is such a thing as authorial 'control' over the way a text is read, and that this must not only be challenged but actively usurped by the authority of the scholar-critic.

This is surely one of the most ridiculously manipulative ideas in the literary postmodern lexicon. How on earth can any author/writer 'control' the reading and/or meaning of their text? Who could possibly believe in such a claim? Even if the author is physically present, or alive and within reach of communication – email, letter, phone – how exactly does/could the author control the mode of reading, let alone the mode and terms of interpretation, evaluation, challenge? If authorial statements about the meanings of their writings were utterly respected, it would put all reviewers, critics and academics out of business. This is yet another disingenuous displacement of critical responsibility onto a spurious notion of unprovable authorial intentionality, blaming the invisible and absent authors for the ways in which other people read their texts.

Additionally, since part of theory's project was to shift from the idea that meaning resided in the text to the idea that meaning resided in the work of the reader, the term 'author' (in the sense of authorial authority) merely becomes a metaphor for 'text'. Thus theory, in its laudable attempts to exploit conceptualised argument, in language which is as precise as possible, in the end falls back on metaphor to prove its point.

Notions of authorial 'control' are also efficiently countered by Andrew Bennett's comment that 'the work of writing involves, precisely, going beyond the conscious intentions of the writing subject, that the writing subject, at some point, somewhere, in some sense, doesn't know what she [*sic*] is doing. . . . The author as unknowing, as not, or as not quite, conscious of what she does, as impersonal or as multiple, are perhaps the most common forms of twentieth- and indeed twenty-first century authors' explanations of their own work.'[12]

---

[11] Ibid., p. 176.
[12] Bennet, p. 80 and pp. 68–9.

Conclusions

Jonathan Culler remarked that: 'To ask of what an author is conscious and of what unconscious is as fruitless as to ask which rules of English are consciously employed by speakers and which are followed unconsciously.'[13] In an echo of Macherey's discussion of what the text does not and cannot 'say', Andrew Bennett pointed out, 'Derrida's work is pervasively engaged with the apparent paradox that an author can always say "more, less, or something other than he *would mean* (*voudrait dire*) . . .".'[14]

Finally, the metaphorical notion of authorial control is belied by recent interest in Bakhtinian theory, and the rationale for renewed attention to the text which this provides. Peter Widdowson, in *Literature*, commented that 'His theory of the "polyphonic" or "dialogic" novel, for example, stresses the presence . . . of various "voices" (heteroglossia) which express different points-of-view and are not subordinated to the author's controlling purpose. The *text*, therefore, articulates liberating and often subversive discourses beyond the author's authority.'[15]

Exposing the contradictions within theory's exploration of the Author does not invalidate the range of discussions which have followed. Ironically, it is perhaps the very fact that theory, often disingenuous, abstruse, as well as difficult and stimulating, could not abolish empirical and theoretical authorship, that lead to some of its approaches being used to form and frame a materialist basis for the pedagogy of imaginative writing.

---

[13] *Structuralist Poetics* (Cornell University Press, 1975), p. 118.
[14] Ibid., p. 82.
[15] Routledge, 1999, pp. 81–2.

17
From Criticism to Theory and On

Elegies

In 1992, Malcolm Bradbury was explicit about one of the hopes behind the MA in 1970: 'that the presence among our own literature students of serious, articulate writers, might have some impact on the bee-swarms of new theory that regularly surge through literature departments, and by which we were also concerned'.[1] In the same year, Stephen Logan, lecturer in English at Magdalene College, Cambridge, wrote in *The Times* that 'literary theory, in its more extreme varieties, was moribund, but that it would take a long time to die'. In 2002 he returned to the same point:

> 'I predict that a period of recuperation will follow . . . the moral and metaphysical disputes conducted under the guise of literary criticism will come out into the open. . . . Theory will be shown to have been a muddled expression of philosophical unease that, lacking the means of expressing itself philosophically, got displaced into the field of literary criticism. Trying to address a profound moral disagreement by literary debate is like trying to cure a stomach ache with aspirin.'[2]

In 2003, Terry Eagleton summarised the fates of those who had spent their lives with Theory: 'The golden age of cultural theory is long past. . . . Fate pushed Roland Barthes under a Parisian laundry van, and afflicted Michel Foucault with Aids. It despatched Lacan, Williams and

---

[1] Malcolm Bradbury, *Times Literary Supplement*.
[2] *The Times Higher Education Supplement*, 26 July, 2002.

Bourdieu, and banished Louis Althusser to a psychiatric hospital for the murder of his wife. It seemed that God was not a structuralist.'[3]

However, even as proto-obituaries are written, more guides to theory proliferate. *Post-Theory*, by Martin McQuillan (1993), *After Theory*, by Thomas Docherty (1996) and *Beyond Poststructuralism*, by Wendell Harris (1996) were followed by *life.after.theory*,[4] edited by Michael Payne and John Schad, which came out in the same year as Eagleton's *After Theory*. Even Eagleton was clear that 'There can be no going back to an age when it was enough to pronounce Keats delectable or Milton a doughty spirit.'[5] A body of knowledge and debate cannot be annihilated, even as its configurations are still on the move.

Theory's triumvirate

One of the most eruditely sceptical and exhilarating books produced in the wake of Theory was Valentine Cunningham's *Reading After Theory*:

> 'Certainly everything that Theory comprises, operates on one zone or another, or in some combination, of what have proved the main continuing focusses of literary theory since poetics and discussion of aesthetics began with the Greeks and Romans. There's only ever been up for grabs, for theory, a simple trio of knowable, thinkable, zones, corresponding to the three components of the basic model of linguistic communication. There is always, and only ever, a sender, a message, and a received – a writer, a text, a reader – the act of writing, the thing written, the reading of the written thing – the literary input, the literary object found to be "there", reader(s) attending to this thereness. Or, if you like, cause, consequence, effect. Only three: but a mighty three for all that. And the whole history of criticism, of theorising, is merely a history of the varying, shifting preoccupation across the ages with these three zones, and with these three alone.'[6]

Cunningham's triumvirate provide a welcome moment of clarity; we cannot unthink theory. Difficult, exciting and frustrating as it may be, it is part of our intellectual and cultural history and heritage. To ignore

---

[3] Terry Eagleton, *After Theory* (Allen Lane, 2003), p. 1.
[4] Continuum, 2003.
[5] Eagleton, op. cit. , p. 1.
[6] *Reading after Theory* (Blackwell, 2002), p. 29.

theory, to pretend it is not there, to claim that CW is, and must be, 'against' theory, is worse than to take issue with it. We must hold the clear triumvirate in our minds – writer–text–reader; but – in applying this thought to CW – we cannot sink into mere empirical appropriation of an imitation of untheorised literary criticism.

The 'difficulty' of theory is both part of the problem and the solution. Recalling Leavis's distinctions between the philosopher and the literary scholar (see Chapter 14), and the later cultural furore caused by the Two Cultures debate, between art and science (see Chapter 7), it is possible to see how CW is part of a continuum in these discussions, whether its practitioners are aware of it or not. It is endemic in the implicit hostility to logical thought and discursive writing, which permeates both the literature and CW's pedagogic practices.

The tension manifest between science and art reappears in arguments about difficult, esoteric language. But 'If "hermeneutical phenomenology" counts as jargon, so does the on-the-job language of dockers and motor mechanics. . . . No layperson opens a botany textbook and shuts it with an irascible bang if they do not understand it straight away. . . . Art, however, seems in principle available to anybody, in a way that knowing about the organic structure of decapods is not.'[7]

What is theory?

Jonathan Culler has succinctly explained how philosophy-derived theory has relevance to literature: 'since the 1960s: writings from outside the field of literary studies have been taken up by people in literary studies because their analyses of language, or mind, or history, or culture, offer new and persuasive accounts of textual and cultural matters'.[8]

'Literary theory is not a disembodied set of ideas but a force in institutions. Theory exists in communities of readers and writers, as a discursive practice, inextricably tangled with educational and cultural institutions. Three theoretical modes whose impact, since the 1960s, has been greatest are the wide-ranging reflections on language, representation, and the categories of critical thought undertaken by deconstruction and psychoanalysis (sometimes in concert, sometimes in

---

[7] Eagleton, *After Theory*, p. 76 and p. 78.
[8] Jonathan Culler, *Literary Theory: A Very Short Introduction* (Oxford, 2000), p. 3.

opposition); the analyses of the role of gender and sexuality in every aspect of literature and criticism by feminism and then gender studies and Queer theory; and the development of historically oriented cultural criticisms (new historicism, post-colonial theory) studying a wide range of discursive practices, involving many objects (the body, the family, race) not previously thought of as having a history.'[9]

Language, the individual subject (the self), meaning and identity

At the centre of theory is the relationship between language, the creation of meaning and the individual, human subject:

'The hallmark of the "linguistic revolution" of the twentieth century, from Saussure and Wittgenstein to contemporary literary theory, is the recognition that meaning is not simply something "expressed" or "reflected" in language: it is actually produced by it . . . we can only have the meanings and experiences in the first place because we have a language to have them in. What this suggests, moreover, is that our experience as individual is social to its roots; for there can be no such thing as a private language, and to imagine a language is to imagine a whole form of social life.'[10]

Ferdinand de Saussure's *Course in General Linguistics*, first posthumously published in 1916, compiled from his notes by his students, is the primary source text:[11]

'Saussure distinguished the system of a language (*la langue*) from particular instances of speech and writing (*parole*). The task of linguistics is to reconstruct the underlying system (or grammar) of a language that makes possible the speech events or *parole*. This involves further distinction between *synchronic* study of a language (focusing on a language as a system at a particular time, present or past) and *diachronic* study, which looks at the historical changes to particular elements of the language. To understand a language as a functioning system is to look at it synchronically, trying to spell out the rules and

---

[9] Ibid., pp. 14–15, and p. 121.
[10] Ibid., pp. 52–3.
[11] Jonathan Culler, *Saussure* (Fontana, 1976).

conventions of the system that make possible the forms and meanings of the language.'[12]

Terry Eagleton articulated the implications of this theory for understanding how the individual was/is 'constructed', and how the individual him/herself constructs meaning through and with language:

'The structuralist emphasis on the "constructedness" of human meaning represented a major advance. Meaning was neither a private experience nor a divinely ordained occurrence: it was the product of certain shared systems of signification. The confident bourgeois belief that the isolated individual subject was the fount and origin of all meaning took a sharp knock: language pre-dated the individual and was much less his or her product than he or she was the product of it.'[13]

This dialectical notion, where the relationship between subject/object, the individual/social, text/context is at the heart of the discussion, makes it impossible to conceive of any simplistic idea of individual identity, of subjectivity itself. In addition, it raises fundamental questions about relatively straightforward notions carried into and through traditional literary criticism about the mimetic nature of literature (as mere 'imitation of life'). In terms of CW's promulgation of imaginative writing as 'self-expression' (i.e. as expressing a graspable, individuated 'self'), the complexity increases: 'We emerge as subjects from inside a reality which we can never fully objectify, which encompasses both "subject" and "object", which is inexhaustible in its meanings and which constitutes us quite as much as we constitute it.'[14] From the point of view of the academy, 'Work in cultural studies has been particularly attuned to the problematical character of identity and to the multiple ways in which identities are formed, experienced and transmitted.'[15]

Interestingly, from a theoretical point of view there is a political slippage in the language. If subjectivity is positioned in a complicated dialectical relationship between *langue* and *parole*, it could blur, if not annihilate, the basis of identity politics: deriving from the cultural movements of the 1970s and 1980s which argued for constituency group identities, whether based on class, gender or ethnic origin.

---

[12] Culler; *Literary Theory*, p. 60.
[13] Eagleton, *Literary Theory* (Blackwell, 2000), p. 93.
[14] Ibid., p. 54.
[15] Culler, *Literary Theory*, p. 45.

'The Incredibly Disappearing Text'

'The Incredibly Disappearing Text' is a phrase used by Valentine Cunningham:[16] 'Theory wipes the textual slate clean. Theory banishes texts.'[17] The implied intellectual Luddism in theory affects the foundations of academic notions of what constitutes the 'subject' and 'object' of study. Frank Kermode and Christopher Norris voiced this concern clearly:

> 'People like myself – old-fashioned people who like texts (we can't even use that word now without bracketing it) – do get worried by the fact that, in our view (and maybe the view is incorrect, maybe there's been a kind of recursive effect), we're getting so far away from the study of literary artefacts, shall we say, that they're in danger of being totally neglected. That's my fear – I'm not afraid of theory, I'm afraid of meta-theory and meta-meta-theory.'[18]

Against this stood Terry Eagleton's broader, theoretically inclusive position on the 'text':

> 'My own view is that it is most useful to see "literature" as a name which people give from time to time for different reasons to certain kinds of writing within a whole field of what Michel Foucault has called "discursive practices", and that if anything is to be an object of study it is this whole field of practices rather than just those sometimes rather obscurely labelled "literature".'[19]

However, while the high and middle theorists took part in these discussions, English departments largely continued to maintain their central focus on traditional definitions of literary texts as objects for study, even when some form of socio-linguistics was added to their approaches. Equally, however, the questions cannot be un-asked.

The Death of the Author and the 'birth' of the reader

The appeal to the reader as the 'creator' and arbiter of meanings created paradoxes of its own:

---

16 Cunningham, p. 69.
17 Ibid., p. 70.
18 'Music, Religion and Art after Theory', in Payne and Schad, op. cit., p. 117.
19 Eagleton, *Literary Theory*, p. 178.

'The work cannot be sprung shut, rendered determinate, by an appeal to the author, for the "death of the author" is a slogan that modern criticism is now confidently able to proclaim. The biography of the author is, after all merely another text, which need not be ascribed any special privilege: this text too can be deconstructed. It is language which speaks in literature, in all its swarming "polysemic" plurality, not the author himself. If there is any place where this seething multiplicity of text is momentarily focussed, it is not the author but the reader.'[20]

Reader-response and reception theory (with their companion in performance studies) developed as custodians of the 'true' sites of the creation of meaning, without in any way removing the text. There must always be something for the 'individual' to read, just as there will always be something which is written by the 'individual'.

The concept of the Reader, then, turns out to be no simpler than that of the Author or the Text, either within theory, or within the practices of writing and reading literature. In a sense, reader-response merely formalised (theorised) the obvious: all critical exegesis can only be based on the process of reading. Theories of reader-response and reader-reception, important as they are, serve primarily to display and rationalise the position of the reader as either critic or academic. While the theorists can comfortably and conceptually annihilate both text and author (since that comes within their self-constructed remit), they cannot annihilate the reader, because to do so would be to annihilate themselves.

From Cunningham's triumvirate, only the Reader remains relatively intact within theory. As Barthes put it, in the closing rhetorical flourish of his seven-page essay, 'The Death of the Author': 'the birth of the reader must be at the cost of the death of the Author'.[21] This should be rephrased (without any necessary hostility being implied) as the birth of the theorist.

However, even for the academic reader there are difficulties. As Cunningham put it: 'What do we readers do, what should we do, what might we do, in the wake – the huge wake – of theory? . . . For better or worse, though, reading cannot ignore Theory, because reading can never ignore its prehistory. . . . Reading always comes after theory. . . . We are all, always post theory, post-theorists. The question for us always is: What then? What follows?'[22]

---

[20] Terry Eagleton, *Literary Theory: An Introduction* (Blackwell, 1983, 1986), pp. 119–20.
[21] 'The Death of the Author', in *Image, Music, Text*, ed. and trans. Stephen Heath (Fontana, 1977), p. 148.
[22] Cunningham, p. 1, pp. 2–3.

Conclusions

What follows is a series of revelations. Literature has remained a contested site, within which there are certain fixed points of reference. The Text never went away, it just had its names changed. The Author never died, because the Author was never there in the first place; the Author was, and is, always Somewhere Else. The whole story is a present-day version of the 'Emperor's Clothes' in reverse. Instead of being naked, without clothes, lacking and exposing, the text was always clothed; and this meant that it could change its clothes (i.e. in variant 'readings'). The Author never went away because the Author was always Somewhere Else, presenting us with a textual Houdini Whodunnit. Now you see it, now you don't, now you do again.

On behalf of the academic reader, Valentine Cunningham asked: 'What do we readers do, what should we do, what might we do, in the wake – the huge wake – of theory?' We can recast this: 'What might CW do, in the wake – the huge wake – of theory? . . . For better or worse, though, imaginative writing cannot ignore Theory, because imaginative writing can never ignore its prehistory. . . . We are all, always post theory, post-theorists. The question for us always is: What then? What follows?'

18
Reconceiving Creative Writing: the Materiality of Imaginative Writing

Author as producer

This chapter sets out a structured cluster of cultural and theoretical positions, which I argue are needed to provide a materialist set of resources for reconceiving CW pedagogy. For classroom practice to be transformed, and for imaginative writing to be taught effectively, teachers and students need to make a decisive break with the impossible ideology of CW as caught in the double bind of the Romantic/therapy axis.

The argument begins with a discussion of the author/writer, not to construct the student as such, but as a preparation for understanding the nature of writing and authorship as a materialist practice, since that is (or should be) at the heart of CW pedagogy. Such a materialist foundation does not deny the aesthetics of the practice, nor does it negate the complexity of understanding the sources and resources of imaginative writing. It provides a conceptual foundation for these.

For Walter Benjamin and Brecht, 'art is first of all a social practice. . . . We may see literature as a text, but we may also see it as a social activity, a form of social and economic production which exists alongside and interrelates with, other such forms.'[1]

The author, therefore, 'is primarily a producer, analogous to any other maker of a social product. They oppose, that is to say, the Romantic notion of the author as creator – as the God-like figure who mysteriously conjures his handiwork out of nothing. Such an inspirational, individu-

---

[1] *Marxism and Literary Criticism* (Methuen, 1976), p. 60.
[2] Ibid., p. 68.

alist concept of artistic production makes it impossible to conceive of the artist as a worker rooted in a particular history with particular materials at his disposal.'[2]

Theory has, through its expanded discussion of author/text/reader, provided additions to the traditional terms:

'Writer; Creative author; Implied author; Artificial author; Author construct; Author figure; Postulated author; Hypothetical author; Author-effect; Created author; Pseudo-historical author; Urauthor; Author-function; Phantasmatic author; Apparitional author; Author; Romantic author; Modern author; Writer; Scribe; Scriptor; Hack; Scribbler; Dramatist; Playwright; Novelist; Poet; Script writer; Auteur; Founder of discursivity; Fundamental author; Auctor; Singer; Troubadour; Vates; Bard; Prophet.'[3]

The author as worker

Some of the more social and industrial aspects of authorship are incorporated above, especially, as Bennett put it, in 'Foucault's notion of the "author-function" and more generally what we might call the "praxis" or "pragmatics" of authorship: the social, historical, institutional and discursive limits on, and conventions of, the author . . . the effects of publishing technologies . . . the history of copyright law and censorship . . .'.[4] This is, in Umberto Eco's terms, also the 'empirical author'.

The writer, like all working members of society, occupies a specific position. Like other 'artists' – painters, composers, musicians, performers – the writer generally has always been a freelance worker. Journalism is the exception. There is no job security – there are no 'proper jobs', indeed, for writers, *as writers*; many journalists, however, do have 'proper' jobs. While writers' unions/organisations have done wonderful work in negotiating contracts and terms, the individual writer–worker is always vulnerable, with little real power in the work process, in the active relations of production in the cultural industries, always auditioning for the next commission.

The professional writer is best defined as a mixture of piece-worker and travelling salesperson. The phrase 'sweated labour' comes to mind; not merely because there is intellectual sweat on the writer's brow, but

---

[3] Andrew Bennett, *The Author* (Routledge, 2005), pp.128–30.
[4] Ibid., p. 5.

because there is a material comparison to be made between the factory outworker, sewing clothes at home for a pittance, and the writer who may take (say) two years to write a novel (or play or poetry collection) and only then may receive payment from a publisher. No writer can ever be certain that their publisher will commission or take on their next book. If there is no commission, the product (the manuscript) is hawked round, often with a literary agent as elegant buffer and door-to-door salesperson.

For tax purposes the self-employed writer is treated like a business; but 'business' is a grand word for such insecurity. In his/her day-to-day work the writer is closer to the pre-industrial craftsperson, making an object by 'hand', and then selling it. Piecework. A writer is considered only as good (just, and not always that) as their last piece of work. The freelance market for all art is fickle and unreliable. Even a commission and money upfront is conditional, not guaranteeing either publication or performance.

Published writers are generally paid in two parts: an advance, and a royalty. The advance is paid 'against' royalties; so the royalty (a small percentage of the sale price of book or ticket) has to earn back the advance money through sales (when the commodity enters the marketplace), before any further payments are made. This aligns the writer with (say) the encyclopedia salesperson, who earns a commission on each individual copy sold. There can be further income from the sales of other rights – translation, film (we all await Hollywood's call), etc. – and this is why copyright law is so important. The writer continues to 'own' the work substantively; each form in which the work appears must be legally 'permitted' (the meaning of 'permissions' clauses), since income comes from sales during the period of copyright. This is what is meant by 'intellectual property rights'. Of course, the big money is there for the very, very few, and operates as a magnet, a fiscal equivalent to the elusive wraith of genius.

In 2007, the Authors' Licensing and Collecting Society (ALCS) commissioned a survey of authors' earnings on behalf of the Society of Authors. The research revealed that 'the typical UK author' earns a third less than the national average wage. Only one-fifth of writers earn all their income from writing, and the top 10% of earning professional writers account for more than half the total income of all authors. Over 60% of writers need other work to earn enough to survive.

Patronage: writer and academic

From one point of view, the expansion of CW in higher education has been/is an extraordinary boon for the published/professional writer. As these new writer–teachers are incorporated into universities, the term 'patronage' is sometimes used for their employment. However, this is not appropriate; writer–teachers are – institutionally – academics, working under the same conditions as other teachers, even though they enter the academy via a different career route. The employment itself is not patronage.

Many career academics, of course, also 'write': scholarly articles and books, poetry and novels – indeed, career promotion often depends on it. However, there are some ironies. First, it is actually *academics* (i.e. those already in academic positions) whose writing work has traditionally been privileged by patronage. This goes under the name of 'research'; academics who write articles and books can be subsidised by research leave (paid time in which to write), sabbaticals, research support (postgraduate students who provide research material), and secretarial help (i.e. in administrative support, typing out manuscripts, bibliographies, etc.).

The academic sector of the publishing industry is thus effectively subsidised by the academy, which indirectly 'pays' academic writers to produce written work. The patronage from which career academics benefit has a serious impact on the professional writer. Advances for academic books are generally derisory; academics tend not to be concerned about this or to join writers' organisations because their incomes already come from their institutions. This means that they are often (if unknowingly) undercutting professional writers. My publisher's advance for writing this book has been spent many times over on books I have needed for my research, and my other writing work has subsidised the time it has taken to research and write this book. Had it not been for a generous Arts Council grant, this book would have taken even longer.

Theory within

Terry Eagleton has neatly combined an understanding of the material context for (professional) writing with a materialist approach to what happens 'in' the writing, drawing on the work of Pierre Macherey and Louis Althusser. For Macherey, 'the author is essentially a producer who works up certain given materials into a new product. The author does not make the materials with which he works: forms, values, myths, symbols, ideologies come to him already worked-upon . . .'[5] Althusser's definition of 'practice' relates to this process of production, the 'process

---

[5] Eagleton, *Marxism and Literary Criticism*, p. 69.

of transformation of a determinate given raw material into a determinate product, a transformation effected by a determinate human labour, using determinate means of production . . .', and, as Eagleton amplified, 'The artist uses certain means of production – the specialised techniques of his art – to transform the materials of language and experience into a determinate product. There is no reason why this particular transformation should be more miraculous than any other.'[6]

Literature (and writing) are therefore, 'not mysteriously inspired, or explicable simply in terms of their authors' psychology. They are forms of perception, particular ways of seeing the world; and as such they have a relation to that dominant way of seeing the world which is the "social mentality" or ideology of an age.'[7] The term 'ideology' is itself complex – now often pejoratively used of a point of view with which someone disagrees, or which has some kind of hidden agenda. However, as Eagleton explained, 'an ideology is never a simple reflection of a ruling class's ideas; on the contrary, it is always a complex phenomenon, which may incorporate conflicting, even contradictory, views of the world'.[8] CW, therefore, cannot, by any stretch of the imagination(!), be mere 'self'-expression.

Lucien Goldmann's critical approach, termed 'genetic structuralism', attempted to engage precisely with this complexity: the relationship between the individual, the literary text, the hierarchies and interactions between ideologies, social structures, and – finally – how these can be understood and discussed in relation to each other: 'What Goldmann is seeking, then, is a set of structural relations between literary text, world vision and history itself. . . . To do this it is not enough to begin with the text and work outwards to history, or vice versa; what is required is a dialectical method of criticism, which moves constantly between text, world vision and history, adjusting each to the other.'[9]

This can easily be appropriated to understand how complex any imaginative writing actually is, and how varied its sources and resources are. The crude 'write what you know' does not begin or end with the individual, and the concept of what one 'knows' is itself inflected as an individual confluence from intellectual fields which ripple outwards from, and back to, each other. Add to this the uncertainties of memory, the sub- and un-conscious, and any reliance on 'intentionality', as expressed by the student, is revealed as another kind of fiction.

---

6 Ibid., p. 69.
7 Ibid., p. 6.
8 Ibid., p.7.
9 Ibid., pp. 33–4.

Fallacies

Critiques of intentionality are not new, and not necessarily always couched in formulations from literary theory. W. K. Wimsatt and Monroe Beardsley wrote a joint article called 'The Intentional Fallacy', first published in 1946.[10] They also collaborated in 'The Affective Fallacy', published in 1949. Their main object was to direct (New Critical) attention onto the text (the 'poem') without ancillary diversions such as attempts to discover the intention of the author, which 'is neither available nor desirable as a standard for judging the success of a work of literary art . . .'.[11] They warned against the 'danger of confusing personal and poetic studies; and there is the fault of writing the personal as if it were poetic'.[12]

> 'The Intentional Fallacy is a confusion between the poem and its origins, a special case of what is known to philosophers as the Genetic Fallacy. . . . The Affective Fallacy is a confusion between the poem and its *results* (what it *is* and what it *does*), a special case of epistemological scepticism. It begins by trying to derive the standard of criticism from the psychological effects of the poem and ends in impressionism and relativism. The outcome of either Fallacy, the Intentional or the Affective, is that the poem itself, as an object of specifically critical judgement, tends to disappear.'[13]

Intentionality is thus clearly, at the very least, an example of wishful mind-reading. Jonathan Culler has expressed this as a 'mis-reading' of the written text 'as if it were spoken and to try to move through the words to recover the meaning which was present in the speaker's mind at the moment of utterance, to determine what the speaker, in that revealing phrase, "had in mind"'.[14]

Intentio operis

Demarcating the conceptual from the empirical, novelist, semiologist and literary critic, Umberto Eco deconstructed the concept of 'intentionality' into three components: *intentio operis* (the 'intention of the

---

[10] W. K. Wimsatt, *The Verbal Icon: Studies in the Meaning of Poetry* (Methuen, 1970).
[11] Ibid., p. 3.
[12] Ibid., p. 10.
[13] Ibid., p. 21.
[14] Jonathan Culler, *Structuralist Politics*, p. 132.

work'), *intentio auctoris* (the 'intention of the author'), and *intentio lectoris* (the 'intention of the reader'). While this, too, is a metaphorical person-ification, it allows for a dialectical solution to the 'classical debate aimed at finding in a text either what its author intended to say, or what the text said independently of the intentions of its author'.[15]

The text

One must be aware not only of what is in the text, but what is not:

> 'For (Pierre) Macherey, a work is tied to ideology not so much by what it says as by what it does not say. It is in the significant silences of a text, in its gaps and absences, that the presence of ideology can be most positively felt. It is these silences which the critic must make "speak". The text is, as it were, ideologically forbidden to say certain things . . . the author . . . is forced to reveal his gaps and silences, what it is unable to articulate. Because a text contains these gaps and silences, it is always incomplete. Far from constituting a rounded, coherent whole, it displays a conflict and contradiction of meanings; and the significance of the work lies in the difference rather than the unity between these meanings.'[16]

This is crucial for the process of categorising literature, as well as reading; it enables us to understand what each genre is not, as well as what it 'is'. Turned inside out, as it were, it also signifies two apparently contradictory phenomena: the first, that the author of any text can never 'know it all', and thus cannot answer to any demands for revela-tion by revealing 'intentions'. Secondly, the very concept of an 'incom-pleteness' based on the limits of consciousness, highlights the importance of final authorial responsibility: the writer selects and organises, deciding (no matter what the cultural, intertextual and historical resources are) of what the text consists: which words in which order. This is very far from the pragmatic incompleteness of workshop pedagogy.

---

[15] Umberto Eco, with Richard Rorty, Jonathan Culler and Christine Brooke-Rose, *Interpretation and Overinterpretation*, ed. Stefan Collini (Cambridge University Press, 2001; first published 1992), pp. 63–4.

[16] Eagleton, *Marxism and Literary Criticism*, pp. 34–5.

The writer and language

Since the 1980s there has been a revival of interest in the work of Mikhail Bakhtin, who attended to

> 'the concrete utterances of individuals in particular social contexts. Language was to be seen as inherently "dialogic": it could be grasped only in terms of its inevitable orientation toward another. . . . Bakhtin respected what might be called the "relative autonomy" of language, the fact that it could not be reduced to a mere reflex of social interests; but he insisted that there was no language which was not caught up in definite social relationships, and that these social relationships were in turn part of broader political, ideological and economic systems . . . since all signs were material – quite as material as bodies or automobiles – and since there could be no human consciousness without them, Bakhtin's theory of language laid the foundation for a materialist theory of consciousness itself. Human consciousness *was* the subject's active, material, semiotic intercourse with others, not some sealed interior divorced from these relations; consciousness, like language, was both "inside" and "outside" the subject simultaneously. Language was not to be seen either as "expression", "reflection" or abstract system, but rather as a material means of production, whereby the material body of the sign was transformed through a process of social conflict and dialogue into meaning.'[17]

Conventions and genre

In *Structuralist Poetics*, Jonathan Culler clarified the relationship between language and literary conventions: 'Structural explanation does not place an action in a causal chain nor derive it from the project by which a subject intends a world; it *relates* the object of action to a system of conventions which give it its meanings and distinguish it from other phenomena with different meanings.'[18]

Linking Saussure's concepts of *langue* and *parole* to Noam Chomsky's notions of *competence* and *performance*, Culler noted that 'The distinction between rule and behaviour is crucial to any study concerned with the

---

[17] Terry Eagleton, *Literary Theory* (Blackwell, 2000), pp. 101–2.
[18] Jonathan Culler, *Structuralist Poetics* (Cornell University Press, 1976) p. 27.

production or communication of meaning.'[19] This is, effectively, what constitutes our understanding of 'genre': 'A genre, one might say, is a conventional function of language, a particular relation to the world which serves as a norm or expectation to guide the reader in his [*sic*] encounter with the text.'[20]

Although Culler developed his ideas in relation to critical reading/thinking, there are clear links with imaginative writing, where 'both author and reader bring to the text more than a knowledge of language ... expectations about the forms of literary organisation, implicit models of literary structures ...'.[21] Culler stressed that 'To speak, therefore, as I shall do, of literary competence as a set of conventions for reading literary texts is in no way to imply that authors are congenital idiots who simply produce strings of sentences, while all the truly creative work is done by readers who have artful ways of processing these sentences ... the line between the conscious and the unconscious is notoriously variable, impossible to identify, and supremely uninterest-ing.'[22]

For CW students this suggests that it is imperative to 'know' about literature: its history, its texts, its conventions, its commentaries. For CW teachers it suggests that they may have to address some of these issues from their own perspective, in order to develop a pedagogy which takes a knowledge and understanding of conventions and genres into account, from historical and theoretical points of view, as well as from the pragmatic stylistic evidence of genre.

A theory or poetics of imaginative writing

Writing, like reading, then, is (can, indeed, only be) based on shared and understood conventions: 'To write a poem or a novel is immediately to engage with a literary tradition or at the very least with a certain idea of the poem or the novel.'[23] Peter Widdowson drew similar conclusions: 'The literary text is the product, first, of a writer, who *elects* to write a poem, a drama or a prose fiction, itself a choice knowingly made within a cultural context which is also known to ascribe meaning to these genres.'[24]

---

[19] Ibid., p. 8.
[20] Ibid., p. 136.
[21] Ibid., p. 95.
[22] Ibid., p. 188.
[23] Ibid., p. 116.
[24] Peter Widdowson, *Literature* (Routledge, 1999), p. 96.

This text is a material object: a published book, a material object consisting of graphic marks on the flat surface of page or screen. This is what finally demarcates the distinction between the conventions of speech and writing: 'The physical presentation of a text gives it a stability which separates it from the ordinary circuit of communication in which speech takes place, and this separation has important implications for the study of literature.'[25] And, we might add, for the study and practice of writing.

Conclusions

It is at this point in the discussion that, even while links between reading/study and the writing/production of literature are made, they must also, conceptually and practically be separated – especially so in the context of discussing the teaching of CW. As Fischer has pointed out, 'reading and writing are separately processed cerebral activities. . . . This is because these processes involve different learning strategies in the human brain.'[26] To adapt Terry Eagleton's comment about form and content, we can see that while reading and writing are, on occasions, and in some respects, 'inseparable in practice, they are theoretically distinct. That is why we can talk about the varying relations between the two.'[27] That is why we must also make clear conceptual distinctions between writing in CW, and the differentiated reading processes entailed at different moments on the literary/critical spectrum. This has direct consequences for reconceived approaches to CW pedagogy.

---

[25] Ibid., p. 131.
[26] Steven Roger Fischer, *A History of Writing* (Reaktion Books, 2001), p. 309.
[27] *Marxism and Literary Criticism*, pp. 21–2.

19
Literacy, Writing and Textuality

The precondition of any literary culture is literacy. While this is utterly obvious, it is still worth emphasising. The consequences of ignoring the importance of literacy at all educational levels cannot be stressed too highly, or too often. We may take for granted the conventions of writing, but even here, a reminder of the material basis of such a vital cultural development is important. All conventions of writing consist of graphic signs inscribed on a flat surface. Our Western conventions derive from 'the Latin alphabet . . . one consonant-and-vowel alphabetical writing system – conveying spatially separated ink-printed letters into divided words from left to right in descending horizontal lines . . .'.[1] The right to literacy was hard-won through the centuries, and remains of fundamental importance in all education.

The crisis in literacy

In 2006 the Royal Literary Fund (RLF) published a report called *Writing Matters*, on their Fellowship scheme, which was launched in 1999.[2] Professional writers are placed in universities and colleges all over the UK, for one or two days a week, available for voluntary one-to-one consultations with students. Hilary Spurling, who set up the scheme, described its initial aims as consisting of: 'help with basic skills, such as how to write a letter, set out an argument or proposal, compose a job application and draw up a CV'.[3]

---

[1] Fischer, *A History of Writing* (Reaktion Books, 2001), p. 11.
[2] *Writing Matters: The Royal Literary Fund's Report on Student Writing in Higher Education*, ed. Stevie Davis, David Swinburne and Gweno Williams (Royal Literary Fund, 2006).
[3] 'A Summary of the Royal Literary Fund's Report' (Royal Literary Fund, 2006), p. 2.

During the first seven years, over 130 writers worked in over 70 univer-sities and colleges. I have been fortunate to be one of these. Our experi-ences in a wide variety of higher education institutions revealed a student need extending well beyond the provision of the functional writing skills described above. As the RLF report summarised: 'Most contemporary British students arriving at university lack the basic ability to express themselves in writing. Growing numbers of students are simply not ready for the demands that higher education is – or should be – making of them.'[4]

Regular headlines and articles in *The Times Higher Education Supplement* (*THES*) all confirm this shocking state of affairs. In the issue of 10 February 2005, Jessica Shepherd explained how the problem of literacy has affected teaching: 'Tutors in despair at illiterate freshers.' This applied to students across the board – in the arts, humanities and science subjects, forcing lecturers 'to postpone courses to the second year of undergraduate degrees to make time for remedial teaching and to develop students' independent learning skills'.

There are serious economic consequences to this: 'employers complain that students lack the essential skills that would equip them for the work place. . . . Research conducted by the Royal Mail concludes that spelling mistakes and poor grammar cost UK businesses more than £700 million a year. A joint report by the TUC and CBI cite figures estimating the cost at £10 billion.'[5]

An Adult Literacy Survey, carried out by the Organisation for Economic Co-operation and Development in 23 countries or regions during the mid-1990s, revealed that 22% of British people 'came into the lowest category . . . [with literacy] levels only better than those of Poland and Ireland among Western Countries'.[6] One in five adults in the UK lacked levels of literacy which should be expected of an eleven-year-old. Along with these relatively low literacy rates in English, in 2005 it was reported that there were 'massive falls in the number of candidates taking languages at GCSE level: 64,000 fewer for GCSE in French, German and Spanish this year compared with last year'.[7] These two developments are linked, since an understanding of grammar is essential in learning a second or third language. The reduction of compulsory foreign-language learning has contributed to poorer language skills in English.

---

[4] Ibid., p. 2.
[5] Ibid., p. 10 and p. 12.
[6] Peter Kingston, 'How Bad are our Basic Skills?', *Guardian*, 29 September 2006.

Knowing grammar and knowing about grammar

That matters of grammar, spelling and punctuation are a general issue of concern was shown by the success of Lynne Truss's witty, exasperated book on punctuation, *Eats, Shoots and Leaves*, based on her series of BBC radio programmes. First published in 2003, the book headed the British hardback non-fiction bestseller list for twenty weeks, and sold over a million copies in its first two years.[8]

The crisis in literacy – because it is that – has come about for a number of reasons. Cultural commentators sometimes blame the libertarianism of the 1960s–1970s, where the very democratising process which encouraged writing from people with relatively limited formal education was also held responsible for influencing educational philosophies in schools: the act of writing was privileged without any necessary regard for formal rubrics. Indeed, some argued that knowledge of grammar, punctuation and spelling could actually get in the way of 'self-expression'. The idea that grammar, spelling and punctuation are, *per se*, tyrannical, links with the odd idea from within theory that the text (or author) are somehow authoritarian, 'controlling' reading. David Crystal also connected resistance to formal conventions, expressed as accusations of elitism, to the legacy of Latin: 'For centuries, the Latin language ruled the grammar-teaching world. People had to know Latin to be accepted in education and society, and their knowledge of grammar was based on how that language works.'[9] Crystal also connected a disregard of grammar to a privileging of spoken over written language; spoken English appears to have 'less grammar', because it is more flexible in use – conversation 'is often inexplicit, because the participants are face-to-face . . . usually spontaneous. . . . The vocabulary of everyday speech tends to be informal, domestic . . . directly addressed to the listener.'[10]

The key point here is the distinction between 'knowing grammar and knowing about grammar. . . . Everyone reading this book knows English grammar. . . . But not everyone *knows about* grammar, so that they could analyse these sentence patterns into their parts, and give them such labels as *subject* and *object*, or *noun* and *preposition*. This is the knowledge which has to be learned specially, as an intellectual skill.'[11] The distinctions between spoken and written language have significant social impli-

---

[7] Roger Woods, 'Speaking in Tongue' (*THES*, 2 September 2005.

[8] Profile Books, 2003.

[9] *The English Language* (Penguin, 2002: first published in 1988), p. 22.

[10] Ibid., p. 94.

[11] Ibid., p. 29.

cations: 'Written language is usually much more permanent and formal than speech. Because of its permanence, it also has a special status, being used where it is necessary to make something legally binding (as in contracts) or to provide a means of identity or authority (as in the sacred literature of a religious tradition). Because of its formality, it is more likely to be used to provide the standard which society values.'[12]

Writing and its conventions

The distinction between 'knowing' grammar and 'knowing about' grammar is partly about the differences between spoken and written language, and the functions implied in each. Both speech and writing are dependent on a complex of systems – conventions – via which meaning is created and conveyed: 'Speech acts are not just sentences. They are linguistic utterances in a given situation or context, and it is through this context that they take on their meaning. . . . The utterance must invoke a *convention* that is as valid for the recipient as for the speaker.'[13]

These shared cultural/linguistic conventions apply to all kinds of written texts, imaginative and discursive. Understanding them involves knowing about other forms of social and cultural 'texts', or systems of signification. The repertoire of textual conventions (genre) is a matter of being able not merely to identify the difference (and relationship) between (say) biography and novel, but also to recognise that each 'text' is more than the sum of its parts: that which in literary theory is called 'intertextuality'. The concept is a theorised development from one of the best known twentieth-century polemic formulations, by T. S. Eliot:

'Tradition . . . cannot be inherited, and if you want it you must obtain it by great labour. It involves, in the first place, the historical sense . . . and the historical sense involves a perception, not only of the pastness of the past, but of its presence; the historical sense compels a man [*sic*] to write not merely with his own generation in his bones, but with a feeling that the whole of the literature of Europe . . . [and] of his own country has a simultaneous existence and composes a simultaneous order . . . And it is at the same time what

---

12 Ibid., pp. 96–7.
13 Wolfgang Iser, *The Act of Reading: A Theory of Aesthetic Response* (Johns Hopkins University Press, 1979; first published in German in 1976), pp. 55–6.

makes a writer most acutely conscious of his place in time, of his own contemporaneity.'[14]

Eliot's essay bears re-reading, not as any kind of semi-mystical gospel on the nature of writing and the writer (though for some it probably will be), but more for the essay's attempt to separate the writer from the text, without destroying the connections, and without denying the writer ultimate responsibility (author-ity) for the text. Indeed, if the concept of intertextuality needed its validation from an alliance between criticism and theory, a comparison between Eliot's position, which seeks to redefine writer, text and cultural history, and Barthes' disingenuous intellectual embroidery which plays with the idea of no writer at all, is worth making.

'The point of view which I am struggling to attack,' wrote Eliot, 'is perhaps related to the metaphysical theory of the substantial unity of the soul: for my meaning is, that the poet has, not a "personality" to express, but a particular medium, which is only a medium and not a personality . . .'.[15] That medium is language, its conventions and uses in particular contexts.

A consciously learned understanding of grammar, spelling and punctuation is the *sine qua non* of CW. Because its usages can entail non-literal (figurative) forms of language, because it engages differently with structure and form, because its relationship with the 'real world' is elusive – because, in other words, it derives from an imaginative mode of thought – 'knowing about grammar' must be the precondition for its pedagogy. Those who think that the CW workshop can somehow compensate for the inadequacies or limitations of students' knowledge of language, or even 'teach' grammar, underestimate how hard it is for students to know what they are really doing when they write if they have little idea about the components and conventions of written language.

Textual production: a theory of writing

The concept which bridges the procedures of knowing about grammar, literature, critical reading and imaginative writing is textual production. This has emerged from committed teachers of literature, in the UK and

---

[14] 'Tradition and the Individual Talent' written in 1917, in *Selected Essays* (Faber & Faber, 1957; first published 1932), p. 14.
[15] Ibid., pp. 19–20.

the US, who are responsive to Composition and CW. 'Textual production', as applied to imaginative modes of thought, begins to allow for a realistic understanding of the objects and practices of CW. These are quite distinct from the processes of the reader-critic; one of the purposes in developing such a pedagogic method to widen ways in which the study of literature can be enhanced. However, the concept of textuality has significant and exciting potential for extended application in the CW classroom/seminar.

Robert Scholes' stimulating and vigorous book *Textual Power* argued for a re-naming of writing-based approaches to literary study as 'textuality'. This provides a realistic starting point for the ways in which linguistic features can be differently applied within discursive and imaginative conventions: through 'poiesis' – making with language, textuality. This encompasses 'textual knowledge and textual skills. . . . Poetry emphasises language itself and the individual subject's relationship to language. Drama emphasises the speech act, dialogue, looking, being looked at, listening, responding. And fiction emphasises the reductive and representational powers of language, the power to give accounts, to tell stories, to turn the world into fiction and history, to narrate.'[16]

Rob Pope's *Textual Intervention* harnesses student writing as an interactive approach to the study of literature: 'The best way to understand how a text works, I argue, is to change it . . . to intervene in it . . . and then try to account for the exact effect of what you have done.'[17] This is a carefully paced classroom textbook, with work meticulously presented – followed in detail, just the opening section could take weeks of seminar work. The procedures entail stylistics-based identification of patterns of words, phrases, devices, analyses of grammatical features, incorporation of appropriate socio-historical features, and discussions of responses, value judgements and the grounds on which these might be based. All the suggested work is structured in relation to specific literary texts, not to students' 'own' writing. The attention, finally, is back to the base literary text, rather than to the development of imaginative writing skills in the interests of discrete student literary production. Whether or not this really is the 'best' way to understand how a text 'works' can perhaps be argued – but in the end, it depends (as do all pedagogic processes) on the ways in which the methods are realised in the working rapport of the classroom.

---

[16] Yale University Press, 1985, p. 20.
[17] Routledge, 2003 (first published 1995), p. 1.

Ben Knights, like Robert Scholes, sees the use of 'transformative writing' as a means of negotiating the 'pedagogic crossover between creative and critical activities'.[18] By engaging students in 'textual production' within literary studies, students return to a close study of language, in an augmentation of 'the established processes of analytic discussion'.

There is a great deal of value in these discussions of transformative or generative or textually interventionist production/writing. While it can, no doubt, produce pleasure, satisfaction and stimulus for students in the active process of writing outwards, as it were, from literary texts, and enhance all kinds of critical and theoretical understanding and reading, this kind of work is primarily framed by its usefulness towards conventional literary objects-texts. Whatever chances it gives students to flex their imaginations as part of literature studies, however enlivening literature teachers may find the experience of teaching via non-discursive student writing, this work must necessarily be delimited by its subject-based context. This is no criticism; it helps to highlight the complex symbiosis that is literary (or English) studies, language and writing studies and CW, each of which call for their own pedagogic spaces and methodologies, while co-dependent on, and integrated with, each other. It shows that, to a limited extent, some teachers of literature can see the benefits of 'learning by doing' – with the support of their own critical/theoretical approaches. The compliment should, perhaps, be returned in the other directions by CW teachers, who might benefit a very great deal from the detailed linguistic and stylistic precision applied in much of this work.

Conclusions: textuality and the imaginative mode of thought

We have reached the point at which the readerly and the writerly must diverge for conceptual, disciplinary and functional reasons. This is not a metaphorical process; it is actual, material and pedagogic. Literary studies address complete, published (canonic or otherwise) books/texts (which then become textbooks) through reading and thinking and a range of contextual, critical and theoretical studies. Their students write discursively – essays, dissertations, theses. CW, on the other hand,

---

[18] Ben Knights and Chris Thurgar-Dawson, *Active Reading: Transformative Writing in Literary Studies* (Continuum, 2006), p. 20.

centrally addresses the production of genres of writing which correspond to modes of imaginative thought: prose fiction, poetry and drama. It is around the production of these convention-framed texts that the work of CW revolves; and within CW courses, this is the practical imperative. If the workshop is to be superseded by better approaches, as I believe it must be, the content of the workshop pedagogy must also be reconceived.

The next three chapters outline a theoretical framework – a kind of 'poetics', perhaps – on the basis of which the content and methods of CW pedagogy in the seminar can be developed by teachers, in relation to the three 'core' genres: prose fiction, drama and poetry. These chapters, along with the rest of the historicising and theorisation in this book, can also provide students with a framework for their genre-based work, in relation to which classroom/seminar work can be structured by teachers.

20
From Elephants to Kangaroos: Prose Fiction

Time

Prose fiction foregrounds three symbiotically related issues: time, narrative, and referentiality. All are important in drama and poetry, but differently inflected. There are three fundamental time scales which coalesce and clash in prose fiction: the time it took the author to write it (uncomputable), the time it takes the reader to read it (mostly uncomputable) and the time scale(s) within the narrative itself (mostly computable).

The singular narrative voice (first or third) which characterises most prose fiction gives the illusion of a transparent 'present'. Even if narrated in the third person and the past tense, the moment of the telling has a 'presence' to it, which belies the textual, writerly and readerly, realities. At the same time, even if narrated in the first person and the present tense, it is already 'past'. As Paul Ricoeur has noted, 'to narrate a story is already to "reflect upon" the event narrated . . .'.[1] Prose fiction deploys a constantly shifting set of illusions about past and present moments, then further compounded in the moment of reading. Part of the thrill of prose fiction is precisely the way in which it teases our very necessary assumptions about the construct of time itself:

'Modern Western commonsense organises time into a linear chronology of hours, days, years, within a structure of shared fantasy. This is held in place by the movement of the sun, together with a mythical

---

[1] Paul Ricoeur, *Time and Narrative*, vol. 2, trans. Kathleen McLaughlin and David Pellauer (University of Chicago Press, 1985), p. 61.

but altogether effective anchoring point, the year of the birth of Jesus (other cultures manage just as efficiently with a different regulatory date-line). . . . .If you believe in it, it works.'[2]

Narrative and causality

The shifting fictional 'present' is woven together into a narrative, into story or plot. To arrange events into a certain order is to construct narrative. In fact, one cannot *not* have narrative, however elliptical the structure may be. The very sentence-structure of language itself implies a sequential accumulation of connective meaning-making. When woven into the genre we call prose fiction, 'No segmenting operation, no placing of functions in a sequence can do without some reference to the plot as a dynamic unity and to emplotment as a structuring operation. . . . Plot was first defined, on the most *formal* level, as an integrating dynamism that draws a unified and complete story from a variety of incidents, in other words, that transforms this variety into a unified and complete story.'[3] This gives us both the linguistic fact of, and the cultural need for, narrative: 'we have no idea of what a culture would be where no one any longer knew what it meant to narrate things'.[4]

Links between moments of narrative may be more or less explicit, more or less predicted and predictable; cause-and-effect(s) are built into the sequential text in many direct and indirect different ways. Narrative may be multiply-voiced, but it can never be eliminated; this is 'confirmed by the category of novels constructed out of a polyphony of voices, where each remains perfectly distinct and yet every voice is posited in relation to every other'.[5] From a theoretical point of view, this is no different from a single-voiced narrative, and thus, self-evidently: 'What is termed the "authorial point of view" is not the conception of the world of the real author but that which presides over the organisation of the narrative of a particular work.'[6]

This does not mean, however, that all fiction writing inevitably constitutes realism or 'must' be 'realistic', nor that cause and effect 'must' always be clearly spelled out. However, sequentiality also implies causal-

---

[2] Anthony Easthope, *Privileging Difference* (Palgrave Macmillan, 2002), p. 7.
[3] Ricoeur, pp. 38 and 8.
[4] Ibid., p. 28.
[5] Ibid., p. 96.
[6] Ibid., p. 93.

ity, direct or indirect, and an awareness of this, as a worked fact in the fabric of the text, is an essential component of developing a grasp on the mechanics of writing prose fiction.

Referentiality: the hopping referent

Prose fiction draws particularly strong attention to language's denotive and connotive qualities, and to the vexed (but inevitable) issue of referentiality. In the nineteenth-century novel, concepts of realism and naturalism corresponded to theorised degrees and kinds of reference to the 'real' world: realism was, and is, seen as 'an easily readable form, closed in on itself, symmetrically arranged in terms of an ending, and based on an easily identifiable causal connection between the initial complication and its denouement; in short, as a form where the episodes would be clearly held together by the configuration',[7] with (to some extent, at least), 'the proposal to establish the most exact correspondence possible between the literary work and the reality it imitates'.[8]

The debate, which still engages all those involved with literature and language, is whether (and/or to what extent) fiction (and language) 'reflects' or 'constructs' or 'imitates' the 'real' world, or aspects of it. This formed part of the disagreement between Henry James and Walter Besant, and it lurks behind all discussions of literary mimesis, particularly so in common-sense assertions that literature is an 'imitation of life'. The conceptual clash is between literary criticism and literary theory, but it is also constantly there in the evaluative criteria used by publishers, literary reviewers, and the common-sense notions of 'sympathy' or 'empathy' (i.e., claimed 'recognition' or 'identification') elicited via the act of reading.

Referentiality doesn't just dissipate as a result of the insights and understandings of linguistics and semiology, however. It remains a site of contradiction. In spoken (and certain functional uses of written) language, consensus on referentiality is crucial for understanding and communication. In literary conventions, it becomes more uncertain, more excitingly ambiguous, but unavoidable.

As Robert Scholes succinctly commented: 'The relationship between text and world is not simply a fascinating problem for textual theory. It is, above all others, the problem that makes textual theory necessary.'[9]

---

[7] Ibid., pp. 8–9.
[8] Ibid., p. 12.
[9] Robert Scholes, *Textual Power: Literary Theory and the Teaching of English* (Yale University Press, 1985), p. 75.

Finding narrative 'plausible', 'convincing', 'believable', on the basis of some supposed 'recognition' of, or allusions to, the 'real' world by the reader is extraordinarily unreliable. It hinges on notions of cause-and-effect which derive partly from subjective experience, partly from literary models, partly from psychological constructs. This creates a relativism which begins and ends in subjectivist assertion.

Referentiality and character

Concepts of 'character' in CW literature are generally built on assumptions that these verbal constructs (representations) are 'real' enough to be liked or disliked, cared about or not cared about. Gerald Prince's 'depersonalised' postmodern account of character as 'an existent endowed with anthropomorphic traits and engaged in anthropomorphic actions . . .'[10] is more accurate (if less sexy).

Actually, in terms of the (literally) constructive function of language, there is no difference between a paragraph about a Chippendale chair, a fish and chip shop, or Jane Eyre (the 'woman'). They are all constructions, 'representations', using vocabulary and conventions which make their allusiveness cognition-friendly – 'recognisable'.

The representation of people clearly always conveys a structural value-laden importance, because commonly 'people' are the active agents in stories, carrying the narrative. The same principle applies, of course, if animals or inanimate objects are the active agents – in which case they become personifications for 'people'/'characters'. These personifications therefore operate as metaphors for the representations of human beings. However, despite the surface appearance of the notion of 'character', the apparent transparency such a concept affords of the relationship between the fiction and 'real life', understanding is not necessarily any easier. For example, to gloss what is or might be meant by commenting that a character is 'convincing' or 'believable' entails a great deal of complex and contentious discussion about the psychological or social norms which provide the measures of convincing-ness. Needless to say, these are not theorised nor, perhaps, even possible, within the frame of CW pedagogy.

The commonly used, and appallingly vague notion that a piece of writing 'works' relies also on certain cultural expectations about narra-

---

[10] Gerald Prince, *Dictionary of Narratology* (Scolar Press, 1988), p. 12.

tive patterns, or on subjectivist responses – i.e., whether this 'would' or 'would not' happen is a judgement based entirely on the patterns of probability assumed by the judge. Life, as many have said is stranger than fiction. Indeed, fiction is stranger than life. That is part of its purpose.

However, referentiality never goes away. Scholes takes issue with any simplistic view that language is 'a system of pure differences ... one cannot rescue the much maligned referent while remaining liberated from the empirical object. The only path that may lead us toward a new secular theory of textuality begins by leading us backward. We shall have to make some attempt to rescue the reference, to rehabilitate reference itself, before moving on to a new textual practice – and we must do this without falling back into naïve assumptions about the empirical object. This task will not be easy for the writer, the reader, or the text.'[11]

This should *not* be taken as an argument (a) for the inevitability or desirability of realism in prose fiction, or even (b) for the reverse: the postmodern pose which argues that realism is inherently 'reactionary', and that therefore the avant-garde is the only thing worth 'teaching' or writing. But it does mean, as Scholes suggests, that 'Texts are just as much a part of the world as kangaroos . . .'[12] and that the kangaroo (the 'referent') was, of course, hopping around long before we had a reference for it.

Referentiality and description

The same principle applies to 'description'; again, the pertinent issue is referentiality and allusion – both of kind and degree. At one level, all prose fiction is no more or less than 'description' – accounts, representations, constructs – of places, times, events and people. All such 'description' alludes to objects, structures of the empirical world, 'recognisable' emotions (based on norms and expectations). This is a huge area, contingent on cultural and emotional assumptions. Indeed, much of the excitement of prose fiction lies in deviating from the 'norm' – exceptional 'people' in exceptional 'situations'. It's all words. It's all language. It's all imagined. It all alludes.

---

[11] Scholes, pp. 105 and 85.
[12] Ibid., p. 105.

In practice: completion

While an undergraduate degree generally 'teaches' the short story, and asks for it as assignments, an MA 'teaches' the novella, and the PhD, the novel. Or should. It is the only logical approach. It is, however, widely accepted that a few chapters and a synopsis (e.g., in the submission of a 'novel' for the MA) is acceptable. This is nonsense.

Synopsis writing is provisional; it has no clear correlation with what *might* be written. It gives absolutely no indication of 'how' the imaginative writing will read. Imaginative and discursive writing come from different modes of thought, as even CW is at pains to stress. The one cannot substitute for the other. A few chapters and a synopsis do not a novel 'make'; a 'synopsis' is a meta-projection of what a novel might be, a discursive fantasy, entailing blurb-writing skills which are very different from imaginative writing skills. This is assessment by prediction. A student might be a poor writer of prose fiction, but a powerful blurb-writer.

No English (or any other subject) undergraduate, MA or PhD student could expect to submit a section (extract) of work, with just a summary of the remander. The word-length of academic requirements allows for a structure within which the architectonic scope of imaginative prose writing is already covered, and which enables the student to develop their work into longer conceptual spans; exactly the same principal which applies in all other subjects.

Part of the reason for this validation of incomplete work in CW is that the dominant literary culture in the UK still privileges the novel over shorter prose forms. Plus, students think they are doing something more important if it is called writing a novel, rather than addressing the fundamentals of the prose fiction genre. The assessment protocol (chapters plus synopsis) seems to mimic the submission process to publishers, and therefore adds the spurious flattery of being part of a professional procedure. This is misleading for the students, and is pedagogically dishonest. It does not in any way mean that the novel is just the short story writ large. It does mean that it is absolutely essential that every piece of writing is complete and completed. No issues of structure, narrative, development can otherwise be adequately addressed.

In practice: structure

The framing of the fairy/folk tale makes explicit what is implicit in all prose fiction. 'Once upon a time' doesn't merely set something in the past. It has a structural function, as does every opening sentence in every story and novel. It disrupts the status quo. The first sentence announces the fiction that nothing has ever 'happened' before this moment and this sentence. Even if the first sentence describes a recurring event, this one moment is singled out as significant. The beginning is where 'it' starts. Not before. The status quo of silence – that which is not narrated – has been disrupted. This concept is based on a cognition of narrative which is part of both individual and cultural memory. The concept of 'back story' is a formulation which only touches the surface of the imaginative process involved in the decisive moment when the narrative 'begins'. This does not mean that the first sentence has to be written first. As professional writers well know, often the beginning is only completed after the end is reached.

The concept of intertextuality supports this, as well as a clear understanding of creativity. In discussing creation myths, Rob Pope has pointed out that 'Practically speaking, there is no "creation from nothing" (*ex nihilo*). There is always something "before the beginning", just as there is always something "after the end". Put another way, everything is "all middle".'[13] While in the beginning there was the Word, even before the word, there was something else: 'All creation myths are strictly *re*-creation myths, and in two crucial respects. Firstly, contrary to initial appearances, every creation myth involves creation from something (whether a prior state of order, chaos, the void or notionally "nothing"); for even "nothing" requires that we imagine "some-thing" in order to negate it. In this sense, so-called "creation from nothing" (*ex nihilo*) is a rhetorical trick and a sleight of mind.'[14]

It is this rhetorical trick which becomes a material reality at the beginning of every narrative. Every first sentence always comes after something else – a something else which is 'not' written. This is more than just the concept of back story. In any case, back story only ever consists of what is useful for the present story. Apart from events explicitly referred to within the narrative itself, all remaining back story is 'pure' (invisible) fiction.

---

[13] Rob Pope, *Creativity: Theory, History, Practice* (Routledge, 2005), p. xv.
[14] Ibid., p. 137.

'They lived happily ever after' heralds the opposite – and the same. After the last sentence, there is, seemingly, no more. However, even here there are implications about what might happen in the unwritten future. For example, we do not know whether 'happily' will really be the case. How long is 'ever after'? Is the narrator telling the 'truth'? There are always potential sequels and more sequels. While there is only ever one final sentence, the unarticulated 'future' of every narrative (also 'not' written) is immanent in the articulated material – in its, however, ambiguous, clues. The imagined future which exists after the 'end' of each prose narrative is partly what determines the critical reading of the narrative itself. The decision of the student or writer about where to end, is also a decision about what to leave for future (undefined) imagining. There can only ever be degrees of closure, never complete closure. All is middle.

In the larger scheme of things, every story is thus shown not to be 'ab nihilo', told from nothing, with no past and no future. In the rhetorical trick that there is 'nothing' before and 'nothing' after; the only thing which can be said to 'exist' with any certainty is the story itself. This is what we call the text, and the clues are always within the text: as Eco formulated it, this is *intentio operis*, something very different indeed from any simplistic notion of authorial or student intentionality.

21
Writing Drama

The title of this chapter deliberately uses the word 'drama', and not script – or playwriting. Screenwriting or scriptwriting are popular, since everyone wants to write movies or for television. That's where the money is. However, despite the mass circulation and importance of film, despite the magnetism of theatre and the ubiquity of television, drama is the hardest of the language-based forms to write.

As any professional dramatist, writing for film, TV or radio, knows, it is essential to know about the way the relevant technology and production processes impact on the conventions and aesthetics of writing, in order to write for any of the dramatic media with any real grasp. Books can't do it, although how-to screenwriting guides (for example) give such highly-formatted instruction that they convey a strong sense that there are rules which can be followed relatively easily. In any case, even where screen or scriptwriting is located in a production-teaching context (i.e. in a film school), there is a great deal to be said for initially developing drama-writing skills quite separately from their application to any specific performance medium.

Modern drama

Official theatre censorship in Britain was in force until 1968. Until then, all plays had to be submitted to the Lord Chamberlain for approval, before they could be rehearsed and staged.[1] Even after a script had been

---

[1] See Kenneth Tynan, 'The Royal Smut-Hound', in *Post-war British Drama: Looking Back in Gender* (Routledge, 2001), pp. 98–111.

approved, representatives from the Lord Chamberlain's office might well visit the theatre incognito, to make sure no untoward *ad libs* or other changes had crept into the production.

Until 1968, therefore, there were strict controls applied to representations of royalty onstage, or of important historical figures, and to explicit references to sexuality, nudity and potentially blasphemous content, and the censorship of 'bad' language. It is extraordinary (and salutary?) to realise that writing for the theatre has thus only had the same in-principle freedoms accorded to the novel and poetry for about half a century. The post-censorship theatrical landscape not only helped transform who wrote and performed what, where it was performed and to whom, but tacitly also made it possible to teach dramatic writing in a climate where there was greater freedom in what was written and produced.

The range and vibrancy of this theatre has been chronicled elsewhere.[2] Called variously 'fringe', 'alternative', 'underground', 'political', it was closely linked with the cultural and political movements of the time: socialism, feminism, the gay movement, avant-garde artistic experiments, in poetry, performance art and theatre, often incorporating moves to democratise theatre-making and theatre-going.

An academic counterpart developed Performance Studies, and performance theory, which utilised semiology to analyse performance and its meanings.[3] This was a valuable reaction against the previous academic convention of just studying plays-on-the-page. However, it also produced a degree of theoretical over-compensation which has helped to fuel serious misunderstandings of what a dramatic text 'is', and as a result, what is appropriate in writing drama. These amount to widely accepted clichés, which call for deconstruction.

Cliché 1: the blueprint theory

The first cliché is that the dramatic text on the page is only a 'blueprint' for performance. The implication is thus that the (written) text on the page is inadequate as an 'object' for scrutiny – in other words, it is not 'meant' (whatever that means) to be read straight from the page. It is only when it is embodied in performance – on stage, in film, TV or radio,

---

[2] See M. Wandor, *Carry On, Understudies* (Routledge, 1986); P. Ansorge, *Disrupting the Spectacle* (Pitman, 1975); N. Khan, *The Arts Britain Ignores* (Arts Council of Great Britain, 1976); S. Craig, *Dreams and Deconstructions* (Amber Lane Press, 1980).

[3] See, for example, K. Elam, *The Semiotics of Theatre and Drama* (Routledge, 1997; originally published in 1980).

says the cliché, that it becomes viably analysable. To suit this, a more subtle distinction is often made between the 'text' on the page and the 'text' in performance. Performance theory thus effectively *reads* the text on the page back via the text of performance, with the latter more highly privileged.

This must mean that the dramatist necessarily writes an incomplete text: 'It is because the playtext is such a strange – incomplete – object – that it seems useful to have a guide as to how someone might get the most out of dealing with this object.'[4] The written 'blueprint' is always secondary, always a lesser offering, only the starting point, a signpost for the 'real thing', for which the director and the rest of the team are responsible – the production. This is a profoundly ironic state of affairs, given that theatre history is still mainly studied in terms of its play-wrights, and in which (minority non-verbal theatre apart) there can be no performance and therefore no theatre without a written text.

Performance theory, exciting as it, is inherently unstable and provisional: no one theatre performance is ever identical to any another – there is never a performance 'object' which can be reliably identified, checked or debated. Any video or film can only ever be a single moment in performance. There is, in fact, no 'obect' for study, beyond the contingent and ephemeral. We need archive records of performances, of course, but the very act of recording means that it ceases to be live and immediate. Not better, not worse, but significantly different. It is far easier to analyse and discuss a film, because its distributed form for consumption is already 'fixed', and multiple, and that is its primary produced form.

Thus, what has been an analytically and historically important distinction between 'dramatic text' and 'performance text', has resulted in both dramatist and written text being seriously demoted and devalued.

The 'incomplete' text

The dramatist as writer of the incomplete is not an incompleteness in the Machereyan sense (with gaps and absences 'written' into the text), but in the sense of something literally unfinished, and *unfinishable*, by the dramatist. While the published, performed and/or canonical (live or dead) dramatist is privileged in the cultural world, s/he is, within theory and performance studies, diminished. The world giveth and the academy taketh away. One might legitimately wonder why any writer

---

[4] See S. Shepherd, and M. Wallis, *Studying Plays* (Edward Arnold, 1998), p. 1.

should ever bother to sit down and write something which is inherently incomplete. Because they're star struck, just plain masochistic or because they are just in it for the money?

However, the Death of the Author is far more than a sophisticated piece of postmodern dismissal for the dramatist: it encapsulates with painful poignancy the way many dramatists experience their involvement in production (in all media). The notion that the only good (because never troublesome) writer is a dead writer has a particularly resonant irony for the dramatist.

Cliché 2: collaboration and production

Drama (in all media) is often referred to as 'collaborative'. In a superficial sense, a play/film/radio is a 'team' production: but then, so is publishing. Groups of people take into the public domain something written by an individual. However the methodological differences, as well as the system of distribution and consumption (drama has mass audiences), have led to associations of the 'collaborative' with cosy and/or stimulating artistic interaction. Of course, the process of dramatic production can be extraordinarily exciting – but the writer is, by definition, always 'outside' or, at best, on the edge of the production process. 'Collaboration', while it may appear to include the writer, actually serves to reinforce the dramatist in their 'incompleteness', masking the real authority structure.

The division of labour: the director

In all drama there are clearly demarcated skills – a division of labour: who does what, and how the skills are co-ordinated. The writer writes, the director directs. The writer acquires skills to do one thing well, the director acquires skills to do another thing well. The division of labour is also sequential. Even where a director and dramatist might be conferring during the writing process, the director's production-based work does not fully begin until the writing is finished. The difference between published and performance media is that in the former, the text is on the page as the author left it, whereas in the latter the written text becomes embodied, spoken, heard and not read, contained within different physical time frames. It is both changed and the same. It is the process of performance-based change which necessitates the director's role.

When a written text goes into production, the writer's job is (or should be) substantially finished. Any major structural rewriting at this point merely attests to the fact that the writer either hasn't finished the job, or been able to execute it with sufficient skill. The director then begins his/her work. S/he not only puts together the final artefact in production (aesthetic), but also co-ordinates all the artistic and technical skills, and is ultimately accountable to the management/producer (administrative, managerial). This gives the director over-arching responsibility, and an inevitable degree of power. Movies and TV are similar, with the director more heavily subject ultimately to the major economic machinery – i.e. the producer/investor. It is not by chance that *auteur* theory developed from cinema.

The director's power is executive, and final. Writers generally have the right to be 'consulted' on casting, etc., but even when consultation is enshrined in a contract, it doesn't guarantee full consultation, participation or agreement. During the 1970s, the Writers' Guild and the Theatre Writers' Union put in place contracts to protect theatre writers' rights, including the principle of presence in rehearsal; for which the writer is minimally, at best, paid. BBC radio drama contracts have an attendance (in the studio) clause in the writer's contract, with a pitifully tiny payment for a day's attendance. In film, the writer has an even tougher time.

Production can, in a very real sense, happen without the writer being present in rehearsal, and more often than not, does. Writers are often actively discouraged from being present. Of course, this becomes a circular problem: inexperienced writers may not understand rehearsal protocol, and as a result, directors might find them disruptive. This simply attests to the need for writers to know and understand as much as possible of the production process, in order to occupy their specific place in the transitional process from page to stage. For pedagogy this raises important questions; at one level, writing for any medium should be studied in a context where the student can also engage with other parts of the process (such as at film school). Classroom-based teaching of dramatic writing can recreate some of the conditions of performance on the spot (its own 'empty space'), but this can never be a fully realised process, even at best.

Cliché 3: the visual and the novel

The combination of clichés that the text is incomplete, and therefore 'unreadable' on the page, together with the idea that it is 'collaborative', produces the cliché that the dramatic text must also be 'visual'. Together, these clichés compound the idea that, compared with the novel, the dramatic text is either 'unreadable' (because incomplete) or, at any rate, harder than reading a novel, because it alludes to a dimension associated with the (performed) visual. This is less a comment on the nature of the dramatic text, than on the fact that in our culture the novel is still the dominant fictional form, and that our dominant reading and critical practices are still primarily derived from the novel.

In the novel, an over-arching singular fictional narrative voice (first or third) determines the act of reading from a certain point of view. Without this, and the conventional elements of 'description' etc. (also via a singular narrative voice), the dramatic text appears to be lacking, to be relatively empty – i.e. a novel with the important bits missing. After all, dialogue in the novel is generally a minor element. This conspires to provide (subliminally) yet more cultural evidence that the dramatic text is incomplete/inferior.

Taken together with the clichés (a) that drama must be 'visual', and (b) that the production is the real thing, we have a rationale for a misconceived approach to the devices which the dramatist putatively uses to incorporate the 'visual' elements: stage directions.

Stage directions

These are – at one level – fragments of *ersatz* novelese, and *ersatz* scenogaphy. In terms of the 'difficulty' of reading a play on the page, the novelese provides shorthand fragments of what might otherwise take up many words in a novel. In terms of production as the primary text of signification, the *ersatz* scenography provides shorthand fragments of what is the province of all those who realise the text in performance.

When one compares the minimal stage directions in a play by Shakespeare with their fulsome presence in the plays of George Bernard Shaw, and then again in the minimalism of plays by Harold Pinter or Caryl Churchill, one can see how historically determined, variable and disposable the phemonenon of the stage direction is. There are historical, genre-centred reasons for this.

British 'high art' drama came back into prominence around the end of the nineteenth century. Plays then carried a transitional legacy (from the dominance of the novel in the nineteenth century) in the way stage directions appeared: with a single-voiced narrator dipping in and out of the dialogue. But even though, as in the case of Shaw, the written texts themselves sometimes appear to be hybrid novel/dramas, the dominance of the dialogue as the aesthetic determinant of narrative, relationships, themes, action, etc., defines them as dramas rather than as novels. Stage directions are aesthetically on the cusp between novel and drama, and from the writerly perspective involve crucially different ways of imagining and writing.

Dialogue has no built-in singular narrative voice. Or, to put it another way, ALL dialogue is, at the moment of its appearance on the page and on the stage, written in the directly articulating existential first 'person', in the present moment of utterance; this is entirely different from a first-person prose-fiction narrative of events which have already happened or are happening elsewhere.

When one reads dialogue in a novel, there is always surrounding written material. In the moment of written and spoken dialogue in drama, there is no surrounding written material. We read the exchange in its present-tenseness, the now-ness of the fictional people speaking. We are able to do this because we grasp the signs on the page which indicate an interactive exchange between people, through the convention/signs of dialogue-speech. These contain, both in the staging and within the fabric of the dialogue, all the significant material which is customarily more fulsomely developed in prose: place, history, etc. Dialogue in novels is always an interlude, a leap into a new kind of 'present' within the narrated fiction. Novels do not have to have dialogue. Plays can have nothing else.

When we read a dramatic text on the page, we may have peripheral questions, but we are actually perfectly well able to read 'just' dialogue. We are not 'filling in' the gaps, but reading *across* the gaps (taking the concept of the novel as the norm for the moment), taking in interactive dialogue, and so, in a sense, there are no gaps. We are, in other words, reading relationships. This is what the dramatist writes: relationships, which are more than the sum of the individual characters/speakers. Drama is entirely composed of, and contingent on, relationships. This is not only an abstract, and complex concept, it is the most difficult to convey in teaching drama writing, steeped as the vast majority of students (and CW teachers) are in traditional notions of character and authorial point of view, based on individuated subjectivity.

We do not visualise, we cannot visualise, because there is nothing to visualise. To read the text on the page is to read the complete text, not just because that is what is written, but because its conventions are completed on the page. I stress here that this is not to return to some outdated way of privileging the written over the production text; not at all. But each is complete in its own terms, and when taken together, their symbiotic relationship becomes fascinating – and supremely complex in its interaction. Most importantly, to write drama at all, the dramatist must conceive in a form which is imaginatively complete in dialogue.

The supremacy of dialogue over other matter can be easily tested. Take away the stage directions in a play by Shaw, and the text will still be complete and stageable. Take away the dialogue in the same play, leaving only the stage directions, and narrative, story, relationships, everything that makes it a piece of imaginative writing, have all gone. The dramatic, stageable indeed, *sensibly* (sense- and meaning-producing) – *readable* – text has gone. However wonderfully visualised, imagined and indicated in stage directions, no drama is ever accepted and staged (or filmed) on the basis of its 'visuals'. In practice, respectful as director/performers etc. may be towards their first reading of stage directions, the latter will be virtually completely dispensed with, once the drama goes into rehearsal/onto the set.

This is not simply because our post-Stanislavski age has created rehearsal norms where director and cast explore the psychological, emotional and gestural ways of delivering lines, but because it is inherent in the signifying conventions of the text itself that all 'directions' are misnomers. Not only are they imprecise (what does 'smiling' mean? What is the appropriate smile? What happens if there is a scowl? How long is a Pinter pause?), but it is evident from the fact that each production of any play varies, that while the dialogue remains the same, the process of production – set, lighting and performances – will always be different. The only real 'directions' in any dramatic text lie in the dialogue: directions to the performers about *what* they have to say, not *how* they could/should/might say it. The *what* belongs to the dramatist, the *how* is the imperative of production.

In their opportunist marginality, stage directions are secondary to the imperative of the dialogue – *intentio operis, pace* Eco. Another way of putting it might be to say the dramatist's 'intentions', as shown by stage directions, will always be (indeed, must be) overruled by the director's 'intentions'; however, this makes for an implied aesthetic battle of wills, which is unnecessary, and distracts from the central focus, which is on what the student or dramatist does in the totality of their responsibility in writing the text dramatic.

Monologue

The monologue (whether it carries the connotations of the Shakespearian soliloquy, or of the Restoration comedy aside, the Brechtian 'alienation' device, the polemical monologue of 1970s political theatre, or the narrative monologue in plays of the 1990s) belongs, as do stage directions, to the writerly convention of prose fiction (the singular, narrative voice) rather than drama (the writing of relationships).

A monologue is a performed short story. From a writerly point of view, it is distanced narrative, in the singular first or third person, even if written in the present tense. This means that however powerful the performance of a monologue might be, it is still someone enacting story-telling, and not performing drama. It is dramatised story-telling. There is nothing wrong with that. However, the monologue makes no useful contribution whatsoever to learning how to write drama.

Monologues are popular with directors and performers, because they are cheap and make good audition speeches. They are comfortable because they allude to the more familiar, accessible, narrative modes of the novel. They are often used by CW teachers, who wrongly think they are the first, or a necessary, step in writing drama. In fact, monologue-writing blurs, rather than bridges, the distinction between writing prose fiction, and writing drama.

The fourth wall

The monologue appears to bridge, or even annihilate, the fourth wall, that invisible divider between performers and audience. Much is made of 'talking to the audience', and this is part of the clever illusion, the suspension of disbelief which constitutes the collusion between performers and audience. The fourth wall never disappears (it never disappeared in Brechtian theatre, or in audience participation pieces, or even in music hall), either in drama or in monologue. It is actually the knowing explicit or implicit negotiations across the fourth wall which help to lend performance its extraordinary excitement and variety.[5]

---

[5] For more detailed discussion of the elements in this chapter, see *The Art of Writing Drama* by Michelene Wandor (Methuen, 2008).

22
Poetry and Form

As befits poetry's status as the most linguistically distilled and distilling literary form, this chapter is the shortest. Poetry is both the most difficult and the easiest to cover in brief. It is the easiest, because it is the genre in which it is not only possible, but essential to quantify a set of formal 'rules' which students can follow, and which can be explicitly 'taught' as a range of convention-based legacies. This doesn't make it easy to teach or practise. But it does mean that classes can be structured in a developmental way, going from relatively 'simple' forms to the more complex. It is easier to talk about quantifiable 'form' in relation to teaching poetry than in relation to the other genres.

Poetry is also the most difficult because it foregrounds the fundamental markers of language – its structures and applied uses in written texts. It reinforces the indispensability of an understanding and application of grammar, punctuation and spelling, precisely because poetry's syntactic possibilities are more variable and multiple than those of prose fiction or drama. It is vital to know how to manipulate sentence structure in order to deal with the matter of space-based decisions in writing poetry: the line.

Knowledge of sentence structure enables access to the very many ways in which the 'rules' can be, and often are, put aside. Poetry demands a command of the most subtle distinctions between discursive and figurative (referential and symbolic) uses of vocabulary. Writing with imagery, metaphor, deploying words with ambiguity as well as with literal sense-making calls for a wide-ranging and complex understanding of the many different ways in which meanings can be constructed, suggested and expanded. It is impossible to teach or learn poetry-writing adequately without these knowledges.

In poetry, other linguistic possibilities have to be explored: sound, pace, rhythms, assimilated and internalised, cross-rhythms, rhyme and rhyming in all its forms, the differential sounds of consonants and vowels, of dialect, echo and sonority. Even these are conditional on a knowledge of language: of basic lexical units, such as syllables, and – in a way which differs from prose fiction and drama – the differences between denotive and connotive language, referentiality, allusiveness, the literal and the metaphorical, the hermeneutically transparent and the abstruse.

Poetry is often seen as the 'highest' art form, not simply because it allows and encourages distillation, or because it lends itself to the deepest and most intimate moments of the 'soul' (in the lyric) or to major aesthetic archetypes (in the epic), but because it combines reference to the most inchoate of faculties and responses (the emotional) with the (literally) 'impossible' – in, for example, the prevalence of metaphor, which can never stand in one-to-one relationship with anything but itself, in language, in its formal context.

23
The Core Genres: Pedagogy

Any accounts of the interior of any pedagogic process are necessarily partial and incomplete. This is true of all live teaching situations and all subjects: seminars, lectures, tutorials. The space, the atmosphere, verbal and non-verbal signs of response and communication are integral to the teaching process, built round the 'extraordinary complex psychic web, impossible to fully represent in words'.[1]

As all teachers and students know, the dynamic, rapport and immediacy of the teaching experience is all. This is entirely dependent on the teacher's ability to create an atmosphere, sustain and develop the process. The role of the teacher in the traditional workshop is as a supposed arbiter-referee, self-effacingly fielding the 'feedback' comments of the students. This is bound to be a slippery exercise, since no given workshop group arrives with shared critical terms of reference, and there can very rarely be a grounded way of developing them within the workshop, in relation to incomplete student writing.

What follows is a set of principles, an outline of my own pedagogic practice, which is very different from received ways of teaching CW. The approach has been developed over a number of years; not consciously from theory to practice, but with the two continually moving backwards and forwards in relation to each other. As I briefly outlined in the Introduction, like other CW teachers, I began by making it up as I went along, drawing on my own professional experience and expertise as a writer. I developed a graduated, cumulative and developmental approach to the teaching of each genre. While what follows is as clear and distilled

---

[1] Peter Abbs, 'The Place of Creative Writing in the Development of Teachers', in *Teaching Creative Writing: Theory and Practice*, ed. Moira Monteith and Robert Miles (Open University Press, 1982), p. 79.

an account as I can offer of a materialist approach to teaching CW, it does not, and cannot, amount to a lesson plan, or a literal structure which other teachers and students can follow. But it will, I hope, provide a structured starting point from which, with a great deal of reading and thinking and different pedagogic practices, everything which I have argued in this book can be translated into understanding and practice.

Aims and pedagogic practice

There are a number of aims behind the way I approach CW pedagogy. These are as follows:

1   to develop verbal acuity in imaginative uses of language in relation to each of the conventions of the imaginative modes of thought realised in the three core genres – prose fiction, drama and poetry;
2   to develop a practical understanding (i.e. through writing and analysis) of the conventions of the above;
3   to become aware of, and understand, what distinguishes each genre from the others, both in the imagining and in the writing;
4   to become aware, *pace* David Crystal, of the difference between *writing* and *knowing and thinking about writing*;
5   to *think* about writing, and to think about *how to think* about writing, through analysing the stylistic features of student writing in the classroom;
6   for each student to develop a greater understanding of how their mind/imagination works; to gain understanding of their own linguistic and cultural resources, and of the necessity of expanding these;
7   to pursue class-based studies which focus on imaginative *writing*, not *rewriting*.

The pedagogic practice which follows on from this is that students literally write their way into each genre. The pattern of work is similar, from class to class, building towards the completion of one or more examples of the genre concerned. Completion is essential in each case, since matters of structure (to take just one example) cannot be explored and understood without the bracketing elements of 'beginning' and 'end' being built into the process. There is a general sense in which this way of working bears comparison with the way music, drama and dance are commonly taught. In these art forms, the work must be 'on the floor', created as an object in the space, as it were, before it can be seen and analysed. In the case of my classes, exactly the same pattern operates: the writing is produced in class, the object is created and then read – it is in the air, as it were.

Value judgements have no place whatsoever at any stage of class work. I explain this very carefully at the beginning, and often have to repeat the explanations, which always make a different kind of sense at other stages of the process. If students weigh in with the good/bad, works/doesn't work, I prefer/don't like, etc., I actively discourage them. We do not engage in 'criticism' or 'feedback'. Students are neither invited nor encouraged to offer textual suggestions to 'improve' another student's writing. There is never any discussion of any student's 'intention', and no-one is ever asked to 'explain' their work, or to discuss its sources or how they 'feel' about its content. Students never bring in extracts from work they are writing outside class, for 'feedback'.

1 All writing is done weekly in class, building cumulatively, section by section, not necessarily sequentially, towards completed examples of the appropriate genre. After each writing session (10–15–20 minutes), everyone reads their piece aloud in turn. Attention to language is thus sharpened through listening, hearing and remembering.

2 Seemingly *ab nihilo*, where there was 'nothing' (i.e. no 'texts' in the classroom), suddenly there are many. This is what builds the practice of writing.

3 All the pieces are heard again, and I draw attention to relevant stylistic/linguistic features, to draw out the aesthetic and convention-distinctive implications of the appropriate genre, and to generate observation of these aspects of the language.

4 Gradually, as part of this process, the possibilities already immanently there within each segment of written text are raised as possible ways in which the writing might develop. Everything we do returns to the written text and derives from it, becoming structurally more complex as the work develops. These observations are not suggestions from which a student can 'choose' or consider for rewriting; they are elicitations of what may be already textually immanent. The students do not rewrite, but *continue* writing, developing their work themselves.

The aural scrutiny of each text reveals what clues or suggestions are already within it, in the language itself, in its structural potential, which leads (not necessarily chronologically or sequentially) to the next piece of writing. Evidence must always come from the text, providing traces of genre-specific elements out of which the piece of writing moves to the next stage. Structure can never be an early point of discussion, since it only becomes directly relevant when there is enough (student) material to be structured. This process reveals the 'gaps' in each piece of writing, defined in terms of its possibilities. Any piece of writing (even a single sentence) can be analysed to reveal a whole range of genre-specific possibilities – narrative, relationships, events, etc.

In terms of a theory of imaginative writing, a *poeisis*, a making, this corresponds most closely to Umberto Eco's metaphor, *intentio operis*, the 'intention of the work'. Except that here, the 'work' is, by definition, always incomplete, ongoing and only ever entails writing, not rewriting, mind-reading intentionality, or second-guessing finalities. This work is entirely separate from the writing which students prepare and submit as assignments; this is in line with the way in which other subjects are taught. This is a vital part of the process, so that the learning procedures and the independent putting-into-practice which each student must undertake are very clearly distinguished. In this sense, then, the CW classroom is different from the music/drama process, where work may be literally 'rehearsed' in class time, before reaching full completion/ production for assessment.

At the beginning of each module/course I ask each student about their own linguistic background; this includes bi-linguality/multi-linguality, as well as opening up the question of their own awareness about the range of 'Englishes' which they each possess, as the 'hard' material on which they will draw for their writing. This is the closest the pedagogy gets to any 'personal' discussion; its focus is entirely on the language, rather than the person or the self.

It can involve dialects, and educational trajectories which affect language use, sometimes involving important distinctions between speech and writing. I always encourage everyone to draw on these languages, and sometimes to mix them. There may well be pieces written in a mixture of English and other languages, or another language and English, perhaps in parallel, sometimes in translation by the student him/herself. Careful discussion of the differences involved in such language interplay enables students to think about their own cultural and imaginative resources, and to see where their options for content and/or subject matter might be. The latter is always entirely up to each student; the foregrounded discussions are always built on exploring and revealing the conventions in all their complexity, and analysing the language in relation to these.

Imaginative writing in stages

Thus, in prose fiction classes, each student constructs one or more complete stories in class during the term/semester. Narrative, its sequentiality, its ordering, its relations (explicit and implicit) between cause and effect form a large part of the work. So also does detailed attention to the language in prose-narrative passages. Work on what is and could be entailed in 'description' takes up a significant amount of time, always focusing on specifics, in order to open up the variety of possibilities in different contexts.

In drama classes, students write a 15-20-minute drama, of between 5 and 7 scenes. Students make copies of each scene between classes, and everyone performs. The classroom is alternately a writing and a performance space. This gives everyone (in principle) an opportunity to experience how imperatives change, from the point of view of the performer, and in relation to the concept and practice of the fourth wall. There are two absolute rules which I impose all the way through: 1. No stage directions; 2. No monologues.

In poetry, the way in is predominantly through the medium of form, beginning with the relative simplicity of the *haiku*. But even this opens up a world of formal and linguistic complexity: there is the relationship between stressed and unstressed syllables, and whether students can hear them, let alone write and read them. There is metre, line-length and rhyme schemes. There are many different verse forms, which generate different workings of content and language. By and large, the emphasis in all three genres is on form and conventions, and there is never enough time to cover all the possibilities.

Materialities of mind, and writing

The central conundrum of the 'invisibility' of the sources of imaginative writing – what is in the mind, the imagination – gives the exhortation to 'write what you know/from your own experience' a very crude, base-line accuracy. However, as soon as the first word is written in class, it has already become something different. It is now marks on the page, and an 'object', with all the weight of its historical, cultural and intertextual determinations. It is no longer in the mind, in the imagination. Something has been made manifest: whether and what relationship it bears to what was/is in the mind is another issue entirely. But concretely, materially, the writing is on the page. Writing is as material an activity as is throwing pots, or painting a picture, or using a musical instrument to produce sounds. The imagination must be given form, in its literal as well as material senses, before it can be 'seen'.

It is only now available for reading. When people talk about 'discovering what you think' as you write, it is to this element of the process that they are (perhaps unknowingly) alluding. There is no other way to manifest what one thinks or imagines, in writing, except by creating/making the object called the text. I say this with all due allowance for the provisionality of texts still being written, and for the provisionalities of the process of reading, creating meaning and interpretation. For the student, the words on the page are both the object and the objective of the pedagogic process.

This is another reason why 'intentionality' is neither relevant nor useful. In particular, the concept of intentionality takes no account of the complexity of consciousness, a matter which continues to preoccupy philosophers and others. As neuroscientist Susan Greenfield has observed, 'let no one be under any illusion that scientists are anywhere near solving the so-called "hard problem" of consciousness: how thoughts and feelings may arise from spaghetti junctions of neurons and squirts of chemicals'.[2]

Comparing the work of the novelist with that of the scientist, Greenfield used a phrase which has important implications for the ethical problems resulting from the workshop's putative linking of writing with therapy: 'To reach the "scientific" conclusion that we "see with our brains not with our eyes" is not to hack into the individual's private world at all, merely to respect its existence.'[3] Hacking into the individual's private world is indeed what is involved when teachers demand (because they are in a position to) that students reveal traumas which may find a place in their writing. Whether or not someone draws on a trauma is between them and the page. It is not the business of the teacher or the rest of the seminar.

CW as incomplete

My CW classes, intensive, hard-working and productive as they are, complete in their own terms as they always are, are also extrinsically

---

[2] 'Minds meet on two-way street', review of David Lodge's book *Consciousness and the Novel*; in *THES*, 6 December 2002, p. 23.
[3] Ibid.

incomplete. It could not be otherwise. Students may themselves connect their literature/theory courses with their writing work; occasionally some students may have taken modules in stylistics or linguistics, but there has never been a shared set of intellectual reference points in any group. This is an enormous problem, both within the current configuration of CW, and in terms of how it might be transformed in the future.

It will not have escaped some readers' notice that there are certain words and phrases which are absent from this book: discussion of emotion, feeling, satisfaction, passion, the urge/compulsion/need to write. This is deliberate. I discount none of these as part of the vital forces which may spur/drive people who seriously wish to write poetry, prose fiction or drama, or anyone who really wants to learn about imaginative writing. Clearly, there are 'subjective' elements to the imaginative writing process, not just because it is an inner, mind-based form of thought. But that is precisely what they are: subjective, 'private', not in a censorious sense, but because the complexity within each mind/imagination does not yield to anecdotal guesswork. Such speculation belongs to interaction between students or friends, or to the discipline of aesthetics, properly studied as such.

In this context, therefore, there is no reason at all why students who want to 'share' their writing (another one of these soft-edged therapy-derived terms) should not or cannot do so in autonomous, self-organised groups. Work in progress can be circulated, discussed, responded to. These augment the more rigorous classroom process, above all keeping the structural clarity of the nature of the seminar, where the roles of teacher and student are clearly demarcated, however enjoyable and rewarding the pedagogic process may and should be.

24
Imaginative Writing: Summary and the Future

The approaches outlined in the previous four chapters are frameworks for an alternative form of CW pedagogy, to replace the workshop principles and methodology. This alternative is based on a cluster of theoretical understandings of the imaginative mode of thought and genre-based writing, with a methodology drawn from linguistic analysis, elements from stylistics, and a seminar-based process that builds students' understanding of the conventions of genre, through class-based writing. All CW roads lead to the workshop, and current workshop practice really must go.

The historical traces responsible for workshop practice come from a number of cultural sources, as has been charted in this book. Part of the imperative for profoundly radical change is the mixture of incompatible ideological strands, at one extreme, that of the double-bind lures of the Romantic muse and the professional writer. The first forewarns all students that the core of CW is unteachable, the second seduces all students (under- and postgraduates) into thinking that they are being 'trained' to become professional writers.

At the other extreme, the notion that CW is 'self-expression', where imaginative writing is primarily a way of discovering and 'expressing' the self, over-identifies the subject with the psychotherapeutic process, transferring what should be a focus on the work and the writing to the self of each individual student. This serves to mask the exciting complexities of the imaginative mode of thought and its various sources and resources from within the mind and memory, and from the pursuit of knowledges and sources 'out there' in the world.

The peculiarly perverse methodology of CW pedagogy is thus fuelled by the incompatible pairing of the Romantic Muse and coercive self-expression. That this should have become such a widespread and accepted form of teaching/learning can only be explained by the background assumption that the training is determined by an aesthetic Darwinism: the survival of the fittest student through the hard-cop/soft-cop scourges of the workshop. This is fundamentally a punitive approach to pedagogy. Even Samuel Smiles, the man who gave us the phrase 'self-help' is very clear about the bankruptcy of such an attitude:

> 'As for Failure, *per se*, although it may be well to find consolations for it at the close of life, there is reason to doubt whether it is an object that ought to be set before youth at the beginning of it. Indeed, "how *not* to do it" is of all things the easiest learnt: it needs neither teaching, effort, self-denial, industry, patience, perseverance nor judgement.'[1]

Justified by the mystique of creativity, whether it is the selective 'genius' or the ubiquitous quality in us all, further screens are created to prevent clear-headed approaches to what CW might be as a subject, and how it might *really* be taught. Genuine learning takes place as a result of doing something properly, and gaining experience of how to do it, as well as thinking about it. If the stress is always on what is wrong, as most CW literature proudly vaunts of the workshop method, everything which CW-as-therapy purports to create (support, encouragement) is, in fact, jettisoned in terms of its opposite: creating insecurity, fear, intimidation, uncertainty, the inability, sometimes, to write at all. The terror of the blank page is its own insidious reward.

This is not helped by the use in CW pedagogy of methods associated with early school education. While they were an important spur in early twentieth-century reforms in Progressive Education, and while they fed into some of the libertarian cultural and educational developments in the 1960s and 1970s, they have become a drawback in CW. The latter's largely hostile attitude to rationality (left-brain activity), to theory and particularly to discursive writing, have led to what Don Paterson complained of as 'the infantilisation of a perfectly serious subject'.[2] The workshop must go.

---

[1] Samuel Smiles, *Self-Help* (Penguin).
[2] Don Paterson, 'Rhyme or Reason', *Times Literary Supplement*, 11 August 2006.

The academic context for CW

Minor reforms to the workshop, such as including some terminology from literary theory, can, of course, be useful and interesting. But this remains superficial, merely responding to symptoms of what is a far more profound issue: the question of where and how CW belongs in the academy. There can really be only one answer to where CW is positioned. Even with CW's own goals (in both senses of the phrase), it can only belong within, or in symbiotic relation to, English literary studies. The dominance of the idea of talent/genius/the Romantic Muse, along with the explicit claims that CW is a training for professional writers, paradoxically secures the argument, even for those who support CW in its current separatist, indeed, isolationist ambitions. The fact that it is a verbal art form links it by analogy to other practice-based arts, of course; but its materials belong in active relationship with those associated with the study of English – literature, language and literary convention. CW's glorious separatism cannot be justified.

Isobel Armstrong made the assessment that 'English has always had a special place in academic study because it carries out its analyses with the same materials which are its objects of study – it is, as Shelley once said, both the materials of the culture and the tools which cut it – texts written in language analysed through language. . . . Language, indeed, is at the heart of our subject, and one could say that the study of the literary text becomes an extension of the study of language'.[3] Related arguments can and should be made for CW.

The arrival of CW in the academy has helped to create a 'subject' which, whether one calls it constructivism or textual production, has a relative autonomy as a subject to be taught (in its own 'write'), by practising, professional writers. The fact that teachers of (and in) English have also developed ways to harness CW as an extension of the study of literary texts, reinforces its importance. At the same time, there is a contradiction between different teaching personnels, as it were, which has created a tension between practising (if not always widely published) writers who teach CW, and teachers of literature who are venturing into teaching CW.

These differences demonstrate even more urgently why CW not only should not, but cannot be separated completely from the subjects which, in a real way, give it history, meaning and context. The academic study

---

[3] Martin Dodsworth (ed.), *English Economists* (John Murray, 1989), p.16.

of imaginative writing, with practice at its centre, separate from English becomes isolated creationism, or creationist isolation, and is therefore pedagogically inadequate, for teachers and students. In the absense of real links with its subject-fellows, the CW workshop is driven by procedures of *re-writing*, rather than any theory of writing. The workshop must go.

There can be no understanding of literary conventions (with which CW students work) without a historical understanding of literature and its forms. There can be no understanding of these without engaging with the field of exegesis as applied to literature: criticism and theory. In other words, any student studying imaginative writing as a practice has to study literature as a body of historical work, along with literary criticism and theory, and realize this work through discursive writing, alongside the imaginative textual production. While it may be controversial to suggest this, the logic of this argument is that all students, both under- and postgraduates, should be required to produce both imaginative and discursive writing, which should be equally graded.

Discursive writing

This means that the diary-based, subjectivist forms of substitute-discursive writing (the journal, the portfolio of notes, etc.), while they may be required as part of the working process, should not be assessed; the reality is that, faced with the massive bulk of portfolios put together over a course, teachers simply cannot and do not read them. All they show – if anything – is that someone has either spent a lot of time jotting notes, or not. There are two repressed issues underpinning the fetishisation of journal/diaries. The first is the stress on such material as a substitute for the conventional academic practice of study – reading and note-taking, while not giving adequate attention to the ways in which such accumulation of material might form resources for imaginative writing. This is a pedagogical issue in its own right, to be developed and 'taught' in a manner analagous to the development of what – in other contexts – are called study skills. The second issue is the focus on such relatively random collections of material as substitutes for the imperatives of discursive writing, and the 'left-brain' rationality of other kinds of thinking – logic and argument-building. From the point of view of academic teaching structures, there may well be a strong case to be argued for an equivalent to America's Composition: generic writing instruction for all first-year students, in both discursive and imaginative writing.

In the context of influences deriving from the adult and community arts movements – the democratisation of access to, and practice of, verbal creativity – the intellectual paths also lead back to literary studies. Rob Pope has argued for reclaiming terms such as 'creativity' and the 'imagination': 'Perhaps the most compelling example of a resource that is extra/ordinarily creative is language: whatever the linguistic model, linguists agree that words are at once an utterly routine and fantastically rich resource.'[4]

However, to make the above arguments is not to suggest that a genuine realignment of CW within its related 'family' of English-based subjects is either ideologically or logistically simple. In the US, where there is already structural potential for connections, English, Composition and CW may co-exist in the same department, but they are as much in argument over status, territory and methodology as they are in collaboration.

A return to some of the origins of CW, and points along the way, serve to show that some of my argument is by no means new. D. G. Myers stressed Foerster's inter-disciplinary work in his CW pioneering: 'Criticism and creative writing went hand in hand at the Iowa School of Letters . . . the aim was comprehension: creative writing was an effort of critical understanding conducted from within the conditions of literary practice. It was the acquisition of a certain kind of knowledge entailed in a certain type of practice.'[5] Foerster was preceded by Quiller-Couch, and followed by other decisive voices: Stephen Potter, Raymond Williams, the Verbal Arts Association, and more recently Composition teachers in the US, concerned about CW's isolationism. Developments within English, welcoming the possibility of textual production, have added their voices and some modified practice. The workshop must go.

CW and its aims

According to D. G. Myers, 'Creative writing emerged over the last decades of the nineteenth century and the first half of the twentieth as a means for unifying the two main functions of English departments – the teaching of writing and the teaching of literature. Instead of greater unity, today's English departments exhibit a growing incongruity and disagreement between their two main functions. In short, creative

---

[4] Pope, *Creativity, History, Theory, Practice*, p. 55.
[5] Myers, *The Elephants Teach*, p. 133.

writing failed to achieve its goals. And one reason is that, after the Second World War, it was put to a different use altogether; creative writing became a means of expanding the cultural role of the American university and thus found occasion for abandoning its original educational goals.'[6]

Paul Dawson agrees with Myers that CW was 'part of an on-going series of reforms to literary education, carried out in response to the intellectual and pedagogical challenges created by the crisis in the humanities'.[7] Augmenting this with a wider cultural role, Dawson titled his penultimate chapter 'The Literary Intellectual', suggesting that 'we must ask what position of literary authority can the writer assume in the academy, not as an artistic practitioner, but as an intellectual.'[8]

Where Myers broadly sees CW's reforming role as a failed enterprise, Dawson posits a model of the CW graduate as the custodian of literature's intellectual, moral and civilising force. The university critic, the outcome of a tradition developed in the early part of the twentieth century, between Matthew Arnold and the Leavises, is to be replaced – if not usurped in an idealised and entirely abstract way – by the CW graduate. David Fenza adds his weight to the latter view. Supposedly, CW 'advances the ideals of a liberal and humane education by inspiring, exercising, and strengthening the efficacy of the human will to do good, to make a meaningful difference in art and in society.'[9] Fenza's manifesto adds further to the colonising and usurpatory role of CW in its claims that it teaches criticism, a way of studying literature, encouraging reading, etc. These totalising claims have come about in part because of the isolationist creationism which has increasingly become the hallmark of CW in the US and in the UK, which means CW practitioners need to recoup the 'civilising' aims once thought to belong exclusively to English.

Such grandiose ambitions and conflicting aims are all different ways of claiming academic 'specialness' for CW. I am not in any way arguing against the specialness of literature – it is, after all, my profession and my passion – but I am arguing for directing attention to its specificity in the academic context in which it now is: whether Myers bemoans its failure, Dawson overestimates its importance, an academic success it certainly is, and will continue to be, for many of the right reasons, as well as many of the wrong ones.

---

[6] Ibid., p. xiv.
[7] Dawson, *Creative Writing and the New Humanities* (Routledge, 2005), p. 155.
[8] Ibid., p. 6.
[9] David Fenza, *The Writer's Chronicle* (April 2000), p. 19.

However, all of these claims make little real sense, in the light of the actuality of CW. It was never, in any concerted way, 'meant' to reform English, or to reconcile it to its differences. Paul Dawson's proposition that CW might produce graduates who are 'intellectuals' with potential cultural power is mind-boggling, given CW's persistent hostility to, and rejection of, anything remotely resembling historical, critical and theoretical study, because they 'belong' to nasty authoritarian left-brain activity. David Fenza's list of claims for CW, amounting to a usurpation of the English department (minus theory), is little more than naïve. In a curious way, the very ambition of all these claims testifies to a need for contact with the very faculties and practices from which CW has isolated itself.

Teachers and students

The early caveat that CW cannot be taught; it can only be learned, is often still proclaimed. This simply lets CW teachers off the hook. The onus is unfairly placed on the individual student; unfairly, because another part of the catechism proclaims that the student can only really 'learn' (i.e. become a professional writer) if the Muse has already visited. The 'problem' of teaching and learning CW, as shared between teachers and students, *must* be addressed. Kelly Ritter spelled out the lack of training comparable to other subjects in US English. CW teachers are either expected to pick up 'tips' by osmosis from workshops they have themselves attended, or to turn up and apply their critical *nous* without any need for other preparation. We have all done it; we all do it. But in so doing, in busking our expertise, as it were, we (CW teachers) have a serious difficulty, which helps to mask the need for change.

We may be widely and deeply read, but we are rarely schooled in teaching literary history, literary criticism and/or literary theory; we are (probably) rarely schooled in linguistics, stylistics. We are employed for our artistic and professional expertise; however, while we may teach what we 'know' as best we can, we are doing so in a sometimes desperate kind of academic free-fall. For us to call for (related) subjects in which we do not have expertise, may look as if we are arguing ourselves out of the very valuable opportunities offered to us by the academy. This is not my argument here at all. It is clear that, just as in the other art forms, professional writers must be the main teachers of CW, and it is equally clear that we cannot do so in isolation from English. In the medium and long run, this must involve structurally integrated courses, which combine elements from the various branches of literary studies. This applies to postgraduate CW study as well; currently, by and large, students tend to be admitted to all courses, under- and postgraduate, on the basis of portfolios of writing alone.

There is not yet a graduated continuum from CW at school through all levels of university of study. This suggests that for some time to come students may well be graduating with degrees (at all levels) which are woefully lacking in literary knowledge, critical understanding and application. This is not satisfactory, however valuable the time thay are able to allocate just to 'writing'. While actively encouraging students to read is good news, it is to ourselves that this exhortation should initially be more strongly addressed. It could be argued that we, as teachers, have the primary obligation to read the history, the theory, the discussions, in order to do more than merely turn up to a 'workshop' and act as critical-feedback umpire. Adjustment for writer-teachers to the academy can be difficult. Apart from the pedagogic demands, there is the routine and procedure of academic work and administration. The writing-as-therapy approach often tempts CW teachers to give high marks just to encourage students.

For students, there are other difficulties too. Just being exhorted to 'read', and being given a short, largely anecdotal reading list, is not exactly to be pedagogically supported or encouraged. A student who expects to discover the Muse within, to be given a set of tips which will magically create a professional writer, or who chooses CW because it's an easy option (you just 'write', and there are no essays) is abdicating their responsibility as a student – which is to participate and to learn. It's a chicken-and-egg situation, in which the teacher is, of course, ultimately responsible. But students also have a responsibility to follow more taxing, intellectual suggestions when they are offered, and not expect (as they are often led to believe) mere encouragement for some self-expression (read Booker prize-winning tips from an agent).

This leaves the workshop in stasis; while many teachers of English have been welcoming and responsive to the presence of CW, there is a new dynamic which has entered the academy. In the context of the traditional creative/critical hierarchy, which still privileges the first over the second, there can be envy and/or resentment towards CW from English career academics who 'really' would like to be seen as novelists and poets, rather than as teachers. One of the paradoxes at the heart of Barthes' 'The Death of the Author' is that 'Author' is taken (tacitly, often) to refer to the author-of-fiction. To have the 'Author' on campus as CW teacher may sometimes, therefore, look like provocation to the career academic, devoting him/herself to what s/he (secretly) believes is a secondary activity – criticism/exegesis. English teachers, while they may well be deploying 'recreative' writing to enhance literary study, also sometimes flatter themselves that CW is light relief from the more taxing business of 'serious' study; if anyone can do it, then why, anyone can do it. Rapprochement is not and will not be easy.

Context: gender and culture

Beneath the banner of the Romantic Muse marches an aspect of literary history and production which has, at particular cultural moments, been contested. If genius/talent are just 'there', if CW cannot be 'taught', then what rises to the 'top', will just appear to be accidental, meant to be, and just 'natural'. While the phrase does not account for every writer and literary product, the Dead White European Male, generally the product of a privileged education, is what is most likely (not exclusively, of course) to emerge.

It could be argued that against this, the belief that creativity is inherent in us all, can become a politically and educationally democratising force, leading to the idea that CW is a truly radical 'discipline', eliding class, gender and ethnic differences. This notion comes up against the idea of CW as a form of self-expression, it may be individually liberating, but what kind of individualness is being liberated? To make any sense of this at all, issues of cultural and social difference must be approached. And, again, this suggests reference out to a varied body of knowledge and cultural theory: feminism and gender analysis, post-colonial studies, etc., etc. Students from cultures with different literary histories taking CW courses in the UK or US, will be (literally) buying in to traditions which differ from their own imaginative and cultural resources. This may not be a problem at all, but it does point to problems in 'teaching' genres that have only one historical and literary provenance.

The relationship between 'thinking' the relationship between gender and literature is a telling case study here. Women had an influential presence in the pioneering of CW in the US. The University of Iowa, one of the first universities to accredit creative work for advanced degrees in the arts, awarded two Masters degrees for musical composition to women in 1925; the following year a woman received a Masters for painting, and in 1931, a woman was the first to receive a similar degree for CW. Ben Knights has pointed out that both at school and BA level, CW female students are in a ratio of 3:1 with male students.

As enthusiastic participants in the advantages of establishing English as a university subject in the nineteenth century, women were active in the adult education movement, and English teaching at university level became one way in to academic life for women. Although Cambridge University did not admit women to university teaching posts until 1926, they were able to teach at the two women's colleges, and there were more women English students than there were men students. There was, however, an ideological struggle which has gradually affected the gendering, as it were, of literary study. A clue to this lies in Quiller-Couch's advice for good writing. His approval for what he characterises as the 'masculine' in writing stands almost as a justification against the early disapproval of imaginative writing as fit only for emotional women, and therefore lesser as a subject for serious study. Gradually, of course, as happens virtually across the arts, the more a 'subject' becomes professionalised, the more it is subject to the dominance of men. In CW, there are generally more female than male students, and, if general academic patterns are repeated, it is likely that the more prestigious academic posts will be dominated by men too.

This cultural imbalance is there in other forms in the interstices of different ethnic and cultural imaginations. This is revealed often in the ways in which students access and develop the languages at their dosposal – their Englishes, as well as other languages. Issues of gender, cultural representation have scarcely been touched on in CW literature in the UK and in the US. It is as if the egalitarianism of the 1960s and 1970s has been taken over without any material attempt to follow-through the practical, theoretical and imaginative implications. These exciting implications apply to subject matter, form, theme, and linguistic choices; it is more than a matter of including some socio-linguistics in the work of the CW seminar. It entails also attention to the theoretical legacies of feminism and gender-analysis, and of post-colonial theory, as well as the demographic configuration of higher education

The Author

The very fact that Myers and Dawson have such diametrically opposed judgements on CW, goes beyond the difference between pessimism/optimism, scepticism/support. Both accept 'the central pedagogical aim of Creative Writing, which is to teach students how to develop their writing skills in order to produce literary works.'[10] From within the AWP, this

---

[10] Ibid., p. 161.

early aim, deriving from Iowa's original postgraduate courses, remains: 'The goal of graduate study in creative writing is to become, first and foremost, an accomplished writer who makes significant contributions to contemporary literature'.[11]

Let us remember that it is not as if contemporary literature 'needs' CW courses to keep its presses and literary journals going. If CW were to disappear tomorrow, it would make no difference to literature, though it would affect the bank balances of many writer-teachers. If there is a genuine case for the importance of CW as the final, verbal, art form to join the other art forms in the academy, it cannot be on the grounds of essential training for the profession of writer. Indeed, while the desire to 'produce' students with writing of professional, publishable standard, was one of the important spurs to CW's arrival in the academy, it has proved to be a counterproductive objective. Some professional writers may emerge from CW courses, but they may equally well emerge from other courses of study, or no formal study at all. The same is true of nuclear physicists, musicians, historians. Some graduates will teach, and many will go on to take all kinds of other jobs. This is true of all academic disciplines, and it does not negate ambition, aspiration, passion.

This book has been written from a passionate commitment (a) to teaching CW, and (b) to seeing CW established on a secure and viable basis in the academy. It is a contribution to the historicising and theorisation of CW; this is perhaps the most important compliment which can be paid to a subject of serious academic standing. The teaching of the imaginative mode of thought (CW) is, indeed, a success story in the academy. Now is the time to begin doing it properly.

---

[11] Fenza, op. cit., p. 13.

Epilogue

An intertextual manifesto

'Like all the best radical positions, then, mine is a thoroughly traditionalist one. I wish to recall literary criticism from certain fashionable, new-fangled ways of thinking it has been seduced by –
"literature" as a specially privileged object, the "aesthetic" as separable
from social determinants, and so on – and return it to the ancient
paths which it has abandoned. . . . I do not mean that we should
revive the whole range of ancient rhetorical terms and substitute these
for modern critical language. . . .'[1]

Textual intervention

'Like all the best radical positions, then, mine is a thoroughly traditionalist one. I wish to recall literary criticism (*creative writing*) from certain
fashionable, new-fangled ways of thinking it has been seduced by –
"literature" (*creative writing*) as a specially privileged object (*separate from
the study of literature*), the "aesthetic" (*self-expression, genius, inspiration,
the imagination*) as separable from social determinants, and so on – and
return it to the ancient paths (*the study of the histories of literature, the close
study of literary texts and their contexts, the study, understanding and practice
of language through different forms of writing, literary and non-literary, discursive and imaginative, figurative and literal, fiction and non-fiction*) which it
has abandoned. . . . I do not mean that we should revive the whole range
of ancient rhetorical terms (*or deny the relative autonomy of creative writing
and other writing studies, or merely use writing as an adjunct to literary
studies, although it can clearly be that too*) and substitute these for modern

---

[1] Terry Eagleton, *Literary Theory: An Introduction* (Blackwell, 1986), p. 179.

critical language (*which would consist of a study and understanding of the history and concepts of literary criticism and literary theory; a writerly study, understanding and practice of discursive and imaginative writing, alongside usefully traditional and readerly-based literary studies, effecting a rapprochement between them all*) . . .'[2]

Intertextual intervention

'Like all the best radical positions, then, mine is a thoroughly traditionalist one. I wish to recall creative writing from certain fashionable, new-fangled ways of thinking it has been seduced by – for example, the idea that creative writing is separate from the study of literature, the idea that the "aesthetic": self-expression, genius, inspiration, the imagination, are separable from social determinants – and locate CW in its real cultural and disciplinary homes: in active relationship with the study of the histories of literature, the close study of literary texts and their contexts, the study, understanding and practice of shaped language through different forms of writing, literary and non-literary, discursive and imaginative, figurative and literal, fiction and non-fiction, in relation to which it is not comfortable, and from which it seeks to maintain its separateness. . . . I do not mean that we should deny the relative autonomy of creative writing and other writing studies, or merely use writing as an adjunct to literary studies (although it can clearly be part of that too), but we should not ignore the legacies and importance of modern critical language, and the forms of literary criticism still being used. Any CW study is seriously incomplete unless it also consists of a study and understanding of the history and concepts of literary criticism and literary theory; unless it is a series of writerly and productive studies which develop verbal acuity and a writerly understanding and practice of discursive and imaginative writing, alongside the readerly-based studies of literature (however categorically defined) which are already in place, thus effecting a rapprochement between them all.'[3]

---

[2] Ibid., p. 179, modified by Michelene Wandor, *The Author is not Dead, Merely Somewhere Else* (Palgrave Macmillan, 2007), p. 229–30.

[3] Ibid., p. 179, reworked in tribute to Terry Eagleton by Michelene Wandor, *The Author is not Dead, Merely Somewhere Else* (Palgrave Macmillan, 2007), p. 230.

Bibliography

Abbs, Peter, *English for Diversity* (Heinemann, 1969).

Abbs, Peter, *English within the Arts* (Hodder and Stoughton, 1982).

Abbs, Peter, *A is for Aesthetic* (The Falmer Press, 1989).

Arnold, Matthew, *Culture and Anarchy* (Cambridge University Press, 1963).

Arnold, Matthew, *The Function of Criticism at the Present Time*, www.kessinger.net.

Aston, Elaine and Savona, George, *Theatre as Sign-System* (Routledge, 1998).

Atwood, Margaret, *Negotiating with the Dead* (Cambridge University Press, 2002).

Ayckbourn, Alan, *The Crafty Art of Playmaking* (Faber, 2002).

Bailey, Jennifer and Clarke, Norma, *Ways with Words* (BBC, 1994).

Bakhtin, M.M., *The Dialogic Imagination,* ed. Michael Holquist (University of Texas Press, 2002).

Bal, Mieke, *Narratology* (University of Toronto Press, 1997).

Barry, Peter, *Beginning Theory* (Manchester University Press, 1995).

Barthes, Roland, *Image, Music, Text* (Fontana Press, 1977).

Barthes, Roland, *Writing Degree Zero* (Cape Editions, 1967).

Barthes, Roland, *Camera Lucida* (Vintage, 2000).

Barzun, Jacques, *Simple and Direct Rhetoric for Writers* (Quill, 2001).

Bassnett-McClure, Susan, *Translation Studies* (Methuen, 1980).

Bell, Julia and Magrs, Paul (eds), *The Creative Writing Coursebook* (Macmillan, 2001).

Belsey, Catherine, *Critical Practice* (Routledge, 2003).

Bennett, Andrew, *The Author* (Routledge, 2005).

Bennett, Arnold, *The Author's Craft* (Hodder & Stoughton, 1914).

Bennett, Susan, *Theatre Audiences* (Routledge, 2003).

Bentley, Eric (ed.), *The Importance of Scrutiny* (Grove Press, 1948).

Bentley, Eric, *The Theory of the Modern Stage* (Penguin, 1992).

Bentley, Eric, *The Life of the Drama* (Applause Theatre Books, 1991).

Bentley, Eric (ed.), *The Theory of the Modern Stage* (Penguin, 1992).

Besant, Walter, *The Pen and the Book* (Thomas Burleigh, 1899).

Besant, Walter and James, Henry, *The Art of Fiction* (Algonquin Press, 1900).

Bildersee. Adele, *Imaginative Writing* (D. C. Heath, 1927).

Birkett, Julian, *Word Power* (A. & C. Black, 1998).

Bishop, Wendy and Ostrom, Hans (eds), *Colors of a Different Horse* (National Council of Teachers of English, USA, 1994).

Blau, Herbert, *The Audience* (Johns Hopkins University Press, 1990).

Blonsky, Marshall (ed.), *On Signs* (Johns Hopkins University Press, 1985).

Bloom, Harold, *How to Read and Why* (Touchstone, 2001).

231

Bloor, Anthony, *A Multidisciplinary Study of Fiction Writing* (Edwin Mellen Press, 2003).

Boal, Augusto, *Theatre of the Oppressed* (New York Theatre Communications Group, 1985).

Bonham Carter, Victor with Curry, William Burnlee, *Dartington Hall, the Formative Years, 1925–1957* (Exmoor Press, 1970).

Borges, Jorge Luis, *The Craft of Verse* (Harvard University Press, 2000).

Boylan, Clare (ed.), *The Agony and the Ego* (Penguin, 1993).

Bradbury, Malcolm and McFarlane, James (eds), *Modernism: A Guide to European Literature 1890–1930* (Penguin, 1991).

Bradbury, Malcolm and Palmer, David (eds), *Contemporary Criticism* (Edward Arnold, 1970).

Bradbury, Ray, *Zen in the Art of Writing* (Bantam Books, 1996).

Bradford, Richard, *Stylistics* (Routledge, 1997).

Brande, Dorothea, *Becoming a Writer* (Macmillan, 1996).

Brayfield, Celia, *Bestseller* (Fourth Estate, 1996).

Brewer's Concise Dictionary of Phrase and Fable, ed. Betty Kirkpatrick (Helicon, 1999).

Brooks, Cleanth and Penn Warren, Robert, *Understanding Poetry* (Holt, 1950).

Brownjohn, Alan, 'Writers in Education 1951–1979' (unpublished, 1981).

Burke, Sean, *The Death and Return of the Author* (Edinburgh University Press, 2004).

Burroway, Janet, *Writing Fiction* (Longman, 2003).

Buzan, Tony, *Make the Most of your Mind* (Colt Books, 1988).

Byrne, John, *Writing Comedy* (A. & C. Black, 1999).

Byron, Glennis, *Dramatic Monologue* (Routledge, 2003).

Cameron, Julia, *The Artist's Way* (Pan Books, 1995).

Carlson, Marvin, *Performance* (Routledge, 2003).

Carlson, Marvin, *Semiotics and Signs of Life* (Bloomington, Indiana).

Cassill, R. V., *Writing Fiction* (Pocket Books, I962).

Casterton, Julia, *Creative Writing* (Macmillan, 1998).

Checkoway, Julie (ed.), *Creating Fiction* (Story Press, 1999).

Chisholm, Alison, *The Craft of Writing Poetry* (Allison & Busby, 1997).

Cluysenaar, Anne, *Introduction to Literary Stylistics* (Batsford, 1976).

Cohen, M. J., *The Penguin Thesaurus of Quotations* (Penguin, 2000).

Collins, John Churton, *The Study of English Literature* (Macmillan, 1891).

Collins, L. C., *Life and Memoirs of John Churton Collins* (John Lane, the Bodley Head, 1912).

Cook, H. Caldwell, *The Play-Way* (Heinemann, 1917).

Counsell, Colin, *Signs of Performance* (Routledge, 1996).

Counsell, Colin and Wolf, Laurie (eds), *Performance Analysis* (Routledge, 2001).

Crème, Phyllis and Lea, Mary R., *Writing at University* (Open University Press, 1998).

Critical Quarterly (Manchester University Press, 1986).

Crystal, David, *The English Language* (Penguin, 2002).

Cuddon, J. A., *Penguin Dictionary of Literary Terms and Literary Theory* (Penguin, 1991).

Culler, Jonathan, *Structuralist Poetics* (Cornell University Press, 1976).

Culler, Jonathan, *Saussure* (Fontana, 1976).

Culler, Jonathan, *Literary Theory: A Very Short Introduction* (Oxford, 2000).

Culler, Jonathan, *Barthes* (Oxford University Press, 2002).

Cullup, Michael, *Brush Up your Grammar* (Elliot Right Way Books, 1999).

Cunningham, Valentine, *Reading After Theory* (Blackwell, 2002).

Curran, James and Seaton, Jean, *Power without Responsibility* (Routledge, 1993).

Davis, Steve, Swinburne, David, and Williams, Gwen (eds), *Writing Matters* (Royal Literary Fund, 2006).

Dawson, Paul, *Creative Writing and the New Humanities* (Routledge, 2005).

Derrida, Jacques, *Writing and Difference* (Routledge, 2002).

de Saussure, Ferdinand, *Course in General Linguistics* (Fontana, 1974).

Dillard, Annie, *The Writing Life* (Harper Perennial, 1990).

Dodsworth, Martin (ed.), *English Economis'd* (John Murray, 1989).

Doubtfire, Dianne, *Creative Writing* (Teach Yourself Books, 1996).

Duff, David (ed.), *Modern Genre Theory* (Longman, 2000).

Eaglestone, Robert, *Doing English* (Routledge, 2000).

Eagleton, Terry, *Marxism and Literary Criticism* (Methuen, 1976).

Eagleton, Terry, *Literary Theory: An Introduction* (Blackwell, 1986).

Eagleton, Terry, *Literary Theory* (Blackwell, 2000).

Eagleton, Terry, *After Theory* (Allen Lane, 2003).

Easthope, Antony, *Privileging Difference* (Palgrave Macmillan, 2002).

Eco, Umberto *The Search for the Perfect Language* (Fontana, 1995).

Eco, Umberto, with Richard Rorty, Jonathan Culler and Christine Brooke-Rose, edited by Stefan Collini, *Interpretation and Overinterpretation* (Cambridge University Press, 2001).

Edgar, David (ed.), *State of Play* (Faber, 1999).

Egri, Lajos, *The Art of Dramatic Writing* (Touchstone, 1960).

Elam, Keir, *The Semiotics of Theatre and Drama* (Routledge, 1997).

Eliot, T. S., *Selected Essays* (Faber, 1957).

Elkins, James, *Why Art Cannot be Taught* (University of Illinois Press, 2001).

Elsom, John, *Post-War British Theatre* (Routledge, 1979).

Esslin, Martin, *The Field of Drama* (Methuen, 1988).

Evans, Colin (ed.), *Developing University English Teaching* (Edwin Mellen Press, 1995).

Fairfax, John and Moat, John, *The Way to Write* (Penguin, 1998).

Fenton, James, *An Introduction to English Poetry* (Penguin, 2003).

Fenza, David, *The Writers' Chronicle* (AWP, April 2000).

Fergusson, Rosalind, *The Penguin Rhyming Dictionary* (Penguin, 1985).

Fergusson, Rosalind and Manser, Martin H., *The Macmillan Guide to English Grammar* (Macmillan, 1998).

Fischer, Steven Roger, *A History of Writing* (Reaktion Books, 2001).

Field, Marion, *Polish up your Punctuation and Grammar* (How to Books, 2000).

Findlater, Richard, *Author! Author!* (Faber, 1984).

Fish, Stanley, *Is There a Text in this Class?* (Harvard University Press, 2003).

Fo, Dario, *The Tricks of the Trade* (Routledge, 1991).

Foerster, Norman, *Towards Standards* (Farrar & Rinehart, 1930).

Fortier, Mark, *Theory/Theatre* (Routledge, 1997).

Friedan, Betty, *The Feminine Mystique* (Penguin, 1968).

Frye, Northrop, *Anatomy of Criticism* (Princeton University Press, 2000).

Gardner, John, *The Art of Fiction* (Vintage, 1991).

Gardner, John, *On Becoming a Novelist* (W. W. Norton, 1993).

Gavron, Hannah, *The Captive Wife* (Pelican, 1966).

Gawthrope, Jane and Martin, Philip, *Survey of the English Curriculum and Teaching in Higher Education*, Report No. 8 (English Subject Centre, October 2003).

Gerould, Daniel (ed.), *Theatre Theory Theatre* (Applause, 2000).

Gioia, Dana, *Can Poetry Matter?* (Grey Wolf Press, 1992).

Goldberg, Jonathan, *Writing Matters* (Stanford University Press, 1990).

Goldberg, Natalie, *Wild Mind* (Bantam, 1990).

Goldmann, Lucien, *The Hidden God*, trs Philip Thody (Routledge, 1964).

Gooch, Steve, *Writing a Play* (A. & C. Black, 1995).

Gotham Writers' Workshop, *Writing Fiction* (Bloomsbury, 2003).

Graff, Gerald, *Professing Literature* (University of Chicago Press, 1987).

Grimes, Tom (ed.), *Seven Decades of the Iowa Workshop* (Hyperion, New York, 1999).

Gross, John, *The Rise and Fall of the Man of Letters* (Penguin, 1973).

Haake, Katharine, *What our Speech Disrupts* (National Council of Teachers of English, 2000).

Hall, Stuart, Hobson, Dorothy, Lower, Andrew and Willis, Paul (eds), *Culture, Media, Language* (Hutchinson, 1980).

Hawthorn, Jeremy, *A Glossary of Contemporary Literary Theory* (Edward Arnold, 2000).

Hayden, Diana (ed.), *Directory of Writers' Circles, Courses and Workshops* (Diana Hayden, 2005).

Henderson, James L., *Irregularly Bold* (André Deutsch, 1978).

Herbert, W. N. and Hollis, Matthew, *Strong Words* (Bloodaxe Books, 2000).

Highsmith, Patricia, *Plotting and Writing Suspense Fiction* (St Martin's Griffin, 1990).

Hobsbaum, Philip, *Metre, Rhythm and Verse Form* (Routledge, 1998).

Hoggart, Richard, *The Uses of Literacy* (Penguin, 1971).

Holbrook, David, *The Exploring Word* (Cambridge University Press, 1967).

Holland, Siobhan, *Good Practice Guide: Creative Writing* (English Subject Centre, February 2003).

Holquist, Michael, *Dialogism: Bakhtin and his World* (Routledge, 2001).

Horstmann, Rosemary, *Writing for Radio* (A. & C. Black, 1997).

Hough, Graham, *Style and Stylistics* (Routledge & Kegan Paul, 1969).

Hourd, Marjorie, *The Education of the Poetic Spirit* (Heinemann, 1949, 1962).

Hughes, Ted, *Poetry in the Making* (Faber, 1969).

Hunt, Celia and Sampson, Fiona, *The Self on the Page* (Jessica Kingsley, 1998).

Iser, Wolfgang, *The Act of Reading* (Johns Hopkins University Press, 1980).

Jameson, Fredric, *The Political Unconscious* (Routledge, 2002).

Kearney, Anthony, *The Louse on the Locks of Literature* (Scottish Academic Press, 1986).

King, Stephen, *On Writing* (Pocket Books, 2002).

Knights, Ben and Thurgar-Dawson, Chris, *Active Reading: Transformative Writing in Literary Studies* (Continuum, 2006).

Kroll, Jeri, 'Draining Creativity: the Teacher–Writer in the Vampire Academy', *TEXT*, vol. 10, no. 2.

Lamott, Anne, *Bird by Bird* (Anchor Books, 1995).

Laurenson, Diana and Swingewood, Alan, *The Sociology of Literature* (Paladin, 1972).

Leahy, Anna (ed.), *Power and Identity in the Creative Writing Classroom* (Multilingual Matters, 2005).

Leavis, F. R., *Mass Civilisation and Minority Culture* (Gordon Fraser, 1930).

Leavis, F. R., *English Literature in our Time and the University* (Chatto & Windus, 1969).

Leavis, F. R., *Towards Standards of Criticism* (Lawrence & Wishart, 1976).

Leavis, F. R., *The Great Tradition* (Penguin, 1977).

Leavis, F. R., *Valuation in Criticism and Other Essays*, ed. G. Singh (Cambridge University Press, 1986).

Leavis, Q. D., *Fiction and the Reading Public* (Pimlico, 2000).

Lewis, C. S., *Rehabilitations* (Oxford University Press, 1939).

Lewis, John, *The Left Book Club* (Gollancz, 1970).

Lodge, David, *Modern Criticism and Theory: A Reader* (Longman, 1988).

Lodge, David, *The Art of Fiction* (Penguin, 1992).

Lodge, David, *The Modes of Modern Writing* (Arnold, 2000).

Lodge, David, *The Language of Fiction* (Routledge, 2002).

Lubbock, Percy, *The Craft of Fiction* (Jonathan Cape, 1966).

Macherey, Pierre, *A Theory of Literary Production* (Routledge, 1988).

MacKillop, Ian, *F. R. Leavis: A Life in Criticism* (Penguin, 1997).

MacKillop, Ian and Storer, Richard, *F. R. Leavis: Essays and Documents* (Sheffield Academic Press, 1995).

Mamet, David, *True and False* (Vintage, 1999).

Mamet, David, *Three Uses of the Knife* (Vintage, 2000).

Mannion, John, *School Grammar* (Collins, 1998).

Mansbridge, Albert, *The Trodden Road* (J. M. Dent, 1940).

Margolies, David (ed.), *Writing the Revolution* (Pluto Press, 1998).

Marshall, Sybil, *Creative Writing* (Macmillan, 1974).

Matterson, Stephen and Jones, Darryl, *Studying Poetry* (Edward Arnold, 2000).

McKee, Robert, *Story* (Methuen, 1999).

Mcquillan, Martin (ed.), *The Narrative Reader* (Routledge, 2000).

Mearns, Hughes, *Creative Youth* (Doubleday, 1930).

Mearns, Hughes, *Creative Power* (Doubleday, 1958).

Minnis, Noel, *Linguistics at Large* (Paladin, 1972).

Mitchell, Juliet, *Woman's Estate* (Pelican, 1971).

Monteith, Moira and Miles, Robert (eds), *Teaching Creative Writing* (Open University Press, 1992).

Morley, Dave and Worpole, Ken, *The Republic of Letters* (Comedia/Minority Press Group Series, no. 6, 1982).

Moxley, Joseph M., *Creative Writing in America* (National Council of Teachers of English, 1989).

Myers, D. G., *The Elephants Teach: Creative Writing since 1880* (Prentice-Hall, 1996 and 2006).

Myers, D. G., 'On the Teaching of Literary Theory', in *Philosophy and Literature*, 18 October 1994.

Nash, Walter and Stacey, David, *Creating Texts* (Longman, 1997).

Neill, A. S., *Summerhill* (Penguin, 1972).

Nelson, Richard and Jones, David, *Making Plays*, ed. Colin Chambers (Faber, 1995).

Neville, Richard, *Play Power* (Granada, 1973).

Newlyn, Lucy and Lewis, Jenny, *Synergies*, vol. 1: *Sea Sonnets* (Chough Publications, St Edmund Hall, Oxford, 2003).

Newman, Jenny, Cusick, Edmund and la Tourette, Aileen (eds), *The Writer's Workbook* (Edward Arnold, 2000).

Nicoll, Allardyce, *The Development of the Theatre* (George Harrap, 1948).

Odam, George and Bannan, Nicholas, *The Reflective Conservatoire: Studies in Music* (Ashgate, 2005).

O'Rourke, Rebecca, *Creative Writing: Education, Culture and Community* (National Institute of Adult Continuing Education, 2005).

Osborne, John, *Look Back in Anger* (Faber, 1996).

Palmer, Tony, *The Trials of Oz* (Blond & Briggs, 1971).

Paterson, Don, 'Rhyme must have reason', *Times Higher Educational Supplement*, 30 June, 2006).

Payne, Michael and Schad, John, *life.after.theory* (Continuum, 2003).

Peers, Robert, *Adult Education* (Routledge, 1972).

Pfister, Manfred, *The Theory and Analysis of Drama* (Cambridge, 1991).

Pike, Frank and Dunn, Thomas G., *The Playwright's Handbook* (Plume Books, 1996).

Plumb, J. H. (ed.), *Crisis in the Humanities* (Pelican, 1964).

Pope, Rob, *Textual Intervention* (Routledge, 2003).

Pope, Rob, *Creativity: Theory, History, Practice* (Routledge, 2005).

Porier, Richard, *The Performing Self* (Rutgers University Press, 1992).

Porter, Abbott, H., *The Cambridge Introduction to Narrative* (Cambridge University Press, 2002).

Potter, Stephen, *The Muse in Chains* (Jonathan Cape, 1937).

Powell, Jim, *Postmodernism for Beginners* (Writers and Readers, 1998).

Prince, Gerald, *Dictionary of Narratology* (University of Nebraska Press, 1987).

Punter, David, *Metaphor* (Routledge, 2007).

Queneau, Raymond, *Exercises in Style*, trans. Barbara Wright (New Directions, 1981).

Quiller-Couch, Sir Arthur, *On the Art of Writing* (Cambridge University Press 1933).

Rabinow, Paul (ed.), *The Foucault Reader* (Penguin, 1991).

Radavich, David, 'Creative Writing in the Academy', in *Profession* (Modern Language Association, 1999).

Reinelt, Janelle G. and Roach, Joseph R. (eds), *Critical Theory and Performance* (University of Michigan Press, 1992).

Richards, Denis, *Offspring of the Vic: A History of Morley College* (Routledge, 1958).

Richards, I. A., *Principles of Literary Criticism* (Routledge, 1924).

Ricoeur, Paul, *Time and Narrative*, vol. 2, trans. Kathleen McLaughlin and David Pellauer (University of Chicago Press, 1985).

Ritter, Kelly, 'Professional Writers/Writing Professionals: Revamping Teacher Training in Creative Writing PhD Programs' (*College English*, vol. 64, no. 2 November 2001).

Roget's Thesaurus (Penguin, 1974).

Roorbach, Bill, *The Art of Truth* (Oxford University Press, 2001).

Rose, Jonathan, *The Intellectual Life of the British Working Classes* (Yale University Press, 2002).

Rosen, Michael, *Did I Hear You Write?* (Five Leaves, 1990).

Royal Literary Fund, *Writing Matters* (The Royal Literary Fund, 2006).

Said, Edward, *Culture and Imperialism* (Vintage, 1994).

Sanger, Keith, *The Language of Drama* (Routledge, 2001).

Sansom, Peter, *Writing Poems* (Bloodaxe Books, 1997).

Sartre, Jean Paul, *What is Literature?* (Routledge, 2001).

Schiach, Don, *Basic Punctuation* (John Murray, 1999).

Schiff, Hilda (ed.), *Contemporary Approaches to English Studies* (Heinemann, 1977).

Scholes, Robert, *Textual Power: Literary Theory and the Teaching of English* (Yale University Press, 1985).

Serle, Chris (ed.), *Stepney Words* (Centreprise Publications, 1973).

Sharples, Mike, *How we Write* (Routledge, 1999).

Shepherd, S. and Wallis, M., *Studying Plays* (Edward Arnold, 1998).

Short, Mick, *Exploring the Language of Poems, Plays and Prose* (Longman, 1996).

Siegel, Ben (ed.), *The American Writer and the University* (University of Delaware Press, 1989).

Simons, Judy and Fullbrook, Kate (eds), *Writing: A Woman's Business* (Manchester University Press, 1998).

Singleton, John, *The Creative Writing Workbook* (Macmillan, 2001).

Singleton, John and Luckhurst, Mary, *The Creative Writing Handbook* (Macmillan, 2000).

Snow, C. P., *The Two Cultures* (Cambridge University Press, 1996).

Soviet Writers' Congress 1934 (Lawrence & Wishart, 1977).

Spencer, Stuart, *The Playwright's Handbook* (Faber & Faber, 2002).

Stein, Gertrude, *How to Write* (Sun & Moon Press, 1995).

Stillman, Frances, *The Poet's Manual and Rhyming Dictionary* (Thames & Hudson, 1982).

Strunk, William and White, E. B., *The Elements of Style* (Allyn & Bacon, 2000).

Tawney, R. H., *Religion and the Rise of Capitalism* (Pelican, 1969).

Taylor, Val, *Stage Writing* (Crowood Press, 2002).

Tennenhouse, Leonard (ed.), *The Practice of Psychoanalytic Criticism* (Wayne State University Press, Detroit, 1976).

Tierno, Michael, *Aristotle's 'Poetics' for Screenwriters* (Hyperion, 2002).

Tillyard, E. M. W., *The Muse Unchained* (Bowes & Bowes, 1958).

Todorov, Tzvetan, *Genres in Discourse* (Cambridge University Press, 1990).

Toolan, Michael, *Language in Literature* (Arnold, 1998).

Trask, R. L., *The Penguin Guide to Punctuation* (Penguin, 1997).

Treglown, Jeremy and Bennett, Bridget, *Grub Street and the Ivory Tower* (Clarendon Press, 1889).

Turner, G. W., *Stylistics* (Penguin, 1973).

Tusa, John, *On Creativity* (Methuen, 2003).

van der Will, Wilfried (ed.), *Workers and Writers* (Birmingham, 1975).

Vogler, Christopher, *The Writer's Journey* (Pan Books, 1999).

Wagner, Betty Jane, *Drama as a Learning Medium* (Hutchinson, 1985).

Wake, Roy and Denton, Pennie, *Bedales School: The First Hundred Years* (Haggerston Press, 1993).

Wallis, Mick and Shepherd, Simon, *Studying Plays* (Edward Arnold, 1998).

Wandor, Michelene, *The Body Politic* (Stage 1, 1972).

Wandor, Michelene, *Carry on, Understudies* (Routledge, 1986).

Wandor, Michelene, *Postwar British Drama: Looking Back in Gender* (Routledge, 2001).

Wandor, Michelene, *Forget the muse, it's hard graft you need* (*Times Higher Education Supplement*, 6 August 2004).

Wandor, Michelene, *The Art of Writing Drama* (Methuen, 2008).

Wellek, Rene, *The Attack on Literature* (Harvester Press, 1982).

Wellek, Rene and Warren, Austin, *Theory of Literature* (Penguin Books, 1970).

Welty, Eudora, *On Writing* (Modern Library, 2002).

Widdowson, Peter, *Literature* (Routledge, 1999).

Widdowson, Peter (ed.), *Re-Reading English* (Routledge, 1982).

Wilbers, Stephen, *The Iowa Writers' Workshop* (University of Iowa Press, 1980).

Wilde, Oscar, *Intentions* (The Unicorn Press, 1945).

Williams, Raymond, *Culture and Society 1780–1950* (Penguin, 1961).

Williams, Raymond, *Keywords* (Picador, 1976).

Williams, Raymond, *Marxism and Literature* (Oxford University Press, 1977).

Williams, Raymond, *Writing in Society* (Verso, 1991).

Williams, Sadie, *Admission Trends in Undergraduate English*, Report No. 1 (English Subject Centre, April 2002).

Williams, T. G., *The City Literary Institute* (Saint Catherine Press, 1960).

Wimsatt, W. K. and Beardsley, Monroe, *The Verbal Icon* (Methuen, 1970).

Writers' and Artists' Yearbook (A. & C. Black).

Writers on Writing (Times Books, 2001).

Writing in Education (NAWE).

Wu, Duncan (ed.), *Making Plays* (Macmillan, 2000).

Yaguello, Marina, *Language Through the Looking Glass* (Oxford University Press, 1998).

Zinsser, William, *Writing to Learn* (Harper & Row, 1989).

Index